W9-CQN-386

Globalizing Ideal Beauty

Globalizing Ideal Beauty

**How Female Copywriters of the
J. Walter Thompson Advertising
Agency Redefined Beauty
for the Twentieth Century**

Denise H. Sutton

GLOBALIZING IDEAL BEAUTY
Copyright © Denise H. Sutton, 2009.

First published in hardcover in 2009 by PALGRAVE MACMILLAN® in the United States—a division of St. Martin's Press LLC, 175 Fifth Avenue, New York, NY 10010.

Where this book is distributed in the UK, Europe and the rest of the world, this is by Palgrave Macmillan, a division of Macmillan Publishers Limited, registered in England, company number 785998, of Houndmills, Basingstoke, Hampshire RG21 6XS.

Palgrave Macmillan is the global academic imprint of the above companies and has companies and representatives throughout the world.

Palgrave® and Macmillan® are registered trademarks in the United States, the United Kingdom, Europe and other countries.

ISBN: 978-1-137-02100-7

The Library of Congress has cataloged the hardcover edition as follows:

Sutton, Denise H.
   Globalizing ideal beauty : how female copywriters of the J. Walter Thompson advertising agency redefined beauty for the twentieth century / Denise H. Sutton.
      p. cm.
   Includes bibliographical references and index.
   ISBN 978-1-137-02100-7
   1. Women in the advertising industry—United States—History. 2. Women in advertising—United States—History. 3. Beauty, Personal—United States—History. 4. J. Walter Thompson Company Women's Editorial Department. 5. Advertising agencies—United States—History. I. Title.

HF5805.S87 2009
659.1092'2—dc22   2009004025

A catalogue record of the book is available from the British Library.

Design by Scribe Inc.

First PALGRAVE MACMILLAN paperback edition: July 2012

10 9 8 7 6 5 4 3 2 1

Transferred to Digital Printing in 2012

For Peter, with love and gratitude.

And, in memory of my grandmother

Esther Dinse Stoskopf.

Contents

Illustrations

Acknowledgments

It is a pleasure to have this opportunity to thank the many people who helped me as I worked my way through this project. This book grew out of my dissertation, and I am indebted to the faculty members at Clark University who served on my committee, Parminder Bhachu, Sally Deutsch, Cynthia Enloe, and Fern Johnson (my advisor), for their unwavering support and intellectual generosity. My committee has also continued to offer guidance for which I am grateful. Robert Clark was a part of this project from the start. This book benefited greatly from his critical insights and sharp editing eye. Thanks to Claire Cummings, who read the manuscript and provided valuable feedback and loving support throughout, and to Anna Balas for creative inspiration. Mona Domosh was kind enough to read a section of my manuscript and provided insights into the international expansion of American businesses, in particular. My brother-in-law, Robert Shoemaker, a retired professor from New York University's Stern School of Business, provided crucial feedback from a business perspective. Bart Astor introduced me to the world of publishing, gave me good advice, and cheered me on.

I owe a special debt to Laurie Harting, my editor at Palgrave Macmillan, for her interest in this project and her care with the text. Her enthusiasm for the ad women at J. Walter Thompson (JWT) matched my own. Many thanks to Laura Lancaster and Erin Ivy at Palgrave Macmillan and to Jennifer Kepler at Scribe, all of whom made this book better. This book also benefited from the suggestions of the anonymous reviewers at Palgrave Macmillan.

Over the last couple of years, I have presented some of this research at academic conferences. In particular, I would like to thank those scholars at the women's history conference at Guildhall University, London, who provided thoughtful feedback on my book. I also learned a great deal from the students in my Advertising Gender class at the New School University, whose interest in advertising was indefatigable. I am grateful, too, for generous financial assistance from Clark University for the support of a three-year fellowship and travel grants. In addition, a research grant from the Hartman Center for Sales, Advertising, and Marketing History at Duke University allowed me to spend time at the JWT Archives held there.

One of the most exciting aspects of writing this book has been the opportunity to dig through various archives. I am grateful to Karen Baldwin and Richard Taylor for introducing me to the thrill of archival research. I have spent years surrounded by boxes of archival material, transported to the world of the women I write about in this book, some of whom, I discovered, had lived only a few blocks from me on the Upper West Side of Manhattan. There were days I expected to see the flash of Aminta Casseres's skirt whipping around a corner on Broadway or to catch a glimpse of Ruth Waldo, in her famous hat, strolling through Riverside Park. Many thanks to archivists Ellen Gartrell, Jacqueline Reid, and Lynn Easton at the Hartman Center for Sales, Advertising, and Marketing History, Duke University. This book would not have been possible without the existence of the JWT Archives. It was truly a pleasure to spend time there. I also wish to thank John Pollack at the Rare Book and Manuscript Library at the University of Pennsylvania, Marcia Bassett at the Barnard College Archive, Dorothy Brown at the Wellesley College Archive, and Nanci Young at the Smith College Archive. A considerable amount of time was spent tracking images and obtaining copyright permissions. Kenneth Leonard at Unilever was helpful and kind, for which I am grateful.

My family and friends have sustained me during the last couple of years—you have my enduring love and gratitude. In particular, my husband, Peter Metzger, provided support and laughter. He tolerated my distracted state of mind, and his presence gave me a life outside of writing and research. I am also grateful to Adele Mauro and Peter at Cullen and Dykman who secured for me a writing room of my own.

I have always been drawn to advertising. As a little girl the lullaby I sang to my Raggedy Ann doll was an ad jingle for panty hose: "our L'eggs fit your L'eggs, they hug you, they hold you, they never let you go!" My mother threatened to put my homework to the tune of an ad jingle since I easily memorized them, unlike my multiplication tables. And later, as a teen, I had a love-hate relationship with *Vogue* magazine. This book tells the story of a group of talented women who were drawn to advertising and went on to develop many of the advertising strategies we still see today. I regret that I did not get the chance to meet and talk with them—many had passed away during the 1960s or earlier. I hope that this book does justice to the complicated story of their work lives at J. Walter Thompson and to what they accomplished there.

Introduction

J. Walter Thompson's Women's Editorial Department

Headline: Women in Advertising—Eighty-five percent of all retail purchases are made by women.

Copy reads: In selling goods to women, you hear much of the women's point of view. It is spoken of as if there were some mystery about women, which perhaps some woman, properly gifted, could divulge. . . . To establish these facts and to base the work of presenting an article to be sold to women on complete facts, the JWT Company has developed a staff of women. . . . Among the members of its creative staff, the JWT Company includes women holding degrees from Barnard, Smith, Vassar, University of Chicago, Wellesley, and Columbia—women who have also gone through the regular course of training in advertising which the company gives.

—An ad created by JWT placed in *Advertising Club News*,
May 6, 1918, JWT Archives

The women I write about in this book were pioneers in the advertising industry. They entered the business world at a time when neither the major business schools in the United States nor the business world accepted women. Many of these women considered themselves feminists: They marched in suffrage parades and had previous careers at major suffrage organizations. They had careers in social work and were part of a progressive urban reform movement, advocating for the poor. Others had careers in publishing and public relations. They were all angling for bigger and better jobs. But once they entered the world of advertising, they promoted the same stereotypical imagery of women that many of them fought against in former careers. Through their wildly successful ad campaigns, these ad women contributed to an image and concept of ideal beauty that traveled beyond the borders of the United States. This is a complicated story because even though they made certain compromises, these women had not given up their feminist goals. They were struggling for their own share of the market in an emerging media—their own place in a business world dominated by men. And in the process, they made *a lot* of money for the J. Walter Thompson (JWT) Company.

The women were led by Helen Lansdowne, an advertising superstar who was raised in a single-parent family in Kentucky and who through force of will and talent as a JWT copywriter made her way into the boardroom of the Cincinnati-based Procter & Gamble Company to present her Crisco shortening ad campaign. Lansdowne was the first woman to appear in a Procter & Gamble boardroom to make a presentation. She remade herself into a sophisticated, modern woman, eventually serving on the board of the Museum of Modern Art in New York City. Side by side, she and Stanley Resor, the president of J. Walter Thompson, whom she married in 1917,[1] created the most powerful advertising agency in the United States, which, by the 1920s, had expanded internationally.

The Women's Editorial Department has received little attention in advertising histories, despite the growing number of scholarly works on the history of advertising in the United States. This omission seems odd considering how much women contributed to the "modernization" of the female consumer—both as women copywriters in the JWT Women's Editorial Department and as female consumers who responded to the ads for women's products by purchasing them. In fact, it appears that more was actually written about ad women during the period covered in this book than in today's histories of advertising. Cynthia Swank, former director of the JWT Archives, said, "Frankly, I was surprised by how much was written about women in advertising in periodicals of the day but how little appears in the memoirs of advertising men or the company histories several agencies have sponsored. . . . Indeed, by the 1920s the JWT company was known as the 'women's agency'—not just because its advertisements often were directed at women but because it had gained the reputation of being the company in which bright, young women would have a chance to succeed."[2]

That chance to succeed was made possible by Helen Lansdowne. As a successful copywriter and, later, the wife of the president, she was in a position to carve out a space for women who wanted to work in advertising. Fortunately, Lansdowne was interested in mentoring women in advertising, and she used the fact that the majority of consumers were women to form her department. She said, "The success of the JWT company has been in large measure due to the fact that we have concentrated and specialized upon products sold to women . . . and I believe that it is conceded in the advertising industry that our agency is preeminent when it comes to advertising articles for women."[3] The conception of the Women's Editorial Department was predicated on the essentialist idea that women knew what other women wanted and that basically all women were after the same thing.

The Women's Editorial Department was successful in creating innovative advertising strategies that appealed to women's desire for sensuality, romance, class mobility, and a modern feminine beauty. In purchasing these newly advertised women's products—from Crisco shortening to Woodbury's Facial Soap to Pond's Cold Cream and Pond's Vanishing Cream—female consumers were buying into the promise of the product. Advancing from straight "reason-why" copy, in which the product's purpose is plainly described, JWT's Women's Editorial Department developed successful advertising strategies that used psychological appeals. By purchasing the product, women consumers felt they could tap into the attributes of the product, whether it was a special kind of feminine allure, a hint of romance, social status, ideal beauty, or all of the above. The revenue brought in by campaigns developed by the Women's Editorial Department helped establish JWT as the most powerful ad agency in the United States and made possible its international expansion during the 1920s.

Popular formulas crafted by the Women's Editorial Department were not merely a projection of their own beliefs and values onto society; rather, these formulas drew legitimacy from dominant ideologies in American society. Yet, I reject what some scholars have called the "reflection hypothesis" or the idea that mass media merely reflect dominant social values.[4] My claim is the more contemporary one that mass media reflect the experience of a minority while making appeals to an imagined majority. The aspirational appeal, in particular, found traction with an audience of strivers and tapped into the still powerful American dream narrative. The women whose lives are reflected in the JWT ads are the very women who created the ads, for it is their desires, experiences, ambitions, and dreams that we find there. They were strivers too, though not in the position of the newly landed immigrant or the working-class shopgirl, factory worker, or seamstress. The ad women at JWT were striving for a place in the emerging (business) profession of advertising.

Of course, advertising men and women were part of a larger society, no doubt influenced by their own identity and place in that particular society. But without considering the specific work of advertisers, ideological processes become faceless and take on the erroneous appearance of a disembodied force. If we accept such an appearance, we gain no real insight into how dominant ideologies manifest and how they are perpetuated. In this type of approach, advertisements just "appear" and are separate from the actual production that takes place in board rooms, copy rooms, and across the desks of men and women who bring their own experiences, values, beliefs, and ambitions to bear on the final result of any ad campaign.

If instead we take the actual tastemakers into account, it is difficult to take "reality" for granted as something having a purely objective existence, which is independent of historical context and human interaction—interactions that include power inequalities. In addition, meaning is not transmitted to us—we actively create it according to a complex interplay of codes or conventions of which we are normally unaware.[5] Recognizing that ads do not reflect an objective insight into society at large is the first step toward uncovering the processes of meaning making. In this book, the process includes discovering who the people were who created the ads and understanding how their beliefs and values were transmitted through the ads in text crafted and images chosen.

In addition, this emphasis on the ad women and their ad campaigns at JWT, as opposed to a focus on how the female consumer received the ads, avoids the assumption that through a semiotic analysis of the text (or ad) one can measure the effect on the reader (or consumer). In this interdisciplinary approach, the effect of the ad is measured by a number of factors: (a) the sales of the product, including analysis of sales figures pre- and post-ad campaign and (b) tracking whether the strategies used in a particular campaign were used in other campaigns, both in the United States and in international markets. In combination with these factors and on a more theoretical level, however, I also analyzed how images and narratives of ideal beauty in the ads created a particular sign system that both drew from and perpetuated the beliefs and values of the ad women and men at JWT. Particular facial and body features are repeatedly used in ads, for instance, and gain (normative) value through repetition and saturation. It is, in part, through this process that a particular form of beauty becomes the "ideal" beauty.

A number of recent studies of advertising have provided some suggestions as to how products gain meaning beyond their utilitarian function and how existing systems of meaning contribute to that process.[6] In terms of the ads created by JWT's women copywriters, a basic insight from Judith Williamson's *Decoding Advertisements* is useful: "The subject drawn into the work of advertising is one who knows. To fill in gaps we must know what to fill in, to decipher and solve problems we must know the rules of the game. Advertisements clearly produce knowledge . . . but this knowledge is always produced from something already known, that acts as a guarantee, in its anteriority, for the 'truth' in the ad itself."[7] In a particular historical, political, and social context, we can determine then at least some of the rules of the game. This understanding, combined with an analysis grounded in archival research on a particular group of ad women and the success of their campaigns, rounds out my perspective.

During the late nineteenth and early twentieth centuries, various ideas, values, and beliefs circulated that affected how people might have reacted to messages in advertisements. A successful ad campaign, with resulting increased sales for the product, means a connection has been made. Though precisely how that connection came about is often difficult to determine. Despite what the ad men and ad women at JWT might have their clients believe (and believed themselves), advertising is not a science. Messages in ads certainly seemed to have a greater effect, especially when connected to narratives of class mobility, race, gender, national identity, and sexuality—things to which people might have an emotional reaction. I argue that these concepts, so intimately related to identity formation, were particularly salient for women (and men) during the early twentieth century. Furthermore, these narratives continue to hold sway in advertising today, since they strike at the core of one's sense of self.

For the most part, we can only speculate how women in the late nineteenth and early twentieth century were affected by images and copy in advertisements. Some scholars have claimed that images of the "new woman," or "modern woman," helped usher in an acceptance of the independent woman who traveled, smoked cigarettes, drove a car, and played sports.[8] Yet, those same scholars also acknowledge that the image of the new or modern woman had limits since many of those images were created within the context of consumerism. The new or modern woman in that context did not seem to threaten the status quo, though her image may have broadened the definition of acceptable behavior for some women.

New scholarship sheds light on the modern woman (or girl) by exploring the development of the modern woman in a global context using comparative methods. Research that focuses on the modern woman in China, France, Germany, India, Australia, the United States, South Africa, Russia, Zimbabwe, and Japan during the interwar period adds interesting new perspectives that complicate histories of modernity and consumption.[9] This research is relevant to and complements the story of the women copywriters JWT, especially since in-depth studies of these various markets add to an understanding of JWT's international expansion and to the ideology of civilization and race and gender formation intertwined with that expansion.

A Developing Mass Consumer Culture in the United States

My argument catches consumer culture at one of its key moments, when magazines such as the *Ladies' Home Journal* and its advertisements were circulated throughout the United States. The development of the first truly national advertising in the 1920s fostered increasingly strong ties among manufacturers, advertisers, retailers, periodicals, and mass media readers. This collaboration multiplied the impact of advertising, further legitimizing women's pursuit of not only feminine beauty but also the attainment of what was then being touted as "modernization." Yet, women worked at those women's magazines as writers, editors, and artists and had an active role in their development, as did the ad women who created ads for these magazines. The Women's Editorial Department, for instance, placed the majority of the ads in the *Ladies' Home Journal* during the 1920s.[10]

The combination of the new forces of national campaigns, mass circulation by mail, and the collaboration between manufacturers, advertisers, retailers, and magazines circulated the notion of the modern American woman, who represented a distinctive ideal beauty, with a force and on a scale never before achieved in the United States. In taking on truly national scope, the image of the "ideal beauty" served to form the consciousness of a nation of immigrants and bolster a class system that also marked the social progress of a growing managerial class.

The construction of an emerging U.S. mass identity (or an "imagined" identity) was channeled through a very narrow concept of femininity that emphasized class and race distinctions. For those women who did not meet the standard requirements of the ideal beauty, consumer culture was ready with instructions for how to achieve the look. This emerging mass identity was facilitated by the large scale and well-known changes of industrialization, urbanization, and secularization in modernity, but it is also identifiable in concrete, everyday experiences such as reading a glossy, attractively written, and edited magazine; reading the newspaper; listening to the radio; or viewing a film. Without the advertising industry, these feminized images of beauty featured in mass media would never have had the impact or reach they did.

As American culture increasingly became a consumer culture, the advertising industry looked for ways to professionalize its field. At JWT, Stanley Resor and Helen Lansdowne strove for respectability within the agency by attempting to make advertising a science. In addition, they shaped a corporate culture to best serve the needs of the agency's most powerful clients: the highly masculinized modern business enterprises (such as Procter & Gamble and General Motors) that were gaining strength domestically and internationally during the early twentieth century. JWT's goal was to legitimize and professionalize advertising by incorporating the new "science" of market research into advertising strategies, making a national reputation for the agency as one that used the most up-to-date scientific approaches. The masculine rhetoric of science appealed to JWT's clients; yet, in tandem with this to sell products to consumers—the majority of whom were women—JWT depended on the intuitive work of the all-female Women's Editorial Department. After all, they *knew* what women wanted.

These major developments affected women and were affected by women: women filled factories with a labor force that supported tremendous industrial growth and middle- and upper-class women filled the stores as consumers. And a few women even participated in the developing new media of women's magazine and advertising (both in-house retail advertising and at agencies). The middle-class housewife went from producing for her home to consuming standardized products for her home. Middle-class, female consumers were just beginning to be bound together as a class by a web of brand identification, marketing, and advertising.

A vibrant media is the essential part of the system for all these changes to create a consumer culture. And in the 1880s, magazines such as the *Ladies' Home Journal* and the *Saturday Evening Post* replaced newspapers as the primary forum for commercial messages. These magazines sold for as little as a nickel, supplementing low subscription prices with advertisements that filled one-quarter to one-third of their pages.[11] Filled with advertisements for cosmetics and other women's products, these magazines became the main medium for reaching the female consumer. In part because of the influence of independent advertising agencies, magazine advertising nearly tripled its volume in the 1880s, and its revenues soon surpassed those from the sale of billboard space, which had previously dominated advertising media.[12]

Pond's Cold Cream and Woodbury's Facial Soap Case Studies

The Pond's and Woodbury's product case studies illustrate how the Women's Editorial Department contributed to the creation of the modern feminine woman and ideal beauty. The chapters reveal how powerful the narratives of race, gender, sexuality, class, and national identity were, especially when cleverly used in ad copy and images to attach particular meanings to products. For instance, because both of these products—soap and face cream—are used on the female body, they function in one of the most intimate yet social aspects of female modern identity. Using psychological strategies that drew on a variety of emotions, the ads cautioned against embarrassing the man in your life by not appearing fresh, they warned against damaging fine and delicate skin, they suggested sensuality and promised a connection to a social class that enjoys the very best. In time, these ad campaigns exported American ideals of feminine cleanliness, appearance, and behavior to international markets.

Sex was highlighted in the Woodbury's campaign with the slogan "A Skin You Love To Touch." Tame by today's standards, it was considered fairly racy at the time and gained market share for Woodbury's Facial Soap. The use of sex is so common in advertising today that one often assumes that it will be a prominent part of the campaign for most products—from beer to airlines, and from cosmetics to cars. The common adage in advertising today is "sex sells," which now extends to men. As Jean Kilbourne points out, using images of men as sex objects in advertising is becoming more common in the twenty-first century.[13] Yet, for the American woman in the early twentieth century, this acknowledgment of their sexuality and sensuality offered the romantic dream of desire. To be desired and to desire was an entirely new mass media message.

The scientific aspects of the campaigns assured consumers that they were buying the latest technology in skin care, just as contemporary ads promise beautiful, youthful skin through the latest technological advances. Circulating the fantasy of perpetually youthful glow, these promises rely on the rhetoric of science that we see in the ads for both Pond's and Woodbury's from nearly a century ago. The current use of retinol, collagen, and alpha hydroxyl in cosmetics can be compared to advertising the special properties of Pond's Vanishing Cream that allowed the skin to absorb it (thus maintaining a youthful glow) and to Woodbury's advice of alternating hot and cold water to wash the face, thereby reducing the appearance of pores. The appeal of science is that it offers a "rational" path to youth and beauty; science legitimizes the pursuit.

This pursuit continues and, in 2009, science offers the latest in anti-aging products, called "cosmeceuticals" by dermatologist Dr. Albert Kligman.[14] This term blurs the line between over-the-counter cosmetics and pharmaceutical grade products that require a prescription. Though "cosmeceuticals" are not pharmaceutical grade and are not reviewed by the Food and Drug Administration, the term alludes to a more sophisticated science and a better result. And, as Fern Johnson says, "the name 'cosmeceuticals' potentially creates a verbal image of exact formulation in the methodology of pharmaceuticals but exists mainly to give status appeal for marketers to use in advertising."[15] The ad women at JWT had perfected this strategy in the early twentieth century.

J. Walter Thompson Expands Its Empire

During the late 1920s, the New York City headquarters of J. Walter Thompson expanded to include a number of international offices (in addition to the London office already in operation by that time). Though the agency had done work for international clients prior to the late 1920s, it was not until they acquired the General Motors account in 1928 that it set up offices in cities where GM had manufacturing plants. JWT male executives were sent to these new offices and began to service the GM account; they approached their international expansion as empire-building. Within this JWT corporate empire, the male executives focused on "virgin markets" filled with "virgin consumers" who needed to be educated in the ways of consumerist desire. JWT archival evidence shows that these executives perceived new markets as uncivilized and, therefore, justified their domination in those markets where, most often, advertising and communications systems already existed.

In an effort to tap into an existing system of consumption, JWT made an overarching appeal to international consumers, overwhelmingly based on images and language that represented American modernity—images and copy polished, tested, and proven successful by the Women's Editorial Department. Sophisticated, modern American men and women were represented in ads as civilized, as having class, beauty, and sex appeal—all attainable through the use of the product advertised. Whether the consumer was a man or a woman, U.S. ads, advertising mostly U.S. and British products, appealed to an ideology of civilization. An American sign system of advertising, with all its inherent meanings, was transferred to international markets through images and text that reflected ideologies of civilization and of ideal beauty—as American trademarks, so to speak.

Recent scholarship has come to examine imperialism in terms of consumerism, not just political and territorial conflict.[16] For instance, in her study of five multinational companies, cultural geographer Mona Domosh shows that "for much of the nineteenth and twentieth centuries, American foreign and economic policy was geared not toward the establishment of formal colonies, but toward the expansion of markets."[17] Domosh reveals an "ideology of civilization" that was crucial to the success of these companies in their pursuit of international markets. The power of the ads was in the ideological messages inherent in the ads—companies aligned their products with images and text that represented American "civilization." Those consumers who purchased these "modern" products could participate in the American dream—just as immigrants in the United States were encouraged to be "modern Americans" by buying Crisco oil.[18]

The companies that Domosh focuses on in her study are multinational "modern business enterprises," as defined by Alfred Chandler. Chandler marks a shift and identifies the "traditional business enterprise" as pre-1850 and a new, "modern business enterprise" emerging post-1850. The key in the change in business was the creation of management arranged into functional and specialized units.[19] JWT served and resembled the new modern business enterprise domestically. In its international expansion, JWT came to resemble the multinational modern business enterprise in building its own empire in service of the multinationals.

The chapter on JWT's international expansion emphasizes the need for a broader conceptualization of imperialism to include the marketing of icons of American experience—so that the United States is not seen as the exception to imperialist nations.[20] This approach shows that JWT's international expansion was fueled not only by economic promise but also by a desire to be seen as cosmopolitan mixed with a desire for adventure in a new "frontier." In addition, as historians Kristin Hoganson and Karen Ordahl Kupperman point out, the United States was not unaffected by foreign cultural production and influence, despite its nationalistic self-assertion—an idea that sheds light on this study of ad men and ad women who interacted with international markets.[21]

The final chapter explores some of the influences of JWT domestic ad campaigns on ads that appeared beyond U.S. borders. Though some variations of ad copy and images did exist,[22] many of JWT international ads resembled the domestic versions. JWT archival records reveal the dominant opinions and attitudes of JWT executives concerning international markets. They believed that the female quest for beauty was a universal desire, and early ads reflect what is either an ignorance about or a resistance to the customs, values, and physical appearance of markets that differed from the U.S. market. After all, despite variation among women in the United States, JWT focused exclusively on a particular ideal beauty—all women are essentially the same and all women desire the same thing. Why would they alter their approach for new markets when their ad campaigns—created by the Women's Editorial Department—had been so successful domestically? It was only later, when they realized they could appeal to a wider market and make more money, that the ads started to vary. In addition, clients (especially those served locally) occasionally pressured JWT to expand their conception of "woman" (and "man") to fit their market.

That Was Then, This Is Now

Studies show that advertising has a negative effect on women. A study done in 2007 found that after viewing photos of models in magazines, the women in the study were equally and negatively affected.[23] More specifically, the study subjects reported a drop in their level of satisfaction with their bodies, regardless of their body size. Can we speculate that the same would be true for those women readers in the late nineteenth and early twentieth centuries? They would have been exposed to women in ads with the "ideal" face and figure. How would that image of ideal beauty affect women who did not resemble that image? And how would women in markets beyond the borders of the United States have responded to an American image of ideal beauty?

Current mass media magazines present unrealistic images of women through airbrushing and computer generation, which impact negatively on women and girls. The late nineteenth- and early twentieth-century images of women were often sketches—ideal beauty as opposed to a real woman. And, generally, any photos used in the 1930s and 1940s were as close as possible to the ideal beauty, with supporting copy extolling the beauty of the endorser or model. Now, airbrushing and computer generation are creating the ideal beauty through total creation (like sketches) or the manipulation of existing images, which often are attempts to make women look smaller in some places and larger in others, blemish free, and wrinkle free, all in accordance with an idea of what is beautiful.

The emerging sign system that mythologized ideal beauty also essentialized beauty. Roland Barthes says, "The disease of thinking in essences is at the bottom of every bourgeois mythology of man."[24] This reaction against essentialism reflects an interest in denaturalizing social constructs, and, in the case of ideal beauty, recognizing the essentialist thinking behind it helps one understand its very construct. But there are a few subtleties to consider.

Diana Fuss explains that "essentialism can be deployed effectively in the service of both idealist and materialist, progressive and reactionary, mythologizing and resistive discourses."[25] For instance, in the case of the myth of ideal beauty, Barthes's reaction against essentialism makes feminist sense. Even Fuss agrees that essentialism can be deployed in the service of myth. Essentialism works against women when they do not have that essential element that would make them part of a privileged group. Consider, however, the women copywriters at JWT and their claim to essential feminine intuition, which worked in their favor as they attempted to enter a male-dominated business world. How does this speak to contemporary women's issues in business?

In a 2003 *Crain's* "Special Report on Women in Business," Nina DiSesa, a McCann-Erickson advertising executive, relates how difficult it is for women who work on the creative side of advertising, which she described as "heavily male." DiSesa says, however, that she owes a big part of her success to being a woman: "Relationships are a female thing." And Linda Kaplan Thaler, CEO of her own ad agency, adds, "If I had to pick one thing that's always helped me, it's that female intuitive sense." Although none of the ad women in this article speak of sexism directly, they do say that they owe their success to their feminine side, which allows them to connect with female consumers.[26]

Charlotte Beers, a woman who has been called the "Queen of Madison Avenue," climbed the corporate ladder by handling accounts such as Uncle Ben's rice and Head and Shoulder's shampoo. During the 1990s, Beers ran two of the largest advertising agencies in the United States: J. Walter Thompson and Ogilvy & Mather. The *Washington Post* ran a profile on Beers in 2001 when she was named the Undersecretary of State for Public Democracy (the public relations office for the State Department) by Secretary of State Colin Powell. Powell said that in her new position Beers will work to "change from just selling us in the old USA way to really branding foreign policy, branding the department, marketing the department, marketing American values to the world."[27] Despite the fact that Beers was one of the most influential women in advertising, the article repeatedly referred to her distinctly feminine qualities and how they served her in a male-dominated field. The article quotes from a *Fortune* magazine article that says Beers is a "flamboyant flirt who calls CEOs 'honey' and darling.'"[28] Perhaps this slant accounts for the placement of the article in the style section as opposed to the business section of the *Washington Post*.

The focus on feminine qualities is not surprising since Beers seems to have consistently used them to succeed in advertising; she did not try to blend in ("I dress with flamboyance. It's half the fun of not being a guy"). Beers seems, however, to have experienced the paradoxical situation of being a woman in a male-dominated profession. "I hate the idea that women are more nurturing than men," said Beers, though she promised to "bring emotions" to the State Department's overseas communications.[29] Beers, DiSesa, and Thaler and the ad women at JWT, from almost a century earlier, share common experiences. These women possessed an edge because of their connection to the female consumer, they marketed a distinct feminine intuition, and they exploited sex appeal, but, at the same time, they rebelled against gender stereotypes that demeaned women by not acknowledging the value and range of their intelligence and experiences.

In one stage of feminism it was important to attack stereotypical views of the qualities of women that held such things as emotionalism, intuition, or nurturance as universal and essential traits in women. Later writers have come to see that some such assumptions on occasion worked in women's favor. Helen Lansdowne and the women at JWT used essentialism as a progressive discourse. They declared a special female intuition as one way to make a place for themselves in a male-dominated work environment. Perhaps women who work in a male-dominated workplace are more apt to claim essentialist arguments as a survival strategy—during the early twentieth century and even now.

I

From Suffrage to Soap

Helen Lansdowne Resor and the Women's Editorial Department

> All women need nowadays is the right soap and the right toothpaste, and the
> world is theirs in a cellophane wrapper. . . . And if they don't use the right
> toothpaste, or soap, the frankness, or, bad manners (according to the taste of
> the reader) of their friends would inform them of their mistakes.
>
> —*Printer's Ink,* October 14, 1937

The story of the all-female department at J. Walter Thompson (JWT)—
women who created famous campaigns that revolutionized advertising
and exported American ideals of the feminine around the globe—appears
to have familiar outlines. The department was started by a charismatic,
forceful, and resourceful woman named Helen Lansdowne (1886–1964),
who rose through the industry in a female version of the Horatio Alger
story. She assembled around her a team of women, many with backgrounds
in suffrage and social betterment movements. Together they overcame—to
some measure—the masculine ideology, customs, and patriarchy of the
advertising industry.

A closer look, however, complicates such a triumphant perspective.
Lansdowne was a southern woman from a large family who overcame not
only sexist obstacles but also wariness about her class, her region, and what
would be an "unconventional" background to the elitist and still Victorian-
tinged assumptions of the early ad business. Perhaps more interesting still,
the women she gathered—and turned into a profit-center enterprise in an
agency that dominated advertising in the United States for decades—are

also irreducible to opponents of the corporate world who were brought in and co-opted.

Many of the immensely talented all-female creative staff were, from the time of their application for employment, in fact, eager and enthusiastic about earning more money and gaining greater social power. They were veterans of the war against oppression and for progressive reform—early examples of women somewhat burned-out and chastened by the hardships of seeking social justice. Not unlike many women today, they were fully aware of the progress that needed to be made in America, but knew from personal experience the high cost of devoting themselves to such causes. But to tell this story of successful female entrepreneurship, the worldwide spread of American culture and its norms for women and beauty, and the complicated loyalties and aspirations of these women, we should turn back to the beginning of the enterprise.

The Women's Editorial Department at JWT was founded during the second decade of the twentieth century by Helen Lansdowne (who would take the married name Resor in 1917). She was a powerful and private woman who worked behind the scenes to give talented women a chance to work in the male-dominated world of advertising. Eventually, her staff would be composed of bright, ambitious women, most of whom already had successful careers in the suffrage movement, journalism, publishing, retail advertising, public relations, teaching, or social reform.

Many of these women were also graduates of elite women's colleges and universities. With only a few exceptions, they already had access to resources virtually guaranteed by their social class, race, and nationality (only one was a first generation immigrant). The socioeconomic background and race of the women in the Women's Editorial Department echoed the background of the majority of men who worked in advertising. This similarity gave them entry—to a certain extent—to an elite man's world.

Lansdowne's early life in rural Kentucky, and her meteoric rise to the top of the advertising industry, hints at why she developed the Women's Editorial Department at JWT and dedicated herself to mentoring other women. Lansdowne was unusual at JWT for not having a college education. She was raised in Covington, Kentucky, by Helen Bayleff Lansdowne, a single mother who worked to support her family as a clerk at her brother's business. Lansdowne was the second youngest of nine children and pitched in with the rest of her siblings to take care of household duties.

The historian Stephen Fox attributes Lansdowne's feminism and self-sufficiency to her upbringing: "You're never going to get caught the way I was," Lansdowne's mother told her daughters. "You're going to learn how to work."[1] Lansdowne listened. She graduated from high school as class valedictorian and immediately found a job. Her mother's wisdom continued to shape Lansdowne's life. She looked for intellectual curiosity and a strong work ethic in the women she hired in the editorial department she created—the same qualities her mother had instilled in her from an early age. Perhaps more revealing, though, is the implicit warning from her mother about being trapped as an uneducated worker and single mother. Everything about Lansdowne's work in advertising—especially her focus on beauty and sensuality—was in direct opposition to the harsh realities of her mother's life. Lansdowne was determined to move beyond her mother's world.

Lansdowne's first job was a brief stint at Procter & Collier auditing bills. There she met Stanley Resor, who was later to become president of JWT and her husband. Lansdowne moved on to write retail advertisements for a Cincinnati newspaper, then wrote copy for a firm that advertised for streetcar companies. When Resor became the head of the new JWT branch in Cincinnati, he remembered Lansdowne from Procter & Collier and offered her the position of its sole copywriter. Against her family's wishes, and despite their warning that Resor would "work her to death," Lansdowne accepted his offer.[2]

In 1910, Lansdowne began to make a name for herself as a national copywriter by creating advertisements for Woodbury Soap, manufactured by the Jergens Company. Her slogan "The Skin You Love to Touch" is considered the first use of sex appeal in an ad. Although tame by today's standards, the ad created a sensation. Under Lansdowne's direction, Woodbury's Soap sales increased 1,000 percent in eight years.[3] In 1911 she moved to New York City to work at JWT headquarters, and six years later she married Stanley Resor.

One of her first big accounts was Crisco, a newly invented solid vegetable shortening made by Proctor & Gamble and called by historian Susan Strasser "an artifact of a culture in the making, a culture founded on new technologies and structured by new personal habits and new economic forms."[4] Strasser's remark underscores that Lansdowne's pioneering work in advertising dovetailed with the creation of a new product—like Crisco shortening that could be conveniently dipped into, stored, and used as needed by homemakers—and a new consumer culture.

Lansdowne consolidated her career in advertising with her work on the Crisco and Woodbury's accounts, as well as with her original ads for Yuban Coffee, Lux soap flakes, and Cutex nail polish.[5] All of these products were convenience aids of one kind or another, items that helped to create the modern, scientific, reduced-labor kitchen and the attractively turned-out homemaker who was supposed to spend her time there. For her stellar work in advertising, Lansdowne was inducted into the

American Advertising Federation's Advertising Hall of Fame in 1967—three years after her death.

Yet as a trailblazer helping to sell a new genre of product, Helen Lansdowne also considered herself a feminist. By the second decade of the new century, she led a JWT contingent in New York's mass suffrage parades.[6] Lansdowne also supported Planned Parenthood, was the committee chairwoman on the babies' ward at the New York Postgraduate Hospital, and served as the president of the Traveler's Aid Society, an organization that provided shelter to homeless women during the Depression.[7] Moreover, her support for women also had a practical purpose. She constructed her department on the common adage in marketing and advertising of that time that "if you are to sell to women, nothing succeeds like a woman's viewpoint." A woman's imputed sixth sense would help her win her rights and help her become a modern woman in every other sense.

Lansdowne said that advertising appeals "must be made with the knowledge of the habits of women, their methods of reasoning and their prejudices."[8] She believed that women would advance further in an all-female environment than one that included men and women. In addition, the growing emphasis on psychology in advertising and marketing may have made the atmosphere of the advertising industry more conducive to considering Lansdowne's approach to reaching women consumers. Lansdowne's comments reinforced the use of psychology already popular in the advertising industry. Yet, despite a modern advertising industry and her own position in that industry, Lansdowne and her advertising women were affected by lingering Victorian notions of gender differences that "sexed" the mind as well as the body.

Advertising Women at J. Walter Thompson

Although some of her employees had once been involved in the suffrage movement, Lansdowne's women were also privileged and maintained notions of propriety that went along with their social positions. Indeed, JWT provided such women with professional opportunities denied them by professional schools and organizations, thereby attracting a white, well-educated, middle- and upper-middle-class staff.

By 1910 nearly 40 percent of all college students were women, and by 1920 nearly 47 percent of all students in four-year colleges were women.[9] Yet occupations for college women at that time were still largely restricted to teaching, nursing, and social work. The Harvard Graduate School of Business kept its doors closed to women until 1963, and when Columbia University offered an adult education program in business that drew as many women as men, Columbia segregated the women into a secretarial program, limiting the business training exclusively for men.[10]

A number of the women who ended up working at JWT in the Women's Editorial Department had earlier careers in traditionally female professions, and some were quite well established. But they were also eager to enter business to make more money and enjoy a greater professional status. Although some women achieved those ends, they may well have lost some of the solidarity—and orientation toward oppositional politics—that they experienced in the service professions. When they took a job at JWT, these women entered an environment with a completely different gender dynamic (the institutionalized masculinity of the business world)—a world different even from their college experiences. Sharon Hartman Strom called the business world during this period "particularly virile."[11] Women were valued at the ad agency but also segregated from men as a group. Their access to male clients was also restricted.

Even so, educational opportunities for women in the early twentieth century were increasing. And although women were still denied admittance to many colleges, universities, and various programs of study, a much greater number of women were enrolling. The colleges that JWT women chose to attend had an impact on their work in advertising and perhaps on their desire to enter the field. Many women at JWT had attended Barnard College, and at about the same time that they would have been enrolled, Barnard was undergoing a dramatic shift in curricula. By the 1920s, Barnard had made classics an elective and replaced classical studies with required courses in psychology, sociology, and economics.[12] Such change established some of the grounds for a career in advertising, which was enthusiastically using newly developed social science methods to determine markets and analyze consumers—female consumers.

JWT was regarded as the best agency for women not only because it hired women but because women were able to work in positions not usually available to them in other agencies. Nevertheless, the Women's Editorial Department epitomized a double-edged concept of a woman's place. On one hand, the women were valued for their gender's alleged intuition and sixth sense for a female market. On the other, they were segregated from the rest of the company in an all-female department and almost never dealt directly with JWT clients. The editorial department was created within an institution that was masculinized to a major extent and that aspired to be a modern, scientifically run corporate enterprise along lines that the still largely male laboratory sciences supported.

Though the women copywriters at JWT struggled for respect in the business world, they still enjoyed a privileged lifestyle especially when compared to that of the average female consumer. Findings from research conducted by Wallace Boren were presented in a JWT staff meeting and reveal the differences between JWT copywriters (men and women) and the ordinary consumer. In general, only one in five JWT copywriters went to church, half never went to working-class resorts such as Coney Island, and more than half had never lived below the average national income level (nor had they known anyone who had). And while only 5 percent of families nationwide employed a housekeeper, 66 percent of JWT copywriters did.[13] In addition, Cynthia Swank notes that in 1930, the median salary of women college graduates nationwide was $1,900. The average salary at JWT for all women—with and without college degrees—was $2,200, more than 15 percent higher.[14]

An analysis of some of the ideological paradoxes for women who strove to enter a male-dominated profession—which was nevertheless key in the development of a consumer culture pitched to women and which also was a cornerstone in capitalist business—makes clear the predicament of the women copywriters. Although they may have once protested corporate capitalism in their political work, they had made a fascinating transition. In effect, the women's editorial department were early "knowledge workers"—selling skills and attitudes, creating styles, and manipulating the emotions of social groups that they had come to understand in earlier careers. Thus, many of the women copywriters at JWT continued the work of shaping society they had undertaken earlier by new means.

The women in the Women's Editorial Department, for example, struggled to envision a "new woman" who challenged popular clichés; and for many of the women at JWT, both market research and feminism argued against stereotyping female consumers. Some women found themselves arguing against using women in ads if it meant they were portrayed in a stereotypical role. But the arguments themselves, made to male executives, were tinged with sexism and lingering Victorian themes such as the notion of separate spheres.

In that way the women who worked at JWT had an active, though complicated, role in the development of the advertising industry. Through their nationally distributed ads, they contributed to the development of an American identity, which reflected and helped to perpetuate the dominant ideologies concerning gender, race, ethnicity, and nationality. Their ambitions and dreams, however, often contradicted the very stereotypes they perpetuated in the ads they helped to create. These women's careers were marked by a certain "double consciousness": a straining between strategy and goals, between what the women said around their male colleagues and what they said to one another, between ad women's professional triumphs and the ideological codings in their copy.

JWT's women copywriters may have been set apart, but some were still often connected to past work as reformers, such as their work in the suffrage movement or previous work in service industries. Jennifer Scanlon suggests a "compatibility of social work and/or suffrage work and advertising work . . . [s]ocial progressives could and did view advertising as a form of social service."[15] Indeed, much advertising directed to women included instructions on how to use modern technology and thereby how to become a modern American woman—resembling and building on the tone of middle-class instruction in the work of social reformers who were teaching recent immigrants the ways of "American" middle-class life. Scanlon is also careful to assert a point raised earlier. That is, working in advertising—the corporate world—offered women higher salaries and greater social respect than working in the suffrage movement or social reform. Through my own research into the biographical files of these women, I found many of them actually had already worked in the advertising industry, albeit in retail advertising, before coming to JWT. A great number of them had also worked in publishing, public relations, at magazines, and in other roles in retail.

The details of these women's work experiences suggest something different or at least more nuanced than the claim that these ad women saw their work as consumer advocates or educators. While there was no doubt about the compatibility between social reform, suffrage work, and advertising work, my argument is that this compatibility was motivated by an identification with consumer culture. It was not purely based on an ideological view of social service and reform. A closer look at the suffrage movement in the United States will show that suffrage activists identified with consumer culture and employed its methods of publicity to win political support. The women who worked in retail advertising, publishing, and in the fashion industries were already invested and well versed in such norms of American consumer culture and brought this experience to JWT.

The women working in the editorial department certainly supported the development of an emerging class of managers and professionals—and aspired to be part of that class themselves. Those who hired them, however, had a different—more limited—plan. The complicated dynamic of JWT's corporate culture was such that even though Helen Lansdowne mentored the ad women, the agency's masculinist culture limited their role in the ways earlier noted. Despite those limitations, these women generated a great deal of revenue for JWT. The Women's Editorial Department wrote all the copy for the agency's beauty accounts, which were substantial. Between 1909 and 1929, the number of American perfume and cosmetics manufacturers nearly doubled. The factory value of their products rose tenfold—from $14.2 million to nearly $141 million.[16] By 1918, the revenue generated by the Women's Editorial Department totaled $2,264,759 out of $3,902,601 for the entire agency.[17]

Yet, rather than perceiving the women of the department as merely being the creation of the senior staff of JWT (that is, to be the passive or co-opted tools of the patriarchal capitalist JWT institutional leadership), I suggest that these women had particular business and cultural objectives of their own. It also appears that they succeeded in achieving at least some of those goals. They succeeded, for example, in reworking some basic assumptions of the masculinist corporate culture of JWT. But in doing so, they must have sometimes felt that disoriented sense of "doubleness" that women experience when existing within a system they want to change and within a sexist system that did not value women. And in the case of JWT, the women copywriters not only outnumbered men copywriters but they also worked on more accounts.

Archival records show that in 1916, for example, ten copywriters worked at the New York City office: six women and four men, all segregated in their own department.[18] By 1925, twenty-two women, including five group heads, worked on sixty-two accounts. In contrast, nineteen men copywriters, including ten group heads, worked on eighteen accounts. The distribution of work is interesting: twenty-two women worked on sixty-two accounts compared with the men copywriters who had more writers than accounts. Furthermore, slightly more than half of the men were group heads. In addition to working on the women's accounts, Frances Maule and Evelyn Dewey also worked on two men's accounts.[19]

The five women group heads listed are among the most prominent women in the department: Ruth Waldo, Augusta Nicolls, Aminta Casseres, Edith Lewis, and Helen Lansdowne. Two men are listed as working under Ruth Waldo on her accounts. The remaining seventeen women include some highlighted in this chapter, including Frances Maule, Margaret King, Monica Barry O'Shea, Therese Olzendam, Gladys Phelan, Pearl Dienst, Evelyn Dewey, Helen Brown, Mary Loomis Cook, Esther Eaton, and Janet Fox Wing.[20]

What is striking about the Women's Editorial Department staff is the underlying story of ambition in the archival materials that focused, most particularly, on their job applications. Women were enthusiastic about gaining entry into the business world and saw JWT as a place where that dream could be realized. Though one would expect this enthusiasm on a job application, the terms in which they expressed it and the universal degree of energy and excitement in the texts they wrote are compelling. Some of the women sounded burned-out in their "helping" professional careers, especially the social workers. An examination of the job applications of approximately forty women speaks to these issues. Stories about these women, gleaned from company newsletters and other archival material, also illustrate how these women navigated JWT's corporate culture.[21]

The JWT job application was extremely detailed and comprehensive. Some of the questions that appear on it would now be illegal, such as questions about religious affiliation, age, children, memberships, and the nationality of parents, to name a few. Other, more standard, questions revealed where the applicant went to college; where the applicant was born; the occupation of her father; her marital status; her previous employment; why the applicant wanted to work for JWT; what the applicant's ambition was; was the applicant optimistic; was she detailed-oriented; did she work best on her own or with supervision; did she have any hobbies; did she have poise; did she have self-confidence; what she thought she lacked; her level of energy, imagination, concentration, patience, manual accuracy, deliberateness; had she been published; and, finally, did she like to write. The application process also involved writing a biographical statement (fully 1,000 to 1,500 words), and choosing three advertisements from two popular magazines (the *Ladies' Home Journal* and *Saturday Evening Post*) and analyzing the ads in terms of effectiveness and aesthetic qualities.

Answers to the application questions also speak to the absence of women in advertising. The form's comprehensive nature implies that there was no industry-wide basis on which to judge women entering the field. The application was also to some extent gendered as female in its questions about poise and self-confidence, which reinforce desirable "ladylike," middle-class qualities. While a college education was not a requirement to work in the Women's Editorial Department, college-level writing and analysis skills obviously were. Furthermore, applicants who were familiar with women's magazines and could articulate the aesthetics of current fashion would have an edge in filling out this application. The whole employment process makes it apparent that JWT—as an institution—was reproducing itself. Women that reflected the class and race of those already working at the agency were the ones most likely to be hired. It is likely that Helen Lansdowne created the application process and, if so, in this instance, took her place as part of the legitimizing body of the agency.[22]

Institutional tools such as the employment application and agency newsletters supported the corporate culture of JWT and helped perpetuate homogeneity among the managerial and copywriting staff. At the very least, these institutional communication tools were instructive to potential and current employees who probably understood the implication of questions on the application and were able to read the subtext of the stories about their colleagues in the newsletter. The presence of questions addressing nationality, religion, father's occupation, and so forth, indicate the importance that JWT placed on family and social position. Furthermore, typical success stories about female colleagues in the JWT newsletters were inspirational and instructive in their tone. It is not surprising, then, that the women who were hired to work in the Women's Editorial Department were from similar, if not the same, socioeconomic class as the male executives—despite some of their more unconventional experiences. While that may be expected, the closeness of the match is striking in a company that purported to place heavy emphasis on scientific management, research, and innovation.

The detailed nature of this job application is indeed astounding and shows how serious Lansdowne was about bringing together a group of intelligent, well-educated, and well-connected women. The stakes were high for Lansdowne because the success of her department would validate her own theories about the potential contributions of women to advertising as well as her value to the company. Through her husband's position as president, Lansdowne had access to what went on at the highest level of the firm. She understood that she could appeal to her husband and male executives with an argument based on business. Through her own business savvy, Lansdowne showed JWT that the company could use her department as a marketing ploy to lure potential clients. If a client gave JWT its account, the Women's Editorial Department would use its supposed collective feminine intuition to appeal to the female consumer, giving that client an advantage in the marketplace. While this may seem contrary to JWT's intended reliance on more scientific methods, JWT made sure to announce that the members of the Women's Editorial Department went through a rigorous training program to prepare them for advertising challenges and to ensure that they were indoctrinated into the JWT corporate culture.

Lansdowne was heavily involved in the hiring and mentoring of the women who worked for her in the Women's Editorial Department. A *Ladies' Home Journal* article by Harriet Abbot in 1920 praises Lansdowne for her business acumen and mentoring: "She not only put manufacturers' products and her own agency on the map; she made a place in advertising geography for women, a place no advertiser or agency ever before had granted them. She pioneered the way for women in advertising, marking a trail for which successful women today are grateful to her."[23] Lansdowne's success in this male-dominated field depended on her ability to create copy that combined scientific reasoning and modern feminine sex appeal.

Lansdowne set high standards for her group of copywriters and warned them that advertising was not glamorous or clever work. Rather, she said, it was persistent hard work that was based on in-depth study of markets and manufacturing, of research and statistics. Of course, this all depended on landing a position as a copywriter, and Lansdowne employed an argument that combined female intuition with marketing savvy. Lansdowne believed that a woman did not absolutely need a college education to work in the Women's Editorial Department (though most did have one), but that she needed a kind of curiosity that would be reflected in how she approached her job. She said,

> The agency searches back into her interests in college. Was she attracted by economics, psychology, sociology, history? Was she a real student; did she really dig out the causes of things, think for herself, enjoy thinking for herself? Or did she learn texts and lectures by rote, pass "exams" with amazing A-pluses, bury her nose constantly in the alcoves of the college library or keep an eye forever over a "scope"? What was her mother like? Was she a constructively minded woman, seeing a big future dawning for women over the horizon, even though she herself stayed at the grindstone to put her daughter through college? Did she breathe this faith of hers into her daughter, filling her young mind with the vision of a new day for women when they should stand squarely beside men on the platform of achievement?[24]

Lansdowne must have asked about an applicant's mother during the interview process, since there were no questions about the mother on the application form, with the exception of her nationality. Or maybe the mother's influence was more of a memory of her own past experiences since Lansdowne seems to be talking about herself in the last part of this passage and the feminist ideals her mother instilled in her. The passage also supports the hiring of college graduates. There is a strong emphasis here on how the women learned in college (Was she a real student? Did she enjoy thinking for herself—was she a critical thinker?), and hiring college graduates would certainly have legitimized the Women's Editorial Department. If a woman applicant had a background in sociology or psychology—with training in research methods—she was an especially valuable addition to the department.

College-educated women, of course, brought other valuable resources to the agency; since many were from the same socioeconomic group, they could tap into the social and political capital, from networking to manners and attitudes available to them. The Women's Editorial Department's connections through families, businesses, acquaintances, friends, schools, and social clubs and organizations contributed an aura of class distinction to the agency. And while not all of the male executives at JWT were happy about working with women, the fact that these women were from the same socioeconomic background as the men made it possible for certain women to enter the advertising business.

Helen Lansdowne's Group of Women Copywriters

Frances Maule was a copywriter at JWT and veteran of the presuffrage women's movement. She was thirty-six years old when she applied at JWT in 1920. She identified her family as "American" (as do many of the applicants when responding to the question of nationality), and claimed that she has no religion "now," though she was baptized and confirmed an Episcopalian. Her father was an attorney, and Maule inked in a space for "Mother's Occupation" and wrote "author." Maule received a BA degree from the University of Nebraska and was married to (and separated from) Edwin Bjorkman, a Swedish scholar and translator of Ibsen and Strindberg, authors then considered radical in their appreciation of female power. Maule worked in journalism, as a reporter for the *New York American*, the *Chicago American, Denver Times*, and the *Colorado Springs Telegraph*, as well as in publishing at prestigious Henry Holt and Company. She also worked for the New York State Suffrage Party in New York City and the National Women's Suffrage Association in New York City, where she was a field organizer and spoke on behalf of each organization. When asked if she was optimistic, she said, "Yes, I believed we could put our women's suffrage in New York State and (by federal amendment) throughout the United States." And in response to the question about why she wanted to work at JWT, Maule said it was "because [she had] heard that it recognizes the special utility that women must have in appealing to women as the chief purchasers of goods."[25]

Maule's answers indicate a certain advertising savvy and confidence. She was older than most of the other applicants, had been married, and had a wide variety of work experiences. She followed her mother's profession by going into journalism—a move that would appeal to Lansdowne. Maule's comment about JWT's recognition of women's "special utility" in appealing to other women also would have caught Lansdowne's eye. This fits with the JWT corporate ideology, which justified women's presence in the commercial world by marketing female intuition. Maule's combination of work experience, education, family background, and knowledge of JWT made her an extremely desirable candidate. She was hired in 1920.

In her first month at JWT, Maule worked as a cosmetics demonstrator at department stores: three weeks at Abraham and Strauss in Brooklyn demonstrating Cutex nail polish, and one week behind the counter as a Cutex demonstrator in a beauty show at the opening of Blatt's new department store in Atlantic City, New Jersey.[26] This was not an uncommon practice for most of the Women's Editorial Department staff. They were trained in retail market research and marketing, with a dose of direct customer service, as well as advertising. Maule developed strong ideas about advertising during her career and went on to write about them for the JWT newsletter, as well as in her own advice manual for women advertisers. Maule criticized the then overwhelmingly male-dominated industry for relying too much on the "good old conventional angel-idiot conception of women" and urged them to remember the old suffrage slogan—that "women are people."

Maule emphasized that it was impossible to pick out a feminine type and call it woman, just as it was impossible to pick out a masculine type and call it man. Maule supports her argument with knowledge gained in her suffrage work and uses that argument to influence the way advertisements with women looked and read. She tried to expand the representation of women in advertising with argumentative strategies she cultivated in the suffrage movement. There are other similarities between strategies used in political movements and consumer culture, as we will see later in this chapter.

In Maule's work at the editorial department, she identified four different types of female consumers, each responding to different appeals: the housewife, the society woman, the club woman, and the working woman.[27] Even though Maule attempted to expand the menu of the ideal woman in the United States, these categories presented their own limitations. They do not fully account for women of color or immigrant women (to name a few of the obvious omissions). Yet one would not expect Maule to acknowledge or include these groups since they were not part of her social or political experience. For example, these women would not have been her peers in suffrage work or classmates in college. In addition, and most importantly, they would not have been considered acceptable subjects for ads in the mainstream white media during this time.

Nonetheless, Maule's conceptions of these limited categories provides a way to explore the social issues of the time by comparing such typing to the age, gender, and demographic niche targeting in advertising according to contemporary norms and social theory. Her categorical conceptions also reveal the paradox or double consciousness of entering a profession that had already absorbed the practices of the dominant male hegemony.

Maule was limited in her own attempts at creating broader, more inclusive categories of the female consumer even as she was attempting to expand her own opportunities in the business world.

Also relevant to Maule's attempt to expand the definition of the ideal woman and the limitations of this effort is an advice manual she wrote for women seeking jobs in the advertising business. Published in 1934, Maule's *She Strives to Conquer: Business Behavior, Opportunities, and Job Requirements for Women* describes the advertising world as full of opportunities for women because advertisers had recognized the importance of a woman's point of view. Even the witty play of the title on the famous play *She Stoops to Conquer* announces a feminist tilt. The book, however, emphasizes personal appearance more than business opportunities and the improvements in the workplace brought about by modernity.

For example, Maule dedicates four chapters to the modification, presentation, and restraint of the physical self—in fact, echoing much of what was popular copy in cosmetic and personal hygiene product advertisements of the day.[28] Victorian notions of ladylike behavior resonate in Maule's descriptions of restraining the physical. Her book is not completely different from the "dress for success" advice of today. Yet Maule's manual should be read as more of a justification for women's presence in advertising than as an advice manual for women who want to enter the industry (though it would be instructive in defense of those women entering the field). Maule and her colleagues must have had to justify their presence at JWT daily. What better way to justify their presence than to use the argument already in existence and the argument that JWT used itself in its ads marketing the Women's Editorial Department? By describing the ideal female advertiser—using language similar to ad copy appealing to the female consumer—Maule attempts to make a space for female advertisers in a male-dominated field. Through a close reading of Maule's work, from marketing and advertising to advice manual, it is possible to gain insight into the way in which these women "advertised" their own feminine touch to their colleagues. In doing so, they simultaneously sold the notion that a feminine presence and intuition were essential in the workplace—even in a workplace that placed much more emphasis on scientific research and methods.

Ruth Waldo, one of the most prominent women at JWT, was a graduate of Adelphi College and Columbia University. She was twenty-nine years old and single when she applied at JWT in 1915. There are no answers to the questions about her nationality or father's occupation on her application, although we know she was a Quaker through other archival materials such as the "Thumbnail Sketch" in the JWT newsletter. She had an extensive background in social work and worked for organizations such as the Bureau of Social Research, the Harlem and Jefferson County offices of the New York Charity Organization Society, and the Russell Sage Foundation. When asked on her application what her ambition was, she replied, "To be always moving ahead, to feel that I am accomplishing something, to be part of a successful business; that is why I wish to leave social work, as I feel in a rut, and why I wish to go into advertising, as I believe that it moves."[29] The accounts she worked on included Pond's, Standard Brands, Lever Brothers, Pharma-Craft, Scott Paper, Pacific Mills, Brillo, Alexander Smith, Libby Glass, Seth Thomas, E. R. Squibb, Sharpe & Dohme, Penick & Ford, Oneida Ltd., Craven A, Fish Advisory Council, and Ballantine Beer.[30] Waldo was the head of the copy department in London by 1922, the chief woman copywriter for the entire agency by 1930, and the first woman vice president of the agency by 1944.[31]

In a feature of the JWT newsletter called "How Well Do You Know Your JWT'ers? Thumbnail Sketch," Ruth Waldo recounts the story of her hiring at JWT: "I was sharing an apartment with Marie Beynon Lyons, the managing editor of *Vogue* at that time and Mr. Resor thought my clothes were much too *Vogue*-ish. I heard later that he laughingly said, 'All right, hire her, but I don't see how anybody with a hat like that and shoes like those could be any good.'"[32] This anecdote is interesting in how it reveals the attitudes of advertisers at this time. Waldo was part of a group of fashionable, sophisticated young women who were trendsetters in New York City. The managing editor position at *Vogue* was—and still is—a high-profile job in which one works with the fashion and business elite of New York City. Immigrant women, women of color, and working-class women did not have access to that position. Waldo was rooming with the managing editor of *Vogue* and was influenced by her attention to style. Stanley Resor's comment acknowledges that Waldo was fashionable—maybe too fashionable—but it does not seem to be a serious matter, for he agrees to hire her despite her shoes and hat. This incident affirms the class and race standard—and at the same time shows that there were limits on how fancy one could dress and still be acceptable in a business environment.

The importance of clothing as class markers at JWT should not be underestimated. What a hat or a pair of shoes signified had implications for the women who worked there. Just as today, these advertising men and women were especially cognoscente of outward appearance since they spent most of their days focusing on selling products that improved outward appearance in one way or another. They were in the business of encoding products, associating meaning with the products they advertised. Stanley Resor, for example, notices Waldo's hat and shoes, comments that they might be a bit too much, yet overlooks the concern—if it was really ever that much of a concern. Perhaps Resor's pause was an adjustment to the image of a woman with a distinct personality who was not going to be working as a secretary—a woman more easily dismissed. Resor seems to be implying that her outfit is not entirely businesslike, but there is also something recognizable to him in Waldo's fashionable outfit—a style (code) that Resor would have seen in his own social circles.

In Russell Pierce's memoir, *Gringo-Gaucho: An Advertising Odyssey*, this former JWT executive describes meeting some of the women copywriters in the New York City office just before his departure to work at the new JWT Buenos Aires office in 1929: "Now and then along Madison Avenue you would hear a catty reference to 'The Thompson Nuns,' . . . [w]hen I met them I saw nothing that would suggest the black habit of the sisterhood. They were all modishly dressed in the style of the 1920s."[33] Perhaps taking the comment about nuns a bit too literally, Pierce's comment does reflect the visual impact these women had, which included a carefully cultivated sense of style. The gossip circulating about the copywriters also conjures up an enigmatic and curiously desexualized group of influential women. Was the desexing a way to take some of the edge off the power these women held? Pierce's description of Lansdowne is worthy of note as well: "She was dressed elaborately, as if for a tea party or matinee, and wore a hat, a custom I soon perceived was followed by the women copywriters on the staff. Her dress was elegant, tastefully accommodating her mature figure. Although she was no beauty, she compelled attention. There was strength in the firm mouth. She wore no make-up. Apparently, she chose not to dramatize the large penetrating eyes nor to downplay a slightly prominent nose."[34] These descriptions of Lansdowne and her women copywriters reveal the conflicting emotions of men at JWT and other ad agencies. It is almost laughable—if only it still were not true of the way powerful women are described today.

Waldo, fully understanding the importance of clothing, used outward appearance as a signifier of class position and attempted to put the fashion system of meaning to her advantage at JWT. Resor's comment about Waldo's hat and Pierce's mention of Lansdowne's hat foreshadows a later incident at the agency involving class tensions between the copywriters and clerical staff. Waldo wanted to differentiate the Women's Editorial Department staff from the clerical staff at JWT. This attempt to mark class boundaries is not so surprising; after all, how many times must have male workers at JWT asked Waldo or her peers to make coffee or type a letter—mistaking them for one of the secretaries? This would have been insulting to the educated and ambitious women who had their own copywriting department at JWT.

In an attempt to mark their own territory, Waldo instituted an agency-wide dress code requesting that all Women's Editorial Department employees wear hats to work to differentiate them from the secretaries. In retaliation, the secretaries started to wear hats to work as well. Since all the women who worked at JWT were "white," no one could tell the difference; the hats enabled the secretaries to "pass" as middle or upper-middle class. This story reveals the class tensions that existed between women at JWT—tensions that were amplified by working side-by-side in an institution that allowed only well-educated and socially connected women to advance. It also reveals the lack of solidarity based solely on gender when issues of class come into play. The privileged copywriters were more interested in aligning themselves with the male executives—the legitimizing body of the institution—than with the working-class secretaries.

As noted, prior to applying for a job at JWT, Waldo was a social worker. In 1964 she told Sidney Berstein, a JWT company biographer, "Social work was different then, consisting mostly of practical actions in emergencies. If a man had tuberculosis we arranged to send him to a tuberculosis sanitarium and we could help his wife with a pension. We helped older people. If someone broke a leg and was in the hospital, we'd help his family out at home. But in many cases it was frustrating and depressing too, situations where it was up to the people themselves and if they couldn't help themselves, what could we do?"[35]

Waldo recounts how she had a friend in Canada who was doing well in advertising and how his enthusiasm kindled her curiosity. She went to *Harper's Bazaar* and talked to people there, one of whom knew Helen Lansdowne at JWT (evidence of Waldo's social connections). Waldo went to talk to Helen and Stanley Resor and, after her interview, was hired. When she went back to tell her social work colleagues, they were very upset with the news: "Ethically and morally, they were scandalized. You see, they thought it was fine to be helping people, but not to work to make money," said Waldo.[36]

The reaction of Waldo's social work colleagues to her career change is a good example of what women were probably up against as they moved into the business world. Not only were they facing the resistance of male co-workers, but also the disapproval of other women with whom they had once claimed a shared identity with in reform and suffrage work. Jennifer Scanlon says when writing about the women copywriters at JWT that "these women often approached their work with a missionary spirit about the consumer culture, a spirit many of them carried over from the progressive politics of their college educations, suffrage activities, or social work experiences. They saw their work not as exploitation but as a positive good."[37]

While this may have been true for a few of the women, it would be a mistake to view these advertising women as extending their missionary spirit from their reform or political careers to advertising. Their approach, more likely, was informed by their experience with marketing and advertising strategies learned during their careers as suffragists and social reformers, and, while they were college students, their exposure to the new fields of psychology and sociology. There was not a simple transference of women's "missionary spirit" from social work to advertising, but rather practical, day-to-day experiences with a consumer culture that influenced other aspects of their lives. Calling ambition a "missionary spirit" does not take into account the goals and desires of the Women's Editorial Department, and ignores the reach and overlap of consumer culture into political and social movements. What skills then did these women carry over from their careers in social work? What did they carry over from their college educations? Could the convergence of these two worlds contribute to their ability to navigate the business world, or did their experiences in traditionally female occupations only make entering the business world more appealing? Or difficult?

Ruth Waldo said that from the earliest days Lansdowne foresaw that the separation of women copywriters was its strength. She felt that women would not have achieved the positions of authority they did at JWT had Lansdowne not continued throughout the years to urge this separation with Stanley Resor:

> When a woman works for a man or in a men's group, she becomes less important, her opinion is worth less, her progress and advancement less rapid. Then she does not have the excitement and incentive to work as hard as she can, nor, in a men's group, does she get the full credit for what she does. . . . But with the knowledge and confidence of Mrs. Resor's support, a woman at Thompson could advance in her own group without having to compete with men for recognition of her ability. She has greater independence and freedom; a woman's ideas could be judged on their value alone. It was one less handicap.[38]

Though many of the women who worked at JWT graduated from women's colleges, Waldo did not. This opinion about separating women from men would have likely come directly from her work experience, including her experience in the female-dominated field of social work. Waldo saw the advantage of a separate department for women, a view she shared with Helen Lansdowne, who never attended college but instead went directly into the advertising field. Waldo and Lansdowne seem to have had other things in common as well.

As told to Sidney Berstein by an anonymous JWT officer, Stanley Resor was a very eligible bachelor, and office rumor had it that Ruth Waldo was a possible candidate to become Mrs. Stanley Resor. When Stanley married

Helen Lansdowne instead in 1917, it did not seem to upset things. The two women continued to work well together for forty years, often combining their forces to get their points across. "Once we were talking about a new product Waldo wanted to propose to Lever Brothers and she and Mr. Resor got into a violent argument, with real temper flashing. Finally, Mr. Resor stuck out his tongue at her and said: 'I'm glad I didn't marry you.' He was joking, but it was like Danny Danker said, 'It was kidding on the square.'"[39]

Nancy Stephenson, another prominent woman at JWT, said that "they [Waldo and Lansdowne] worked beautifully together; sometimes they worked together even against Stanley Resor. Waldo was lively, specific, an extrovert, determined, a fighter."[40] Those women—who had access to both Resors—thus had access to the top. And, Lansdowne's willingness to form alliances with some of the Women's Editorial Department staff to manipulate her husband gave the department an influence at the agency.

Aminta Gomes Casseres was also a copy head in the Women's Editorial Department. In a JWT newsletter profile of Casseres, a Colombian who grew up in Jamaica, she is described as *paradoxical*: "Believe it or not—Miss Casseres, the timid—shy as Madame Curie—quiet as a mouse—likes prize fighting and (during the suffrage campaign) was whole-heartedly for window smashing."[41] She is described as both "exotic" and as rejecting this exoticism: though she is different from the other women in the Women's Editorial Department in that she was not U.S. born, she was "educated by English people and has always been reticent about speaking Spanish," claims this article. Casseres was a graduate of Barnard College where she achieved a reputation as a brilliant writer who claimed that "American girls seemed queer to her." However, Casseres claimed that she liked "queer places, queer people and queer things." Perhaps she also fit into the environment at JWT because she "belonged to the landed gentry." Her home in Connecticut is described in detail, as is her attention to detail in home decorating and in her personal style, which is described as "straight out of *Vogue*."[42]

The complexities of identity are personified in this profile of Casseres. Despite her timidness, she is passionate about suffrage. Despite being born in Colombia, brought up in Jamaica, and speaking Spanish as her first language, she insists that she prefers to speak English (not a surprising comment considering the audience of this piece—her peers at JWT). And despite her ambition and interest in smashing traditional sex roles, she made a rather unusual argument against using a pretty woman in a Simmons Mattress ad that featured a man. In 1930, at a staff meeting, Casseres tried to dissuade a group of her peers from taking a stereotypical approach to the ad, which was about sleeping positions. Some in the meeting asked Casseres, "Why don't we have a pretty girl pose in these postures?" Casseres explained, "I am against having a pretty girl because I think the pictures we have are very scientific, really laboratory pictures; they have a scientific significance that a pretty girl in pretty pajamas will not have. I am willing to grant that the male of the species is the species and the female is just a variation. I feel that we should show men in the illustration if the advertising is to be sincere and true."[43]

Is it surprising that a well-educated woman, passionate about suffrage, would make an argument that women are a variation of the male species? In this context it was a smart way to sell a product—not based on sex, but based on a warped sense of science (and using the masculinist, scientific rhetoric learned at JWT) that would appeal to the senior men advertising executives. It may also have been another way of arguing against using a "cheesecake" model in the ad, which was Casseres's method of facing the challenge of navigating an ideology that both privileged women, such as her, and oppressed women, in general, faced. She seems to have been quite successful in this; as evidence of her success in navigating JWT's corporate culture, Casseres was called a "swell advertising man" in a JWT company publication.[44] A high compliment, but again, the ad woman is desexed—or, to be more precise, resexed.

Casseres worked in the London office in the early 1930s, where she oversaw the development of the Pond's campaign. In a letter from Stanley Resor dated February 18, 1931, Resor asks Casseres to stay in London to get Pond's off to a good start. In this same letter, he goes on to say that he agrees with her about taking the Pond's campaign to Berlin. In a letter from Sam Meek, dated one day prior to Stanley Resor's, he outlines Casseres's work in London: "Miss Casseres completed her review of Pond's material . . . she is acting as a member of the Review Board while she is here . . . and has recently completed her review of Lux Flakes, Rinso and McVitie and Price. As soon as these are out of the way she is planning to review GM [General Motors], Lloyd's Bank, Cutex, and Kraft Mayonnaise. She is also working on the solicitation of the Gillette business."[45] In her international work, Casseres seems to have moved beyond working strictly on accounts for women's products, as her work on GM and Lloyd's Bank indicates.

Casseres's ability to finesse an argument and navigate office politics at JWT enabled her, like Waldo, to work on accounts other than cosmetics and household products. Her position in London attests to the fact that she had the respect of Stanley Resor, who trusted her to develop the Pond's campaign there. Though she is described as timid, shy, and quiet in the JWT newsletter article, she nonetheless had the ability to get her point across in a way that worked in this particular corporate environment. The

JWT newsletter, a tool that maintained and perpetuated agency culture, presents Casseres as fiercely opinionated (she is all for breaking windows in the name of suffrage) yet timid. It balances out her more obvious ethnic and radical attributes so that her story is appropriate to circulate throughout the agency. Casseres was surely aware of how best to present herself in this article, as is seen in her remarks about preferring to speak English and bringing up important cultural markers of class (Barnard, landed gentry, personal style straight out of *Vogue*). Despite being Colombian, Casseres fit in with the other women at JWT because of her privileged background. And, it appears that in Casseres's case, this background superseded ethnicity and race.

Others among the women at JWT lived a woman-centered life in Greenwich Village. Copywriter **Edith Lewis** lived there for many years with her longtime companion, novelist Willa Cather. Lewis was born in Lincoln, Nebraska, where her father worked in real estate. She described her nationality as "American" and her religion as "Christian."[46] These answers to the two questions about nationality and religion, common in the majority of women in the Women's Editorial Department during this period, were the "correct" answers, so to speak, for anyone applying for work at JWT during that time. Of course, there was no question about the applicant's race, an omission that signifies the agency's complete confidence that no one of color would apply.

Lewis earned a degree in French literature and history in 1903 from Smith College, and her job application shows that she already had a fair amount of experience in publishing and in the magazine world before coming to JWT. She worked for Cromwell Publishing in New York City as the managing editor of *Every Week* and prior to that worked at *McClure's Magazine* as the literary editor and acting managing editor. At *McClure's* she also held positions as proofreader, art editor, and makeup editor. Lewis must have learned quite a bit about advertising in these jobs since she responded to the application question, "What experience especially fits you for this position?" by saying, "My thorough knowledge of every branch of advertising work."[47] Edith Lewis probably was not motivated by a "missionary spirit" at JWT, where she worked from 1919 to 1948. Her many years of advertising experience in publishing and in magazine editing served as the basis of her qualification and desire to join the women at JWT.

Just as some of the JWT women lived outside of the middle-class convention of their times, Lewis's relationship with Willa Cather showed her dedication to living a woman-centered life. Both Frances Maule, who also lived in Greenwich Village, and Lewis shared their apartments with women lovers or friends while several other applicants listed women as housemates as well.[48] Lewis lived with Cather in Manhattan for forty years. JWT archival materials describe Lewis as one of the best copywriters and as being "devoted" to Cather, and it is with pride that JWT mentions the works of Cather. Lewis was a group head and handled a number of large beauty accounts, including Pond's Cold and Vanishing Creams.[49]

Women-centered relationships may have been even more important for these copywriters as they navigated the masculinist corporate culture of JWT. Frances Maule and her sister, novelist and suffrage lecturer Florence Maule Updegraff, were members of Heterodoxy, a "band of willful women" in New York City. According to some historians, Heterodoxy members were among the first to use "feminism" in a self-conscious and deliberate way.[50] The group also included women more well-known than the Maule sisters: feminist lecturer and writer Charlotte Perkins Gilman, lawyer and social activist Crystal Eastman, and black leader and National Association for the Advancement of Colored People member Grace Neil Johnson.[51] Part of the already established Greenwich Village community of artists and intellectuals, the Heterodoxy women pushed the boundaries of middle-class womanhood in the early twentieth century, which included living women-centered lives.

As indicated earlier, Barnard College was in the background for many of these women. For example, **Margaret King**, JWT's second female vice president, attended Barnard before taking a job in the research department at JWT and prior to moving on to the Women's Editorial Department. JWT copywriters Aminta Casseres, **Janet Fox Wing**, and **Jean Graham Townley** graduated from Barnard as did **Isabel Black**, whose "inclination for the ordered sentence, complete with punctuation, was developed to zealotism" there. Black was also group head of the large Lux soap accounts.[52]

Evelyn Dewey, who started work as a copywriter at JWT in 1922 at the age of thirty-three, enrolled at Smith College but transferred to Barnard one year later, where she studied psychology and education. She worked at both the Lincoln School and the Russell Sage Foundation in New York City, where she investigated and wrote about working girls. One of her jobs after graduating was as the director of a psychological study conducted in New York City by the Russell Sage Foundation. She started as a "mental tester" and statistician, and, as she says on her application to JWT, she "contributed to the accuracy of the science of mental testing and to the criticism of such data."[53] While Dewey obviously benefited from her background in psychology at Barnard and went on to put her knowledge to use in her subsequent jobs, she ultimately had a desire to work in the advertising field. This career choice was not so far afield from conducting psychological surveys since the advertising industry was already using findings from psychology in marketing. These women may have had an interest in the suffrage movement or social reform, yet it may not have been the dominant force in their work life.

Many of the Women's Editorial Department staff, for example, went directly from college to working in the business world—albeit in the more female-oriented sectors. **Esther Eaton**, a 1905 graduate of Vassar, worked at Wanamaker's department store in advertising and in public relations for the Girl Scouts national headquarters in New York City. **Annette Anderson** graduated from Wellesley in 1922 and came to work at JWT in 1939. Prior to JWT, Anderson worked at *Home, Inc.* magazine as a writer and editor. **Ann Blackshear**, who worked for Aminta Casseres as a copywriter, had a background in retail advertising at B. Altman and Macy's department stores. **Helen Brown** came to work for JWT in 1924. A University of Cincinnati graduate, Brown worked at Procter & Collier in Cincinnati as a copywriter and for the *Cincinnati Post* as a reporter and editor of its women's page. **Mary Loomis Cook** attended Miami University and the University of Pennsylvania before going to work at Wanamaker's and Marshall Field's department stores as a copywriter. **Margaret Brown**, a Wellesley graduate, worked at Bamberger's department store. She started at JWT as a copywriter in 1919. **Helen Buckler** attended the University of Illinois and worked as a secretary at *The Nation* and as a feature and general news writer for *The Paris Times*. **Monica Barry O'Shea** graduated from Bryn Mawr then worked at the Butterick Publishing Company in advertising and as a correspondent. **Mary Tucker** went to Northwestern and Columbia University. After graduating, she worked as an associate editor at *Designer Magazine*, in advertising at Saks & Company in New York City, as an editor for *Vogue*, and in public relations for the Greenbriar Hotel in White Sulfur Springs, West Virginia.[54]

No doubt their experience in writing and editing in publishing and public relations enabled these women to do well at JWT. And, moving out of retail advertising into an advertising agency was a step up in their careers. In reading the names of magazines and department stores at which these women worked, one gets the "small world" sense of a group of connected women; for example, Mary Tucker was at *Vogue*, as was Ruth Waldo's roommate. Waldo heard about the Women's Editorial Department through friends in both advertising and magazine publishing. The information she gained through her connections enabled her to do well in the application and interview process, and this was probably true for many of the women who applied to work in Lansdowne's department. Basically, there were two streams of talent coming into the Women's Editorial Department: women who worked in publishing, retail advertising, public relations, and journalism, and women who had careers in the suffrage movement or social reform.

Though Frances Maule is probably the most well known woman at JWT with a former career in the suffrage movement, other women came to JWT with a background in women's politics. JWT copywriter **Agnes Foote Campbell**, a graduate of Vassar, worked as a field organizer for the New Jersey branch of the National Women's Party and the Congressional Union for Women's Suffrage in Washington, DC. **Lucille Platt** studied political science at Mt. Holyoke before working at the Rhode Island League of Girls' Clubs as a fund-raiser. **Therese Olzendam** graduated from the University of Vermont, then worked as a secretary at the National Women's Party in New York City and as the circulation manager of *The Suffragist* at the National Women's Party in Washington, DC. **Helen Thompson**, a graduate of the University of Chicago, worked as a social worker making family visits, which she described "as pretty depressing." She also worked at Marshall Field's department store in Chicago as a copywriter, an event planner, and fashion show coordinator. It seems that Thompson found her work at Marshall Field's less depressing than social work since she decided to make a career for herself in the world of advertising and promotion. **Gertrude Coit** graduated from Smith College and did graduate work in social work at Columbia University and the New School for Social Research. She worked as a supervisor at College Settlement, as well as an executive manager at Madison House, both in New York City.[55]

Many feminists during this period were interested in consumer culture—and not just as advocates of consumers, but as consumers themselves and of users of advertising and public relation strategies for their causes. It is not surprising then that some of the women who went to work at JWT had careers in the suffrage movement where they accumulated experience as advertisers for their movement. For example, Frances Maule on her employment application writes about her experience in general promotional work for the publication of the National Women's Suffrage Association and her work in the creation of suffrage literature and in a small line of suffrage novelties. Maule's experience with promotional work in the suffrage movement is not uncommon. Though not commonly acknowledged by historians, there was overlap and connection between the suffrage movement and consumer culture.

Feminism, Suffrage, and Consumer Culture

The appropriation of the women's movement by consumer culture is most famously portrayed by Virginia Slim's slogan: "You've come a long way, baby!" This ad plays on women's rights with photos illustrating, for example, a nineteenth-century woman hiding behind the barn to have a smoke only to have a bucket of water dumped on her head. The message is that women have come a long way since it was considered unladylike to smoke—now women have the "right" to smoke. Advertisers have learned to appropriate the political power of personal choice for women to the consumerist power of choice in deciding which cigarette to buy.

The ideology of consumer culture in the twenty-first century has, in fact, widely absorbed the messages of the feminist movement and appropriates the language of choice for female consumers. The women at JWT who had careers in the suffrage movement and social reform experienced consumer culture in a different way, but they incorporated some of the marketing and advertising strategies that they had used in their suffrage work.

The Women's Editorial Department staff who had careers in the suffrage movement exemplified the adaptation of activist women to an increasingly urban, commercial, consumer capitalist environment. In many ways this adaptation developed into full-scale appropriation. Historian Margaret Finnegan points out that during the 1910s suffragists incorporated modern methods of advertising, public relations, mass merchandising, and mass entertainment into their fight for voting rights. They adopted commercial standards of design and display. Suffragists also added their own slant to capitalism's consumerist thrust by reworking basic assumptions into their ideology. For example, when industries tried to sell goods by extolling women's public presence, suffragists turned this approbation into a justification for expanding the boundaries of women's space into the public realm of politics. And when department stores, manufacturers, and a changing society made consumption central to middle-class women's lives, suffragists turned their roles as shoppers into arguments for granting women the ballot. Blending political aspirations with everyday duties, suffragists redefined both voter and shopper, making both terms synonymous with responsible, rational, and empowering action.[56]

The overlapping boundaries of commercial and political culture are evident in the lives of the women who worked in the Women's Editorial Department at JWT. In an age of mass culture and consumerism, neither the women who were politically active nor the women who worked in the culture industries (publishing, public relations, retail advertising, and so forth) could escape the effects of that culture.

In fact, the women who had careers in the suffrage movement and in social reform were quite savvy in the way they appropriated consumer ideology. The Women's Editorial Department certainly appropriated the concept of female consumer in arguing that by possessing female intuition women had the upper hand when writing ads for women's products. In other words, since the female consumer represented the majority of the market, space should be made for women in advertising to specifically address the needs of that market—to tap into the hearts and minds of the female consumer. Though it is unlikely that this argument alone—without the backing of Helen Lansdowne—would have worked.

We have seen how Frances Maule used this strategy in her advice book to women advertisers by focusing on the physical appearance of women and using the language commonly used in ads targeting female consumers. Maule appropriated the ideology of consumerism to argue for women's presence in advertising. JWT women had worked in retail advertising as well, and suffragists were emulating some the department stores' merchandising tactics in their own work. Both groups of women, although at different ends of the spectrum, were trained in merchandising. Lansdowne not only understood these women—both the copywriters who had been suffrage workers and the copywriters who had worked in retail and publishing—but also shared their politics and ambition.

Helen Lansdowne's secretary later remembered the day that Lansdowne organized women at the JWT office to take part in a large suffrage parade in New York City: "Mrs. Resor got us all big campaign hats to wear of various colors—green, purple, white. Mine was white." Lansdowne's secretary also recounted that Augusta Nicoll, one of the Women's Editorial Department staff members, dressed in white and rode a white horse in the parade.[57] In getting her female staff hats with the colors used by the suffrage movement, Lansdowne acknowledged the brand of the movement and showed the movement's successful branding efforts.

The use of these three particular colors demonstrates the influence of the British Suffrage Movement since purple, white, and green were the colors used by the Women's Social and Political Union (WSPU). The WSPU was headed by Emmeline Pankhurst, who is generally considered to be the most influential of all the British suffragists.[58] Actively participating in consumer culture is the thread that connects the women at JWT's Women's Editorial Department during the early twentieth century. The effects of a capitalist consumer culture and the politics of suffrage are seen in the ways that the women at JWT struggled in and adapted to their roles as advertisers—and especially in how they came to work in the advertising field.

In terms of their political outreach strategies, nonradical suffragists adapted and appropriated consumer ideology to the benefit of the movement. Mainstream suffrage publications, such as *Woman Voter*, invited department stores to advertise in their pages. *The Woman's Journal* employed advertising agents.[59] Suffragists emulated advertising strategies and purveyed the "art of publicity," as JWT copywriter Frances Maule did in her suffrage work and mentioned in her job application. They devised suffrage billboards and posters, calendars and movies, and conducted great parades and pageants, in which the women at JWT participated.

Like liberal and leftist political activists in other countries, American non-radical feminists relied on an aesthetic politics of mass spectacle that imitated the practices forged by the urban merchant class. Suffragists used advertising space in streetcars, where they tacked up vivid placards. Stores everywhere volunteered their windows and their interiors for suffrage advertising. Wanamaker's set a precedent by permitting all female employees to march in suffrage parades during working hours. In 1912, suffragists chose Macy's in New York as the headquarters for suffrage supplies, including marching gowns, bonnets, and hatpins.[60] Many of the JWT women copywriters actually had worked in these very department stores, some of them participated in the suffrage parades, and it is possible that others created the displays for the suffrage supplies while employees there.

Women's rights leaders published magazines that reflected the clear merger of feminism, marked by a secular, international perspective, with the cosmopolitan, heterogeneous culture of consumption. The magazine *Madame*, printed in Indianapolis as the official organ of the National Council of Women, appeared in 1903. Similar to *Harper's Bazaar*, *Madame* mixed articles on jewelry, cosmetics, food, theater, and department stores with descriptions of woman's advancement in public life. Also in 1903, the short-lived *American Business Woman's Magazine*, the first of its kind in America, was published in Denver, Colorado. It was followed in 1915 by a hardier version, *Business Woman's Magazine*, a Manhattan periodical that was kindred to the official bulletin of the National Federation of Business and Professional Women's Clubs, the *Independent Woman*, in print four years later. These magazines promoted a liberal, individualistic feminism and described the businesswoman as the "new feminist" who sought to release herself from all restraints and to enjoy life to the fullest. "The businesswoman is who extracts from life its best flower and romance. The modern girl wants to come into contact with the live forces of the busy old world which is moving every day."[61] This quote also describes the women who worked for Helen Lansdowne at JWT. It certainly expresses their desire to be part of a busy world that is "moving every day" and that offers them the possibility of liberation from traditional female occupations. The Women's Editorial Department staff aspired to be businesswomen and to create new roles for women in the business world.

Many feminists had some connection with the commercial world, and still others were attracted to urban centers. In 1916, Elsa Maxwell and Alva Belmont, the president of the Congressional Union for Woman Suffrage, wrote a fund-raising operetta, *Melinda and Her Sister*. Alva Belmont, who had strong connections to consumer culture, as a suffragist and through marriage into the elite class, was later signed by JWT copywriter Edith Lewis to endorse Pond's Cold Cream in a JWT testimonial ad. Maxwell acquired fame as a columnist and party giver.[62] Recognizing the connections between the commercial and the political helps to explain how Edith Lewis was able to convince Alva Belmont to endorse Pond's Cold Cream—an endorsement that, on the surface, seems antithetical to a feminist ideology. The connections between consumer culture, suffrage, and feminism add up to a larger continuity of culture—not only a new space in the public realm but a "new woman's world."

The career paths of the JWT women reflect their increasing interest in advertising, public relations, and the business world in general. Whether they were working in department stores, at magazines, in publishing, social reform, or in the suffrage movement, they were affected by, creating, and contributing to consumer culture in the United States—and by the end of the 1920s at JWT, globally. Their educational backgrounds, which were influenced by the institution of sociology and psychology as academic disciplines, were instrumental in that they provided a base for their work in advertising. Findings from psychology and sociology were already incorporated into advertising and marketing strategies by the time the Women's Editorial Department was formed.

Some of the JWT women who had former careers in social work found that work depressing and longed for higher pay, greater respect, and excitement. Some of the women who were already writing copy at department stores or worked as editors at magazines or in publishing houses seemed to long for a work environment where women were mentored and given a chance to do the same work as men. JWT and Helen Lansdowne provided this environment. By the time the advertising women at JWT entered the industry, some universities and colleges had already created opportunities for women and altered women's expectations in important ways—ways that broadened freedom for women and gave them a more open-ended sense of their own capacities. Many women learned in college that they could indeed compete with men on an intellectual level.

The suffrage movement—a major force in the lives of the JWT women—also employed methods of advertising, public relations, and merchandising to win political support. The women at the forefront of the movement, after all, were faced with designing and coordinating mass public relations campaigns. They had to educate themselves in the ways of marketing both to reach a wide audience and, on more local levels, to orchestrate parades, create advertisements for public display, design suffrage literature, and publish suffrage magazines. One could certainly imagine Frances Maule supporting the image of the businesswoman as the "new feminist." Helen Lansdowne, also a supporter of the suffrage movement, combined her feminist beliefs and business acumen to create a space for other women to enter the advertising world.

The women who worked at JWT in the Women's Editorial Department lived through a time of tremendous change in the United States. As historian Alice Kessler-Harris argues, at the turn of the nineteenth century, public life was male and individualism was a male aspiration. By 1915, that paradigm had been weakened by the transformation of work. It must have been exhilarating for these women to be part of an advertising department led by a woman who championed their role in the department. During their tenure there, the women at JWT made valuable contributions to the agency and enabled it to grow into the largest advertising agency in the world.

Yet although opportunities for women were expanding, there were limits on the gains women were able to make in the business world. Conflicting forces at work in the business world (women entering the public male-dominated business world) resulted in paradoxical circumstances (the "need" for women in advertising to tell advertisers what women want). Women found themselves arguing against sex stereotypes while reinforcing others in their own work. They faced the limits of their own social and economic backgrounds while they struggled to find beauty and comfort in a consumer world.

2

"Good Looks Supremacy"

Advertising an American Ideal Beauty

If people of color ruled the world, white people would curl their hair and darken their skin.

—Chandler Owen, editor of the *Messenger*[1]

Among the Nigerian Wodaabes, the women hold economic power and the tribe is obsessed with male beauty; Wodaabe men spend hours together in elaborate makeup sessions, and compete—provocatively painted and dressed, with swaying hips and seductive expressions—in beauty contests judged by women.

——Naomi Wolf, *The Beauty Myth*

Americans spend more each year on beauty than they do on education.

—"The Beauty Business: Pots of Promise," *The Economist*, May 22, 2003

By the time the women who worked as copywriters at J. Walter Thompson (JWT) graduated from college, they had already been exposed to a relentless focus on the female body. In securing a place in academia, women in the late nineteenth and early twentieth centuries were subject to extreme bodily surveillance by parents, college administrators and faculty, and physicians. This surveillance carried on the tradition of a monitored and regulated female body through a Victorian "cult of domesticity" and "true womanhood" that insisted on female demureness in the public sphere for middle-class women.

Dr. Edward Clarke, a retired Harvard medical professor who was especially concerned about women's admittance into higher education (particularly Harvard Medical School), had put forth a widely accepted idea in his book *Sex in Education; or, A Fair Chance for the Girls*, that "a girl could study and learn but she could not do all this and retain uninjured health, and a future secure from neuralgia, uterine disease, hysteria, and other derangements of the nervous system."[2] Clarke's claim was ostensibly supported by case studies from his own practice that illustrated the negative effects that overtaxing the brain had on a woman's reproductive system, which, of course, also disrupted women's prescribed social role.

The surveillance of female college students' bodies on campus came about as a way to prove that Clarke and others who shared his views were wrong to say that educating women would harm them. College students wrote home, sometimes daily, filling their letters with details about their food intake and daily exercise programs, aches and pains, and physical exam results. College presidents also reported on students' health: Reverend L. Clark Seelye, Smith College's first president, included a report on the status of students' health on the first page of every annual report from 1875 to 1910.[3] Historian Margaret Lowe shows in her study of college women during this time that—not surprisingly—the concept of "body image" emerged.[4] The developing and proliferating mass media—such as women's magazines—during this period supported the focus on women's bodies and their faces and contributed to building a kind of panopticon[5] of bodily surveillance. This echoed the surveillance already in place at women's colleges and in most women's lives.

By the early twentieth century, the hypervigilant focus on women's bodies due to the belief in part that academic pursuits would interfere with reproduction began to subside. Yet other anxieties about women's bodies would soon take the place of the Victorian anxiety about women's reproduction. New anxieties developed out of a focus on preventing social embarrassment often associated with class position, which many products promised to do.

The first group of influential women copywriters at JWT (Edith Lewis, Aminta Gomes Casseres, Isabel Black, Ruth Waldo, Margaret King, and Elizabeth Devree) had graduated from college after the turn of the twentieth century just as this shift was taking place. Many of the Victorian customs were still in place, however, and these women had been exposed to them in college. For example, Greek-inspired games at Barnard were a popular annual event, and at other women's colleges there were extremely strict rules about deportment. Helen Lansdowne gave them all a chance to become real "New Women," not just the image of a concept in the pages of a magazine.

These pioneering ad women were pulled in two directions. On the one hand, there were still people of influence like Dr. Clarke, and a wider debate about women's health and abilities was raging. On the other, these women were influenced by the growing consumer culture. In both cases, middle-class white women were the center of attention. We know how engrossed the JWT copywriters were by consumer culture because in their interview at the company they were asked to write a comprehensive analysis of advertisements in current magazines to convey what made those ads appealing. Their familiarity with women's magazines means that they were also aware of the "New Woman" who began appearing in magazines around this time. This "new" woman was a college student, she was an athlete, she drove cars, and she socialized with her friends in public places. Though Victorian restrictions on behavior and dress still had influence, those old-fashioned ideas were beginning to lose power.

The influence of women's magazines on the ad women at JWT cannot be underestimated. Isabel Black had worked as an assistant fashion editor at *Vogue* before starting at JWT in 1929. Ruth Waldo's roommate, Marie Beynon Lyons, was the managing editor at *Vogue*, which seemed to have an effect on Waldo's style. Waldo was known for her love of hats, and even Stanley Resor commented on her fashionable appearance saying that Waldo's clothes were "too *Vogue*-ish."[6] In 1922, the Paris editor of *Vogue*, Madame Lucien Vogel, was the guest and speaker at the New York JWT office,[7] bringing, no doubt, the style and influence that position still exerts in the world of fashion and design. To one copywriter, *Vogue* seemed to be at the top of the food chain of consumer influencers. Mary Tucker said, "I can't honestly say that *Vogue* changes for anybody or anything."[8]

Vogue, indeed, has been a force in promoting fashionable desires for more than a century. Pick up the latest issue and experience the full force of consumer culture—aspire to look like the models, to wear the designer clothes, to live the lifestyles of featured celebrities. This making of aspirations to another life in women's magazines works in conjunction with the aspirational tone in many of JWT's beauty and household product ad campaigns. The same psychological appeal was apparent in ads as well as the editorial content of women's magazines in the early twentieth century. This desire to transform oneself in line with an image of beauty, sexual allure, and stylishness is still a dominant appeal in ads today. Although many other companies and forces contributed to the supremacy of this appeal, JWT's ad women, mentored and led by Helen Lansdowne, can be credited with breaking ground in making it so.

As students, the influential copywriters became part of a consumer culture that effectively told women exactly what was wrong or right with their faces and their bodies. Once they graduated, many of them had careers in the emerging American media before making their way to JWT. In a sense, perhaps they always had been in training for their role as copywriters. By virtue of being female, they were subject to close examination of their appearance and behavior. Many of the copywriters undoubtedly brought the focus on ideal beauty that the magazines and other media so consistently illustrated in their ad campaigns. The female copywriters at JWT knew more than just what women wanted—they knew women's fears, their ambitions, their desires, and their insecurities. They knew the pressures, first hand, of being a "modern woman." Although, if becoming a modern woman in the early twentieth century had its liberating aspects, the flip was the limitations imposed by a dominating consumer culture that in part thrived on human insecurities in a changing landscape.

The Seductions of Shared Identity through Consumer Culture

To varying degrees, college students, immigrants, the working class, and African American women were all able to imagine themselves as part of a homogenous consumer community through consumer culture. Many of these women, for example, could afford a ten-cent jar of Pond's Cold Cream or to flip through the pages of an inexpensive woman's magazine and dream of a new dress. Women who cleaned houses or worked on the factory line could share in a consumer identity with the wealthy women who endorsed Pond's creams through the purchase of those creams at retail outlets or by ordering sample sizes through the mail. Many women experienced this community as a member of a burgeoning middle class that marked its territory, so to speak, through consumption. But others who were not middle class also participated in the new mass production and democratization of consumer goods. In that way, they answered the hopes of the product manufacturers and marketers of beauty who wanted to gain as broad a share of the market as possible without losing the sheen of satisfying aspirations.

The construction of an American mass identity by way of marketing accelerates rapidly at the turn of the twentieth century. This identity, however, was narrowly defined, yet for those women who did not meet the standard requirements of the ideal beauty, consumer culture was ready with instructions for how to achieve the look. Although the emerging mass consumer identity was facilitated by the large scale and well-known changes (industrialization, urbanization, and secularization in modernity), it is also identifiable in everyday experiences such as reading a glossy women's magazine, reading the newspaper, shopping in a department store, or viewing a film.

Those experiences are on-the-ground examples of the working of such forces with the advantage that they can be understood in quantifiable and concrete terms on the level of individual women as well as large groups of women. The advertising industry is especially important because of the alertness of its star workers to a wide variety of cultural bellwethers such as fine art, movies, magazines and because the ad business, through constant contact with diverse business clients, is attuned to the newest of the new in many industries.

Creating the American Beauty "Type"

Women had a hand not only in advertising an ideal beauty—as JWT's women copywriters did with their work on ads for beauty and household products—they also had a hand in the creation of images that supported an ideal version of feminine beauty. These images included the cover art that appeared on popular women's magazines in the mid-nineteenth to the early twentieth century. The proliferation of these images introduced variations on iconic female images and contributed to a system of signification highlighting the modern woman. The cover art of a magazine is its most prominent advertisement for ideal beauty, and the images and text within the magazine in articles and ads supports and echoes the cover art.

Historian Carolyn Kitch's research traces the origins of visual stereotypes in mass media and shows that women illustrators were responsible for much of the cover art of women's magazines. Kitch claims that during the late nineteenth century a kind of "visual vocabulary" of feminine beauty, that now seems natural, was created.[9] Just as Helen Lansdowne and her group of female copywriters contributed to an American concept of ideal beauty through ad images and text, women artists such as Alice Barber Stephens (*Ladies' Home Journal, Scribner's, Cosmopolitan, Life, Century, Leslie's Weekly,* and *Harper's*), Jessie Willcox Smith (*Good Housekeeping*) and Neysa McMein (*Saturday Evening Post, Woman's Home Companion, McCall's*) created magazine cover art that contributed to an ideal beauty that the whole of the magazine embodied. Jessie Wilcox Smith was the exclusive cover artist for *Good Housekeeping* from 1918 all the way to 1933. Neysa McMein was the exclusive cover artist for *McCall's* from 1923 to 1937. She helped to create the image of the confident and independent "New Woman" depicted as "an individual in a modern world."[10]

These were not the only women whose artwork shaped the vision of women and femininity during the early twentieth century, however. While women at JWT were neither art directors, nor account representatives, advertisers did employ female illustrators on a freelance basis.

Mary McKinnon was one of the first female illustrators hired by JWT. She worked on the important Lux Soap Flakes campaign during the mid-1910s. Elizabeth Shippen Green, Lucille Patterson Marsh, Maude Tousey Fangel, and Helen Dryden all worked on a freelance basis for JWT and produced award-winning illustrations for JWT clients during the 1920s.[11] Women illustrators and copywriters at JWT worked in tandem to produce some of the most well known and successful ad campaigns in the twentieth century for national and international companies. Elite tastemakers and entertainers mingled in this emerging world of new media. As important as magazine illustrators were, they had a great deal of help creating the imagery of women that in altered form still prevails in much media, and the contribution of the ad women at JWT is important to the story.

The new images appear out of the imaginations of artists and advertisers and the ideological beliefs and values held by them and their clients. The symbiotic relationship between advertising and women's magazines, however, extended beyond business to shaping ideas about what it meant to be "American." That vision was styled to prop up a consensus on identity, not controversy, because as noted earlier, in this period advertisers' goals were still primarily to broaden the market for a product as much as possible. And advertisers were quick to seize on spreading a consensus view of the American image through all media open to them. Once radio became a popular medium, advertising ruled there as well. Advertising became a part of the American landscape from billboards to newspapers, from the airwaves to the highways.

In her study of American beauty, Lois Banner identifies the ideal woman of the early nineteenth century as the "Steel-Engraving Lady."[12] This icon of ideal beauty got her name from mass-produced lithographs marketed by Currier and Ives and personified in magazines such as *Godey's Lady's Book*. The image of a delicate lady, petite, white, young, thin, with a heart or oval-shaped face, was supported by a plethora of beauty and etiquette manuals, medical advice books, and women's magazines—all of which lent legitimacy to the idea that women were destined by nature to be passive and dependent.[13] The Steel-Engraving Lady represented passivity and dependence, which was in that era presented as woman's "natural" role.

Banner traces the lineage of this image of ideal beauty to the late Middle Ages, "a product of Eastern influences brought home to Europe by the crusaders and of the veneration of women that was central to the cult of chivalry."[14] An understanding of the context of this creation reveals the connections between nations and women, which are ultimately consumed by a large audience through popular culture. Without representation in mass media, however, this image has no power, no influence.

Historians have traced images of ideal beauty in the United States that appear in popular culture. Some have identified various types from Banner's "Steel-Engraving Lady" (Antebellum years) to the post-Civil War "Voluptuous Woman," to the "Gibson Girl" (1890s) and the "Flapper" (1910s).[15] In an evolution toward the "New Woman," the height of the "American Girl" image (1895–1915) was represented by social types such as the "Beautiful Charmer," the "Outdoor Pal" (Figure 2.1), the "Winged Angel," and the "Amazon Queen." As abstractions and symbolic forms, these types actually represent national values: woman as "virtue," woman as "civilization," and woman as "progress."[16] Eventually, these types evolved into the "New Woman" image that appears in the early twentieth century in cover art and in advertisements.

The cultural construct of the "New Woman" stood for changes in women's lives as well as changes in the United States. The New Woman seemed to alter perceptions of what women could be and do. She was active, often shown playing sports or riding a bicycle; though not explicitly voting, one could imagine that her new independence might include that as well. She also has various manifestations, which, according to Kitch, reveal "opportunities for upward social and economic mobility while she also embodied fears about *downward* mobility, immigration, and the urbanization and corporatization of the lives of white American men. And she conveyed new social, political, and economic possibilities for womanhood. At many historical moments she seemed merely to 'mirror' what was happening in society. Yet she (and the visions of masculinity that accompanied her) also served as a model for that society and as a cultural commentator through whom certain ideals came to seem 'natural' in real life."[17] This is quite a bit of information for one image of a woman to convey, yet in this definition of what the new woman stood for, one gains insight into why a certain image of ideal beauty is constructed.

Ideal beauty at this time, then, is a cultural typing that transformed the American female into a set of powerful iconic images. Obviously, the artists who created these images were influenced by Western art and literature,[18] just as the women copywriters at JWT were influenced by a liberal arts curriculum and the custom of appropriating art and design for business purposes evident in the advertising industry.

Helen Lansdowne, for example, encouraged her group of copywriters to rent paintings and sculpture from the Museum of Modern Art, to appreciate fashion and good design.[19] Lansdowne was for many years a trustee and supporter of the Museum of Modern Art. She and Stanley Resor had amassed one of the "most outstanding collections of modern art in the world," which they often loaned out for public exhibition.[20] It was not

Figure 2.1.   Pond's, "Avoid Sunburn, Freckles and Chaps"

uncommon for the copywriters to mention that they got the inspirational advertising ideas while visiting a museum.

As a case in point, in the March 1922 issue of the *JWT News Bulletin*, a writer reports on a recent exhibition of current work by manufacturers and designers at the Metropolitan Museum of Art in New York. A special case was devoted to several products advertised by JWT for Pond's and the Andrew Jergens Company. The showcased designs for product containers included "a cake of Jergens bath soap and two powder boxes that were inspired by designs on Greek pyxides and pottery from the Museum. . . . A different style powder box, with its origin in French snuff boxes was designed for the Pond's Extract Company."[21] The newly powerful advertising industry, and those who ranked as its leaders, drew from familiar classical art and Western notions of beauty that were then transformed into iconic images that spoke to a nation of strivers.

The Lux Flakes and Cutex Campaigns

The White Man's Burden: The first step toward lightening is through teaching the virtues of cleanliness. Pear's Soap is a potent factor in brightening the dark corners of the earth as civilization advances while amongst the cultured of all nations it holds the highest place—it is the ideal toilet soap.

—Ad for Pear's Soap, *The Cosmopolitan,* May–October, 1899

The ad women at JWT were picking up on beauty "types" already circulating in media when they created their ads. They contributed to the concept of ideal beauty by perpetuating the beauty types most appealing to them, their own desires, and their own fantasies about feminine beauty. Two ad campaigns show, through images and text, American Girl/New Women types that appeal to an aspiring consumer base. By the 1910s and 1920s women of all classes were bent on improving themselves through consumer goods. The immigrant woman, especially, was invited to "pass" socially, economically, and racially; she could aspire to higher status through clothing, manners, and posture. Together, those two groups make up the demographic for Lux Flakes and Cutex nail products.

The Lux Flakes account came to JWT in 1915 from the Lever Brothers Company in Cambridge, Massachusetts (the American branch of Lever Brothers Ltd., a British company). Lever Brothers was described by copywriter Elizabeth Devree, who worked on the account, as "one unit of a tremendous international organization—an industrial empire of colossal dimensions."[22] Founder William Hesketh Lever, later known as Lord Leverhulme, established a model plant and community in 1884 near Liverpool,

England, and named it "Port Sunlight."[23] They were a company that, in their origins, at least, had an aspiration toward remaking society.

By 1932, Lever Brothers placed $4 million worth of advertising through the New York City office,[24] up from an advertising appropriation of $684,000 in 1918.[25] Lever Brothers Ltd. had a tremendous international presence, most particularly on the west coast of central Africa, the Philippines, and in the south Pacific Islands where millions of acres were devoted to the production of palm oil and coconut oil (necessary for making soap).[26] Helen Lansdowne and her copywriters handled the Lux Flakes, Lifebuoy Soap, and Lux Toilet Soap accounts. The success of their campaign for Lux Flakes was extraordinary.

Lansdowne and her team created a campaign that educated women as to the uses of Lux Flakes, a new laundry product (previously, women had to chip off pieces from a large block of soap and work it to dissolve into water to do their laundry). Lansdowne was certainly experienced in creating ads that educated female consumers to the use of a new product. She had a great success in her ad campaign for Crisco shortening, positioning it as a "modern" product for the "modern woman." So, Lansdowne and her copywriters took the Lux ad campaign from its former slogan of "Won't Shrink Woolens," and created a new "modern" campaign that positioned Lux Flakes as a detergent safe for all fine fabrics. This new campaign increased sales from ten thousand cases sold in 1915 to over one million cases sold in 1918.[27]

Some of the elements that went into the creation of the Lux Flakes campaign are familiar, such as the appeal to the "modern" woman (the New Woman). The images and text used in the ads worked in concert to appeal to women who aspired to be (a) modern, (b) beautiful—like the women in the ads, (c) American, (d) managers of a beautiful home, (e) good wives and mothers, and (f) fashionable.

In her presentation to JWT employees at a Creative Staff Meeting, Elizabeth Devree said, "Anticipating a swarm of competitors, JWT built up an added appeal for Lux. They exploited it as something magical, mysterious and in some way synonymous with fashion. Fashion and style, always belonging to the upper class, were becoming the prerogative of the middle class. And Thompson tied up with fashion and rode it through years of success."[28]

One of the early Lux ads (1916) illustrates those points (Figure 2.2). The headline reads, "The Modern Soap Product: Not a soap powder— not a chipped soap—not a cake—but pure essence of soap in flakes." The image at the top of the ad shows a young white woman in a maid's uniform standing at a large basin of steaming water filled with clothes; she is adding Lux Flakes. The room is a modern washroom with a tiled wall, a clothes wringer, and hanging racks—clearly the scene of upper-class domesticity. The image anchoring the bottom of the page shows two fashionably dressed women in a music room—a grand piano sits in the background next to a large picture window. The women portrayed in the ad, including the maid—all have those familiar "American Girl" features: they are young, white, have "regular" Northern European features, they have a "pure" bloodline, and are most likely Protestant.[29] By 1916, this "type" had been around for awhile—at least since the Steel-Engraving Lady. Those facial features and the things that this "best" type implied (e.g., religion) developed out of ideas associated with physiognomy, a pseudoscience that attempted to classify physical traits and determine superior and inferior types.[30]

The particular types of ideal beauty developed by those who supported the basic concepts of physiognomy, though informed by a racist system of classification, fueled the imaginations of illustrators, advertisers, and magazine editors. The types of ideal beauty showed what a true American looked like; of course, the image was about more than regular features, it was an amalgamation of all the things considered "American" at that time. People who exhibited those external traits would receive favorable reactions while those who did not exhibit those traits would be considered inferior.

Other Lux ads bolstered the image of ideal beauty through scenes showing nurturing mothers caring for children. One Lux ad (1917, *Ladies' Home Journal*) shows two fashionably dressed women with children in tow (Figure 2.3). They appear to be on a seaside boardwalk enjoying a leisurely stroll while children play with balloons. Images at the bottom of the ad show a maid bringing the mistress of the house, who is sitting at her dressing table, her fine silk blouse. And the image in the middle of the ad shows a woman washing her stockings with Lux Flakes. The scenes in this ad address the upper-class woman with a maid, the mother, and the housewife who washes out her own stockings. All the women have the features of the American Girl or New Woman.

The Lux Flakes ads are consistently colorful and consistently show beautiful clothes and homes. The children are healthy and impeccably dressed. The women exhibit those common regular features of the New Woman; even the maids have those features. The images, up until the 1930s, are all sketches and show great detail in textiles, as well as in objects such as furniture, jewelry, dishes, and other home accessories. One ad, which was designed to show other uses for Lux Flakes (1925, *Delineator*), has the headline "Won't redden your hands—won't coarsen or roughen them . . . Lux suds free you from that tell-tale-in-the-dishpan-look." The illustration is of two fashionably dressed women, perfectly coiffed, standing at

Figure 2.2.   Lux, "The Modern Soap Product"

Wonderful for Sweaters! Blouses! Stockings!

And all these are things that you have found it most difficult to launder!

Even the greatest care could not bring them from a tubbing without their softness, freshness, and loveliness gone!

You have become so used to it, that you expect your prettiest things to be half spoiled when laundered—you wear them as long as possible before their first laundering, and try not to look at them too closely when they come back.

Keep your sweater soft and woolly

You need not be resigned to ruined things, you can dare to look closely at your flimsiest blouse, your furriest sweater, even after they have been laundered many times.

For it is not that your sweater or silk stockings cannot stand a rubbing—but that they cannot stand the kind of soap you use.

Even the best cake soap should not be used on woolens or on delicate fabrics.

Rubbing the soap on the garment, more rubbing to get the soap out, makes the wool fibers shrink and grow harsh, makes your silk blouse turn yellow, wears through the threads in your very nicest stockings.

Do not let your loveliest waist be spoiled

The fragile Lux flakes do away with every bit of rubbing. They melt into a bubbly lather that contains more cleansing value than is possible with any other form of soap.

You dip your softest woolens, your sheerest waists and silk combinations through it a few times—and the dirt is gone!

Your woolens will come from their little laundering like new, if you will use Lux and very hot water. The hotter the water the more quickly the dirt will loosen and fall out into the thick suds.

For silks the water should be just lukewarm—and in

No rubbing to break the threads—no discolored or faded stockings.

lukewarm water, too, the Lux flakes bubble into the same creamy, cleansing lather.

Thousands of women all over the United States could hardly believe it when they first heard of the wonderful results Lux gives.

Thousands and thousands now say that they cannot afford to be without Lux. They wonder how they managed before they found it, how they bore to see their things lose their beauty and wear out so quickly.

Everywhere that Lux has been introduced, women have recognized its wonder at once. No woman who has tried it is willing to be without it ever again.

Even the frailest things

Their "difficult" laundering is no longer difficult! They buy the most fragile looking waists, the most elaborate camisoles, and wear their most expensive sweaters every day, without a qualm about their getting dirty.

They know that their own and the children's sweaters will be as soft and well shaped as ever, that their silk blouses will stay white and lovely, that fine lace collars, and sheer, embroidered baby dresses can be cleaned, and yet stay whole and beautiful.

At grocers' and department stores

Your dealer has been instructed to return your money if you are not satisfied. But it never happens. One ten cent package of Lux will prove to you what wonderful results it gives.

If you are unable to purchase Lux in your town, we shall be glad to send you a package by mail at the regular price, 10c. In order to have you try Lux, we shall be glad to pay the postage, but cannot send more than one package to any one customer. Send us your dealer's name with the 10c and we will see that he is prepared to supply you hereafter. Lever Brothers Co., Dept. E, Cambridge, Mass.

LUX 10¢

Won't turn silks yellow!   Won't shrink woolens!   Won't injure even chiffons!

When your nice blouses come from their Lux laundering, one comfortable glance tells you that they are not only clean again, but are still as lovely as when they were new.

The creamy Lux lather is so cleansing that it does away entirely with that rubbing which is so hard for you, and so ruinous to fine garments.

Figure 2.3.   Lux, "Wonderful for Sweaters! Blouses! Stockings!"

a kitchen sink full of dishes (Figure 2.4). One woman is inspecting her friend's hands. They must meet the approval of the inspector since they both look absolutely serene. This scene is especially revealing in its portrayal of women inspecting other women. The critical eye is your friend's eye, not just your husband's or father's. And perhaps the most critical eye is the eye of the reader who may, at that moment of reading this Lux ad, look down at her own hands for signs of redness or coarseness.

While many of the Lux ads show maids waiting on their mistresses, a strong appeal in the campaign are the messages of frugality and cleanliness—surely American values. By using Lux Flakes, the housewife extends the life of her fine silks and chiffons, her stockings and delicate undergarments. By using Lux, sweaters and other woolens keep their shape, stay soft, and stay new longer. Lux ads from 1915 to the late 1920s promised the reader a beautiful, modern, American domestic life. The design of the homes featured in the ads perhaps inspired the reader to create beauty in their homes, the images of healthy, well-dressed children would hopefully inspire women to take pride in their role as mother, and the fashionable women with the perfect hair would hopefully inspire the reader to emulate beautiful women . . . and, of course, buy Lux.

Yet, all these social tableaux[31] were instructive well beyond the utilitarian purpose of teaching women about a new soap product. While the utilitarian appeal of the Lux ads draw on the frugal housewife, the emotional appeal of beauty, the approval of peers and husband draws the reader or consumer into an imaginary world where magically she is transformed through the use of a simple household product. There is no mistake that the intent of the ad women was to imbue Lux soap with magic and mystery, as Devree says and as the ads illustrate. And, while doing so, the ad women also gave practical reasons for buying the soap—a winning combination.

In accordance with these images, in 1927 Lansdowne and her copywriters created a series of testimonial ads. Devree notes that for the Lux dishwashing ads they "used realistic artwork—ultimately only photographs—and they introduced sex appeal. Men appeared in many of the pictures, and emphasis was placed on the romantic value of *white* hands free from any trace of that dishpan look" (emphasis added).[32] By the 1930s, Lansdowne and her copywriters focused on campaigns that showed how Lux preserved elasticity in stockings and, as Devree says, "a new version of the perspiration story and the social ostracism that follows from this offense" (headline: "She never omits her daily bath yet she is guilty of this offense").[33] Devree notes how these ads were distributed with care as to the particular demographic they wanted to reach: they ran fashion copy in *Vogue* and *Harper's Bazaar* that included endorsements from the "swankiest" New York shops; copy focusing on baby's clothing was sent to *Child*

Figure 2.4. Lux, "Won't Redden Your Hands"

Life and *Parenting Magazines*; and testimonials from farm women were sent for publication in *Master Farm Homemakers.*[34]

The imagery, class, and racial significance of beauty ads have a slightly different resonance in the case of the Cutex campaigns. Cutex brought its business to JWT around the same time Lansdowne was creating the

Lux Flake ad campaign. The Cutex nail business was started in 1912 by Northam Warren, a pharmacist who had devised a solution for the removal of dead cuticles. Just like Crisco and Lux Flakes, Cutex was a new product. Lansdowne and her copywriters prepared ad copy that was educational, giving advice to women on how to manicure and care for their nails. Again, the appeal was that the "modern" woman paid attention to the appearance of her hands and they purchased nail care products to achieve that look of elegance. As in the Lux ads, women were concerned with the appearance of their hands—if they were too coarse and red, the woman could be mistaken for lower class or couldn't pass as a middle-class woman.

When the Northam Warren Company came to JWT in 1916, the company's total business was $150,000 ($60,000 of which was the Cutex line). Sales of the company doubled in the first year JWT took the account, and by 1920 sales totaled nearly $2 million. The Northam Warren Company eventually expanded to international markets, and, by 1963, its business outside the United States represented a substantial portion of its total volume of sales.[35] The Cutex story is a good example of just how fast the beauty industry was growing in the early twentieth century. New products were introduced and, if advertised effectively, could make the success of a company. Women bought into the promise and hope of a new and better "self" through products. In 1912, only one out of four women used products for the care of their hands and nails. By 1936, three out of four women used such products.[36]

Early Cutex ads stressed the dangers of cutting the cuticle, and the copy detailed just how to properly care for damaged and abused cuticles. Images showed delicate white hands—no attached body or face—treated with Cutex. Aminta Casseres worked with Lansdowne on the Cutex campaign and, by 1923, they were creating ads that used a psychological appeal: "Embarrassed fingers that shrink from scrutiny—or charming fingers that seek the light!" This ad appeared in the *Ladies' Home Journal* and featured a fashionably dressed woman, with hat, who, again, looks the ideal beauty type: young with "regular" features, small bee-stung mouth, and lovely white hands. "You need not have unattractive hands, unless you wish," the ad copy reads, "even if they lack 'sculptured lines,' your hands can still be fascinating, if they have that something which the French call 'chic.'"

The psychological appeal of the ad is powerful: embarrassment at unkempt fingers and hands; shame—it's your own fault! The reader is encouraged to look like the woman in the ad and to desire her life of carefree devotion to fashion and skin care as well. The consumer may even be on par with the universal master of chic, the French woman! As comical as this may sound, one only has to recall recent best sellers, such as Mireille Guiliano's *French Women Don't Get Fat*, in the last few years about how French women's diets, cigarette smoking, and a few other customs capitalized on in spin-off books were still convincing as unimpeachably fashionable.[37]

Testimonials using actresses were used in Cutex ads as early as 1917. One that appeared in the *Ladies' Home Journal* featured three women, all actresses "noted for their beauty": Janet Beecher, Mary Nash, and Gladys Hanson. Beauty specialist and beauty schools also provided endorsements for Cutex. In a 1924 ad in the *Ladies Home Journal*, the headline reads, "The way Beauty Experts keep the cuticle smooth and Lovely." Half the page is filled with a photo of a young, white woman artfully posed at a table with full light on her forearms and hands, which are draped swan-like. She lightly rests her chin at the bend of her wrist, and her head is tilted down so the reader can only see her nose and mouth. Her eyes are mysteriously hidden under the brim of her fashionable hat.

The images of these elegant yet delicate hands are reminiscent of the nineteenth-century Steel-Engraving Lady. She too was delicate, she represented what a lady should be during that particular time. Viewing image after image of perfectly manicured hands in the Cutex ads makes it difficult to imagine those hands hoeing a garden, pulling weeds, holding a picket sign, running fabric through a machine in a sweat shop, or spending day after day cleaning houses, changing diapers, and doing laundry. Those activities of real women—especially groups of real women—were, in the imaginary world of the ads, overwhelmed by such alluring visions of individual beauty.

Connections between the "New Woman," Ideal Beauty, and Discourses on Race

Commonly accepted ideas about ideal beauty, which gained traction throughout the nineteenth century, were asserted in relations to people of color around the world. Kathy Peiss notes that "nineteenth-century travelers, missionaries, anthropologists, and scientists habitually viewed beauty as a function of race. Nodding in the direction of relativism—that various cultures perceive attractiveness differently—they nevertheless proclaimed the superiority of white racial beauty. . . . And because appearance and character were considered to be commensurate, the beauty of white skin expressed Anglo-Saxon virtue and civilization—and justified white supremacy in a period of American expansion."[38] The importance of constructions of and debates over shifts in concepts of women's ideal beauty is thus crucial to understand since these shifts often correspond with fears related to immigration, race, attempts to maintain class status, and, of course, power.

Discourses on race—including the social construction of the "white" race—were already widely circulated in nineteenth-century United States. The facial ideal, dominating much of American popular and commercial culture by the early twentieth century, was still reminiscent of the Steel-Engraving Lady: fair and white skin, blushing cheeks, bee-stung lips, "regular" (Northern European) features, and youth—markers of class as well as race. It is not surprising then that skin whiteners were the most popular cosmetic on the market during the nineteenth century and were used—to varying degrees—by women of all classes and races.[39] JWT advertisers, male and female, consciously tapped into these ideologies of ideal beauty using not just racially feminized ideas but also classed feminized ideas.

While there are vast differences between white and African American women's magazines, there are also some similarities. Noliwe Rooks has shown that in publications created for an African American audience, such as *Ringwold's Afro-American Journal of Fashion* (1891–94), fashion is shown as an opportunity for racial uplift, though this fashion was sometimes connected with whiteness—or a "likeness to whiteness" in light-colored skin, white features on models, and in the articles of the magazine. In addition, the aspirational tone clearly present in mainstream white women's magazines was present in magazines for African American women—though altered by politics of race, differing ideas about respectability, and narratives of slavery in African American publications.

These parallels underline that, just as the New Woman was being created, the "New Negro" image was created during the massive migration north after the Emancipation Proclamation. Both images were connected to urbanization and an emigrant woman might identify with migration and making a home in a new place. But the emigrant or immigrant woman might well be absorbed into nativist white culture and was encouraged to assimilate. She might read *Ladies' Home Journal* or *Woman's Companion*. The African American women's magazines were addressing issues specific to African American women, including the effort to transform the slave narrative's focus on rape, promiscuity, and enslavement into something more inspiring and aspirational. The writers and editors of African American women's magazines (many of which were edited by women, unlike white women's magazines) offered models for behavior and physical appearance that, if followed, would improve the conditions for black women.

For the African Americans who migrated north, a new urban African American culture emerged. The image of the "New Negro" held appeal as a replacement for racist images of African Americans such as the "Sambo" or "Mammy" that appeared in mainstream media and in advertisements for rice, cereal, and maple syrup.[40] Their efforts, of course, were not successful in obliterating images such as those of Uncle Ben and Aunt Jemima, still ideologically laden American brands. Interestingly, Uncle Ben has been recently promoted to "Chairman of the Board" as part of the Mars Company's 2007 Uncle Ben's Rice ad campaign. Unfortunately, there has been no promotion for Aunt Jemima, though such a promotion would no more undo the old stereotype as that of Uncle Ben. The promotion campaign for Uncle Ben rings hollow in light of real racial issues in the United States.

In the world of real persons and magazines, it took quite some time for an African American woman to even appear on the cover of a mainstream (white) women's magazine, when, in 1974 Beverly Johnson was featured on the cover of *Vogue*. Despite Mary Tucker's (JWT copywriter) remark about the unchanging nature of *Vogue*, it apparently was affected enough that years after the height of the civil rights movement the magazine could offer that "Black is Beautiful."

In all events, "native" white, immigrant, and African American women all were encouraged to become modern through consumption. In fact, an interesting transition in African American women's magazines took place that did not occur in mainstream white media. In the late nineteenth century, *Ringwood's Journal* offered an "uplift strategy" put forth by an elite group of writers that linked fashion with "bodies of light-skinned African American women with white features." The magazine featured exceptional women, those who were elite, and those who had light skin and white features. *Half-Century Magazine*, in the early twentieth century, broadened the visual representation of women to include African American women who were not just members of the elite or those with light skin and white features. In *Half-Century*, large-boned, dark-skinned women were featured as being fashionable—a significant departure from the representation of women in *Ringwood's*.[41]

Underlying the philosophy in both magazines, however, was a political agenda: uplift and respect for African American women who were bound through their experiences in a racist society. One wonders how much of a difference it made that the editors of these magazines were women. Would the image of ideal beauty have been any different in white, mainstream women's magazines if the editors had been women? If women controlled media, would those images of beauty have been more inclusive? The African American magazine world indicates that the hegemony of whiteness and patriarchy might not have crumbled even with women in charge, at least not during that period.

Good Looks Supremacy: Women as the Locus of National Anxieties

In white women's magazines, the range of images used by both advertisers and artists were (and still are) limited—they reflected the elite group that created or chose them to represent the modern woman. Kitch makes the point that "by searching for beauty standards specifically in the small world of the native-born, white upper class, the press created a selective view that paralleled President Theodore Roosevelt's public worry about 'race suicide.' His concern—that whites were having fewer children while millions of eastern European immigrants arrived in the United States each year and bore large families—was echoed by the 'scientific' arguments of eugenicists in newspapers and magazines and was justified in terms of the strength of the country as a whole. Physical beauty was a measure of fitness, character, and Americanness."[42] One can also see how easily Dr. Clarke's argument about the dangers of women entering higher education and its adverse effects on reproduction would accord nicely with similar propaganda of bigotry and fear.

Naomi Wolf points out in *The Beauty Myth* that "the [beauty] myth like other ideologies of femininity, mutates to meet new circumstances and checkmates women's attempts to increase their power."[43] During the nineteenth century in the United States, the Victorian ideologies of femininity focused on motherhood—women's sexual reproduction—and the cult of domesticity, hence the focus by Dr. Edward Clarke on the negative impact on women's reproduction by their entering male-dominated institutions of higher learning. This critique was also a result of deep paranoia about the supposed decline of the white, "native" race in the United States and fear about growing immigrant populations and the migration of freed blacks to the north. These fears determined the perceptions held about women's bodies and had real implications for just how much they could do, experience, or enjoy—not too much learning through formal education, not too much time spent in the public sphere, no sex except for procreation, since, for Victorian women, sexual desire for pleasure's sake was seen as a disease.

Once women started to successfully alter those institutions, however, the Victorian ideology started to "mutate." The focus shifted from the value of women's reproductive organs to the value of women's beauty. The Victorian concept of beauty was intricately linked to motherhood (for the white, nativist woman). That is not to say that women were not also judged on physical appearance, but they also were not judged solely on physical beauty. There was some redemptive space in the home for the morally superior mother—she could be protected to a certain extent from harsh judgments about her appearance.

Once admitted to institutions of higher learning, the ideologies of the cult of domesticity began to lose its hold over young women. No longer able to limit women's desire for an education equal to that of their brothers, the male-dominated institutions of an emerging media helped transform an ideology of femininity from the cult of domesticity to the "modern" cult of ideal beauty through consumption.

Wolf convincingly argues that "the qualities that a given period calls beautiful in women are merely symbols of the female behavior that that period considers desirable: *The beauty myth is always actually prescribing behavior and not appearance*" (emphasis added).[44] Generally speaking, in the nineteenth century, the morally superior mother with children tucked securely in the home was considered beautiful. Still, though, an image of ideal feminine beauty circulated though magazines, etiquette manuals, and advice books of the Steel-Engraving Lady: dainty, with small feet, delicate hands, white skin, a bee-stung mouth, and often on the verge of fainting from a tight corset.

In the twentieth century, the modern woman—deodorized, cosmeticized, slimmed, youthful, urban, then suburbanized, consumerized—was beautiful. Today, the highly sexualized, wrinkle-free, silicone injected, anorexic, vaginally reconstructed, adolescent woman is "beautiful." Though these descriptions are generalizations, one gets a sense of the arbitrary nature of the changing criteria for beauty. Unfortunately, a focus on surveillance and control remains consistent.

The cult of domesticity in the nineteenth century mainly harnessed the white "native" woman who achieved a physical beauty in part through goodness. The Steel-Engraving Lady, for example, was named so because of the use of lithographs but also because of an implied morality associated with the strength of "steel." The commercially focused ideal beauty of the twentieth century targeted the growing middle class and strivers who tried to achieve the ideal beauty as shown to them by an increasingly powerful new media.

The modern woman of the early twentieth century was told her liberation would come through cosmetics, a challenge to the Victorian notion of beauty, which was derived from morality and character as opposed to a new focus on "personality." She was also told that her sexual liberation signaled her sexual power—but as so often happens, that sexuality has been cruelly distorted by recommended regimens of starvation, surgery, and a strange mixture of adolescence and an illusion of eternal youth. As Peiss notes, "Ironically, a period that began with cosmetics signaling women's freedom and individuality ended in binding feminine identity to manufactured beauty, self-portrayal to acts of consumption."[45]

3

Selling Prestige and Whiteness

Pond's Cold Cream and Pond's Vanishing Cream Case Study

It is estimated that every second of every hour, there is a woman somewhere in the world buying a Pond's product. The cosmetic industry has grown tremendously in the past 50 years and Pond's has kept pace with this growth, often breaking new ground and setting new trends and standards, for the entire industry.

—William M. Peniche, "Beauty From Bangor to Bangkok: A Brief Review of Chesebrough-Pond's World-Wide Advertising," a presentation before an international seminar, April 18, 1961, Sam Meek Papers, JWT Archives, Duke University Library, Durham, North Carolina

One of Helen Lansdowne's protégées, Margaret "Peggy" King, said in an interview that Lansdowne "encouraged me to rent paintings and sculpture from the Museum of Modern Art, to have very good clothes, to work with top decorators at home and in the office."[1] Lansdowne had a proprietary air concerning her group of women and gave them advice on everything from writing copy to managing their homes. This interest in style that extended beyond the walls of J. Walter Thompson (JWT), hints at Lansdowne's strongly held belief that how one approached style and art permeated all aspects of life. Her attitude toward high art illustrates two interconnected points: (1) she was fluid in the language and attitude of social mobility (a female Horatio Alger character, in effect, a Ragged Jane), and (2) she cultivated style and taste by identifying the proper art (high art) to revere as being the domain of the upper class, closely linked herself to that art, and stressed the importance of that art to her staff. Perhaps Lansdowne had a particularly developed sense of the appeal of social prestige because she had worked so hard to lift herself out of the poverty she experienced as a child. This understanding and ambition would have contributed to the highly effective psychological appeal of social prestige used in the Pond's testimonial ad campaigns. Viewed another way, after Lansdowne improved her fortunes, she was very willing to entice others with ambition that success and status were one and the same.

The women who worked for Lansdowne handled the majority of the soap, food, and cosmetic accounts that were JWT's mainstay. Their ad copy, to some extent, logically would reflect some of their personal beliefs and values, while of course also being designed to win over and influence their audience. This chapter focuses on the work that Lansdowne and the Women's Editorial Department did on the Pond's advertising campaign and reveals the processes by which a product gained meaning and became gendered and laden with an ideology of race and class. Products such as Pond's creams were designed by the Women's Editorial Department to have a special status for women consumers—in part because they were engineered and advertised to be applied to the face, where a woman's beauty, youth, and style were supposed to reside. Moreover, the facial cream industry is an especially rich ground for the study of the role of skin color, social class, and personal identity in the late nineteenth and early twentieth centuries—a time when mass consumer culture took hold in the United States, as suggested in earlier chapters. Finally, those products today continue to be among the most popular and heavily promoted ads for consumer goods designed and advertised by ad agencies. The Pond's Cold Cream and Pond's Vanishing Cream case study shows that the advertisements we see today pull from a rich history of advertising strategy, such as the testimonial advertisements that were such a successful part of the work the women copywriters at JWT did for Pond's.

Lansdowne and her department at JWT were innovative in developing Pond's "pitch." They were clever and thorough in developing what were then state-of-the-art marketing research techniques in understanding consumers' view of themselves and their aspirations—including notions of feminine and masculine ideals inseparable from ideas about class and race. The carefully selected and managed team developed by Lansdowne, and its willingness, rightly or wrongly, to conceive personal feminine style as an element in every aspect of life and identity, was critical to the immense success of the Pond's campaign. Such tactics, now very familiar, were innovations in their day: (a) differentiate the product from competitors (as a two-part system and as affordable), (b) identify and compete in an upscale market through celebrity and social prestige endorsement while retaining large popular market share, and (c) hone in on an expressly gendered psychological appeal of the product.

Advertising and selling were two of the first areas in which modern psychology could be applied—initially used in developing an effective salesperson and then to understand people's desires and buying behavior. Advertising historian Juliann Sivulka claims that, in the early part of the twentieth century, "advertising with a psychological appeal mainly revolved around class appeal and gender."[2] A psychological appeal came to replace the reason-why copy, which simply and basically described the product as opposed to extolling the pleasure and social status it would provide the purchaser.

JWT's development of this changing strategy is an early example of advertisers—in this case, the Women's Editorial Department—taking an ungendered consumer product, deliberately gendering it, and thereby creating an increasingly more intimate relationship with the female consumer. The Women's Editorial Department staff took Pond's from a "utility and cost" market strategy to positioning facial cream as an intimate psychological need—a product enhancing personal feminine beauty.

The psychological appeal was well suited and especially appropriate in a society geared toward social mobility, a society of immigrants, and a society with increasing racial and cultural diversity. Just as Lansdowne advised her Women's Editorial Department staff to emulate the upper class through interest in art, home decor, and fashion, the ads that made a psychological appeal in Pond's testimonial ads implicitly advised the consumer to emulate the upper classes. Pond's testimonials used a powerful, though subtle argument that tapped into basic human drives for elite peer association by using such words as *aristocratic, exclusive,* and *distinguished.*

By using these class- and race-coded words, the Women's Editorial Department accomplished two things. First, it connected the image (woman) to the product (Pond's) by using text that makes a meaningful relationship between the image and product. In an analysis of print ads, it is important to note that images are placed within framing boxes and are situated in such a way as to highlight their presence. These images become partially unhinged from their previous meaning locations, so the reader looks to the text to discover how they might be recombined. The use of class-coded words with an image of a white woman implies that white women are upper-class (effectively erasing any class distinctions among whites) and that Pond's is a product for those who have higher aspirations, for those who want to be like the women portrayed in the Pond's ads. The ads are arranged in the frame to accomplish the transfer of value from one sign system (female, white, upper-class) to another (Pond's).

Second, the Women's Editorial Department staff "hailed" (called out to) particular readers in their Pond's ads. In her analysis of how ads work within an ideological framework or sign system, Judith Williamson shows how consumer ads hail and name the reader, inviting the reader to step into the commodity mirror.[3] The ad hails in terms of what Williamson calls "alreadyness"—the woman who can relate to the white, upper-class image in the ad. Sometimes the ad hails in terms of what a person aspires to be— the woman (such as Lansdowne) who has ambitions of social mobility, for example. Or the ad hails through a connection the reader already feels with the message and image in the ad ("I have that dress!"). Although it is not as clear cut as hailing a "type" of woman—for how every type of woman responded to these ads cannot be determined in this discussion—these testimonial ads drew from a system of meaning that gained value from its particular cultural and historical context.

As historians attest, early twentieth-century women readers were especially anxious about class mobility and race, and the Pond's ads were highly effective, as evidenced by sales increases.[4] The processes by which these ads gained meaning in this context can be analyzed to show how certain myths naturalize systems of power that are in fact social constructions. But the ads should not be viewed as separate from the people who created them, which is why it is important to understand who the JWT copywriters were and the particular institutional culture in which they worked.

Even though these advertisements produce knowledge that feeds the myth of ideal beauty (Pond's is a quality product used by attractive, white, upper-class women), that knowledge draws on values and beliefs already functioning within society. That meaning is produced from something already known illustrates that signs in media texts are read in relation to other signs and other texts in a social and cultural context. Generally, the reader, drawn into the work of advertising, is one who knows how to fill in gaps, how to decipher, and what to fill in from her experiences in a sexist, racist, and class-bound society.

In other words, the reader knows the rules of the game—the system of meaning. Specific to the period, the reader would know the value of whiteness, the accoutrements of the upper class, the preference for fair skin, and its prerequisite for beauty. Since the women copywriters were part of this particular historical and cultural context, they too knew the rules of the game. They were conscious of putting together ads with images and texts that had the most impact in bringing the significant sign system associated with beauty and class into conjunction with their product.

An example of how this played out in the creation of ads is JWT copywriter Edith Lewis's comment on the importance of "outside sources," which refers to the connection between the signified (woman in the ad) and signifier (product advertised). She explained that where a product faced great resistance, or where it had strong competition, the copywriter sometimes had to draw on outside sources in order to reinforce the emotional quality. In other words, she says one "has to invent a situation or create an interest outside the product itself or its uses, in order to awaken an emotional response."[5]

Lewis describes a key concept in all modern advertising copywriting: how important it is to differentiate one face cream from another, one bar of soap from another, one can of fruit from another, and so on, by placing the product in a larger narrative. For the copywriter, in the case of Pond's, this meant drawing on the appeal of social prestige—a prestige that is reflected in a white, upper-class woman with a flawless complexion—to connect one type of sign to another. For the female consumer, this meant buying into, in more ways than one, an ideology of beauty, that has at its core the value and belief in the superiority of whiteness and the striving for upper-class accoutrements.

William O'Barr points out that throughout the early twentieth century, advertising "has tended to treat the American public as a colorless, English-speaking mass audience of rather uniform tastes, preferences, and sensibilities."[6] This is certainly the case with Pond's, which contributed to and reinforced the system of meaning that produced and gave value to "ideal" beauty first in the United States and eventually on a global scale as these ads were exported overseas.

T. T. Pond Company History

In 1846, chemist Theron T. Pond extracted a healing "tea" from the bark of witch hazel for use as a topical salve for wounds and purported remedy for numerous other ailments such as nosebleeds, sunburn, skin disease, and "women's complaints." Pond was among the first to create a commercial product from witch hazel, long used by herbalists in many countries as a mild topical remedy; his formula became known as Pond's Extract. One history of the development of witch hazel claims that Pond was taught by a medicine man from the New York Oneida Tribe to identify the witch hazel plant (Hamamelis) and how to brew the extract. According to this source, Pond considered the Oneida medicine man to be a partner in the business, though he is not mentioned in any other company history.[7]

In 1849, Theron Pond, Alexander Hart, and Edmund Munson formed the T. T. Pond Company, and after the Civil War, the company added soap and toiletries—a move toward repositioning the firm from promising healing to promising "beauty." In doing so, the early executives of the Pond's Company moved to deepen the gendered identity of their product. By attaching beauty to a healing product, these businessmen were expanding their market to even more women—not just those with "women's complaints." The company moved its laboratory and manufacturing facilities from Utica, New York, to Chester (later to Clinton), Connecticut, for its apparently unlimited supply of the witch hazel shrub and its access to Long Island and the shipping lanes. Pond's also had a laboratory in Toronto, Canada. In 1872, Pond's Extract sales efforts reached out across the Atlantic where Pond's Extract Company Limited opened in London. This was the company's first overseas depot, and from there sales of the extract spread to Continental Europe. The Pond's sales office was located in New York City.[8] By 1923, Pond's had international depots in Paris, Brussels, Florence, Buenos Aires, Johannesburg, Shanghai, Sydney, and Dunedin.[9]

Pond's began its first national advertising campaign in 1886, using the services of the J. Walter Thompson Company. Even though the Pond's company began creating other products based on its extract in the 1890s, it advertised only Pond's Extract until 1910. Around that time, owing to the broader availability of witch hazel at a lower price, it became clear that Pond's Extract had no future. An advertising survey in 1891 identified a growing demand for skincare preparations, and Pond's wanted part of that market. In 1906, the Lamont Corliss Company[10] began to operate the Pond's Extract Company with an option to buy, exercising the option in 1913. By that time, William Wallbridge, a chemist who worked in the Pond's factory, developed a formula for two creams—Pond's Cold Cream and Pond's Vanishing Cream. He later became a vice president and director of Lamont Corliss. Another young man in the factory, Clifford Baker, learned to make, market, and sell Pond's products and was later put in charge of Pond's advertising. Baker eventually became chairman of Pond's board of directors.[11]

In 1916, the successful Pond's advertising campaign "Every Skin Needs These Two Creams" was started, and eight years later the social prestige testimonial campaign was rolled out. Pond's Tissues and Pond's Freshener were put on the market in 1927 and were often included in the Pond's Creams advertising campaigns. In 1930, Lady Esther, a new, competing, all-purpose cream, entered the market with aggressive advertising on a "depression" theme that only *one* cream is necessary—an obvious counter to Pond's successful two-creams campaign. Pond's advertising adjusted: in the social prestige testimonial ads, society leaders showed how to save money through beauty care at home.

Pond's Face Powder was introduced in 1932 and Pond's Liquefying Cream came out the following year. In 1934, Pond's began to advertise the Vanishing and Cold Creams separately, and in 1935 a Pond's Cream Lotion was test-sold with no advertising. In 1937, this cream was introduced as "Danya" but was discontinued in 1943 because of disappointing sales. In 1940, in tune with the U.S. "good neighbor" political catchphrase, Pond's international society beauties were highlighted: "Beauties over the Americas." That same year Pond's "Lips" was introduced, and in one and a half years it was the best seller in Woolworth and Kresage stores. And in 1942, "She's Engaged! She's Lovely! She Uses Pond's!" featured Pond's endorsers-turned-war-workers, adding younger women to the campaign. Pond's "Cheeks" compact rouge was introduced in 1942, and in 1943, "Make-Up Pat" was developed. Neither product was advertised. And, finally, in 1946, Pond's "Angel Face" (cosmetic foundation) was introduced.[12]

During World War II, Pond's temporarily curtailed the production of new beauty products, instead focusing on special products for the armed forces. Its most successful product was a two-toned camouflage cream in stick form that was produced in a number of color combinations to blend in with the soldiers' surroundings. Pond's manufactured more than six million tubes of the camouflage cream for the U. S. military.[13] Pond's used its own particular knowledge about cosmetics to contribute a creative solution to the war effort, demonstrating Pond's resilience and willingness to adjust to market forces and interruptions. Interestingly, even though the products became less medically oriented over time, chemists, not just salespeople and marketers, still were part of top management. Perhaps the fact that the company had a history of chemists in leadership positions enabled them to think outside of the box when it came to developing new products while the women copywriters at JWT kept pace with changes related to competitors' products and consumer research.

With the introduction of these new products throughout the years, Pond's had added to its 1949 domestic sales $8.1 million over and above the Vanishing and Cold Cream sales. Sales on these two products alone had increased from $1.6 million in 1923 to $4.3 million in 1949.[14] International sales of Pond's products were substantial; from 1923 to 1948, Pond's total world sales increased 8.8 times as compared with 7.6 times for the U.S. only. Sales outside the U.S. increased 12.7 times.[15]

On April 1, 1950, Pond's Extract Company took over distribution of its products from Lamont, Corliss & Company, becoming an independent firm until it merged in 1955 with Chesebrough Manufacturing Company.[16] Pond's has been owned by Unilever since 1987 when Unilever bought Chesebrough. Business historian Geoffrey Jones calculates that the Unilever brand, which includes Pond's and Lux, two ad campaigns the Women's

Editorial Department created, "can now be found in one of every two households in the world."[17]

JWT Develops a Modern Advertising Campaign for Pond's

JWT created ads focusing on the glycerin-based vanishing cream in 1910— Helen Lansdowne was responsible for the creative aspect of the Pond's account. In the early ads, Pond's Extract and Cold Cream were often mentioned briefly at the bottom of the copy. During the years 1910 to 1915, a competing product called Elcaya was the leading vanishing cream on the market; Daggett & Ramsdell and Pompeian were the leading cold creams. Other cold cream competitors included Hind's and Pacquin's. Sales of Pond's Vanishing Cream in the United States were less than $100,000, and sales of Pond's Cold Cream were negligible. Sales increased for Pond's Vanishing Cream, due, it seems, to JWT's advertising efforts. Sales trend figures available for the years shown were as follows (Table 3.1):[18]

Table 3.1.   Sales Increase Figures for Pond's Cold Cream and Vanishing Cream, 1910–15

1910	29% increase
1911	49% increase
1914	19% increase
1915	58% increase (started advertising vanishing and cold creams together)

Kicking off this impressive and sustained growth, in 1914, a new campaign was initiated by JWT Pond's account representatives and the Women's Editorial Department—it was rolled out the following year. The campaign promoted vanishing cream and cold cream together in ads with the theme noted earlier: "Every normal skin needs these two creams."[19] JWT research had shown that women were confused about the intended purpose of each skin cream. This new campaign set out to educate the consumer, to teach her the modern way to properly care for skin. The new ads drew a clear distinction between the intended functions of the two products: cold cream to cleanse, vanishing cream to protect the skin. According to a JWT report, "The success of this strategy was immediate," with the 1915 sales showing a 58 percent increase for the cold and vanishing creams and a 47 percent increase the following year as shown (Table 3.2):[20]

Table 3.2. Sales Increase Figures for Pond's Cold Cream and Vanishing Cream, 1916–23[21]

1916	47%
1917	47%
1918	51%
1919	32%
1920	46%
1921	4% decrease
1922	18%
1923	16% (total sales volume $1,600,000)

This two-cream campaign theme was consistent for about six years, after which sales gains began to slow, though both creams still were leaders among the numerous brands marketed in the same product categories. The promotion had the distinct mark of Helen Lansdowne since it is similar to the Crisco campaign she had worked on in 1911. For Procter & Gamble's Crisco, Lansdowne worked to successfully market and advertise a product for which there was no real need. Using two skin creams together as part of a skin care regimen was new in the cosmetic industry. The claim that "every skin needs two creams" is highly debatable, but the campaign was successful nonetheless.[22] The creation of an additional cream for Pond's echoes a particular advertising strategy—to convince women that they should take advantage of the latest technology and join the modern female consumer. By purchasing and using Pond's creams, this modern female consumer took advantage of so-called advances in skin technology that necessitated an additional cream to care for the face, neck, and hands. This association with technology hinged the meanings associated with modern technology to the brand: rational, tested, modern, and scientific.

In a phrase, the notion of two creams as necessary for proper skin care and beauty enrolled women in an apparent "system" of care that had the aura of protocol using various scientifically tested elements. Another aspect of the advertisement was that women were not just systematic but in the know about a regimen to which less informed souls were not privy. They were active and insiders.

For eight years, this same basic appeal to use the two creams for special purposes was retained. Sales of Pond's two creams in the United States rose from $307,000 in 1916 to $1.6 million in 1923, passing all its competitors. But after World War I, new competition emerged. JWT surveys showed that with increased incomes, women were buying expensive face creams at three to four times the price they paid for Pond's (such as Helena Rubenstein and Elizabeth Arden creams) but that those creams were not necessarily, according to JWT, "better in quality." An unidentified man at JWT suggested, "Tell women that Pond's is just as good but costs less. Women go for bargains." In reply, an unidentified woman, who may have been Helen Lansdowne, at JWT said, "Yes, but remember this: a woman's own glamour is beyond price. She wants the brand of face cream she thinks will make her more beautiful. Our job is not to sell Pond's down the river as a bargain, but to convince the woman that she just can't buy a better face cream than Pond's."[23] Clearly, the anonymous woman had the more psychologically shrewd approach, a legacy still evident in late twentieth- and early twenty-first-century campaigns such as L'Oréal hair dye ("Because You're Worth It!") and similar strategies that equate higher price with higher quality and higher spending with higher personal self-esteem.

In addition to a psychological approach of showing ad illustrations of women, often in intimate surroundings such as bathrooms or bedrooms, and choosing particular women's magazines in which to place the ad, the Women's Editorial Department employed the earlier noted ideological practice of "hailing" or "interpellation," which occurs when a targeted person recognizes the person being addressed (as in "that is who I am" or "that is who I aspire to be"). The Pond's ads addressed particular women (those who aspired to a middle-class lifestyle); by addressing these women, the ads place them within a social relationship between the idealized beauty (at one end of the spectrum) and women of color (the other end of the spectrum). The addressee aspires to ideal beauty with the knowledge of who represents the opposite of ideal beauty. In recognizing herself as the addressee, and in responding to the communication of the ad, the woman reader participates in her own social and ideological construction.

The flexibility of the construction of a female identity, in this case, explains why this same ad might be appealing to working-class and immigrant women. By purchasing and using Pond's creams, they could take the initiative and join those being hailed as white and middle-class. For while the ads hail the white, middle-class woman through illustration, copy, and magazine placement, the affordable product is actually accessible to many of the working-class and immigrant women who were striving for the middle-class status and being pressured to assimilate.

The tactic of hailing the female consumer, in part, through a psychological appeal would be the prevailing one for the JWT Women's Editorial Department and an advertising appeal that would appear in many of the international ad campaigns that JWT created for its clients. Inherent in that psychological appeal is an ideology of race and a particular idealization of fair skin. Through advertising, then, the Women's Editorial Department contributed to a system of meaning in which a product comes to signify a plethora of dominant ideologies through an advertising strategy that brings significant signs from these ideological codes into relationship with the product. These are the roots of an ideal beauty that circled the globe through cosmetic, food, and household product ads created by the women copywriters at JWT.

The "Problem of 1923" and the Development of the Social Prestige Testimonial Ad

It pays to be personal now;
It brings in the shekels—and how!
If you want to sell drugs,
Or Baluchistan rugs,
Or revolvers to thugs,
Or a spray to kill bugs—
You've got to be personal now.

—Printer's Ink, October 10, 1929

By 1923, Pond's Cold Cream and Pond's Vanishing Cream had been nationally advertised together for eight years (the vanishing cream alone was advertised for fourteen years). By then, these creams had excellent distribution, a positive consumer reputation, and had shown an unusually high annual rate of increased sales over time. Despite this, a JWT study of sales showed that the high rate of increase was weakening. Concerned about the sales slowing down and changes in the competitive environment, the JWT research department (staffed by men and women) and women copywriters undertook intensive market research. This study revealed very active competition from 320 other cold and vanishing creams of about the same price and merit.

More important was the entrance into the popular market of higher-priced products formerly sold chiefly through exclusive beauty salons, but now rapidly gaining sales even at the higher price—if not in fact to a large extent because of the higher price (the "Because You're Worth It!" strategy). The higher cost of these creams, mostly imported, was regarded as an indication of their social prestige. It was apparent that Pond's two creams—leaders in their field—had begun to suffer. Their enormous popularity had brought them "loss of caste; they lacked exclusiveness, social prestige."[24] The Pond's campaign success eventually resulted in the overexposure of the product. The product needed a reworking of the appeal.

Most likely due to sales figures and discussion with the executives at Pond's, JWT executives and copywriters decided that the message that "every skin needs two creams" had been thoroughly learned by women, and that, likewise, the definite uses of each cream were well known and commonly accepted. Moreover, Pond's competitors had for some time been using the same publications as JWT, and exactly the same copy appeal— often even to the very same phrases.

Pond's executives asked Helen Lansdowne to develop an advertising campaign that would at least allow Pond's to maintain its lead among cold creams, and perhaps strengthen it. However, JWT executives and the Women's Editorial Department staff were much more ambitious: they sought a method of presenting Pond's two creams to the public "so startling as to lift them out of the class of the three or four active competitors and to give them a prestige which would place them on a level in public esteem, as they are in actual merit, with the higher priced and imported products of the exclusive beauty shops."[25] Since many of the Women's Editorial Department staff worked on the Pond's account, it is reasonable to assume that they were part of this planning process. In addition to coming up with the idea of making Pond's a "high-class" product, Helen Lansdowne and her women copywriters were directly responsible for identifying, contacting, and persuading various well-known women to endorse Pond's in a testimonial ad.[26]

This campaign may have been one of the most successful advertising strategies ever executed: a testimonial campaign including the endorsements of three of the reigning queens of Europe, six princesses, titled ladies, and leaders of American society. According to Alva Johnston of the *Outlook* (a newspaper also known as the *Outlook and Independent*), "the modernization of the testimonial was completed by Pond's. Directed with audacity, tact, and imagination, backed up by a well-filled war chest, the Pond's cream campaign made endorsing not only respectable but glamorous."[27] Here Johnston credits Pond's with creating the modern testimonial ad, but, in fact, it was the women copywriters at JWT who developed this campaign under the direction of Lansdowne.[28] What makes the Women's Editorial Department's testimonial campaigns "modern" includes many factors: the mass production of the testimonials with consistent themes including design, copy, magazine placement, and endorser story; JWT institutional support; national reach and the eventual spread of the testimonial ad from the United States to international markets; and the gendered, classed, and racialized aspects that represent dominant U.S. ideologies.

As a result of the scope of the Pond's campaign, a new department at JWT was soon created to handle endorsers for testimonial ads: the

Personality Department. The Women's Editorial Department worked closely with Lucille Platt, head of the Personality Department, to identify and contact potential endorsers for Pond's, and, eventually, other products such as Simmons Beds, Martex Towels, and Cream of Wheat.[29] Lucille Platt, a graduate of Mount Holyoke College, was described as "knowing more about the social register than the editors."[30] Like other women at JWT, Platt started out as a social worker but later created her own business, Hostesses, Inc., which arranged parties and did shopping for clients. Serving on her board of directors were a Vanderbilt, a Belmont, and a Whitney—her business experience and contacts were a perfect segue into her work at JWT.[31]

As the group head of the Pond's account, Aminta Casseres and her team, under Helen Lansdowne's supervision, decided to pitch the products as connected to social prestige. And they did so by giving evidence of the results of their use by the endorsements of beautiful and distinguished women. The Women's Editorial Department staff may have been counting on their theory that American women would be so impressed with the endorsers that they would not dare challenge the authority of Queen Marie of Roumania, Lady Diana Manners, Mrs. Alva Belmont, and other well-known women presented. But along with that theory, they also were counting on some desire on the part of American women to imitate those women. Or perhaps the success can be attributed to something more subtle and basic—simply that the consumer would remember the endorsement and the advertisement. These campaigns surrounded Pond's two creams with prestige, distinguished them in the highly competitive field that their popularity had partly created, and opened up the way to further rapid increases in sales as shown (Table 3.3):

Table 3.3.   Sales Increase Figures for Pond's Cold Cream and Vanishing Cream, 1923–30[32]

1924	27%
1925	28%
1926	16%
1927	7%
1928	11%
1929	12%
1930	5%

Pond's Marketing and Advertising Plan in Detail

This section shows the level of involvement the Women's Editorial Department had in the Pond's campaign, in its market research, and in creating the most important aspect of the campaign—the social prestige testimonial. Casseres and her team worked with the research department traveling out of the city to perform fieldwork (door-to-door interviewing), they spent time behind the counters at major department stores, and they performed in-house research and development using themselves and other female staff to test products. Most often, the research of these women, guided them in creating a winning strategy.

The steps by which this campaign was conceived and carried out included (a) consumer investigation, (b) trade investigation, (c) analysis of the product, (d) analysis of buying motives, (e) the copy, and (f) the artwork. The consumer investigation began in August 1923 and examined the extent and use of creams by women in all parts of the country, conducted by means of 1,800 questionnaires sent by the JWT research department by mail under the letterhead of the service department of a leading women's magazine to its readers.[33]

The results of the questionnaire JWT developed showed that 86 percent of the women used a cold (cleansing) cream, 60 percent of women used a vanishing (powder-base) cream, and that of the three leading creams on the market, Pond's Vanishing Cream was first in rank, with Pond's Cold Cream a close second in rank, and that 150 other cold creams and 170 other powder-based creams were being used. Another consumer investigation conducted in August 1923 was a house-to-house inquiry in chosen localities, with many of the Women's Editorial Department staff participating in the door-to-door campaign in and around the New York City area. Of 392 women interviewed in Cincinnati, Ohio, and nearby towns (Covington, Kentucky, and Hamilton and Middletown, Ohio), it was found that 52 percent of the women used cold cream, and 40 percent of the women used a vanishing cream, giving first rank to Pond's for both creams. The third consumer investigation was done in rural and small towns, house to house, in October 1923, in Putnam County, New York, and showed a similar percentage of the use of vanishing creams. And finally, 100 women were interviewed in Topeka, Kansas, in August 1923, which gave yet another cross-section of ages and classes. This investigation showed the habitual use of different creams for different purposes, a familiarity with the higher-priced beauty products, and an occasional feeling that Pond's were "good old products but not 'up-to-date'" but still ranked first in volume among all creams.[34]

The trade investigation also included JWT female employees (from the research department and the Women's Editorial Department) spending two weeks as salesclerks behind the toilet goods counter in each of two leading stores of different "class" in New York—a Fifth Avenue store, Lord & Taylor, a Third Avenue store, Bloomingdale's, and the leading store in Chicago (not identified in account history, perhaps Marshall Field's). JWT's research found that women had a thorough understanding of how the two creams worked, that women were in the habit of using two or more creams, and that there was a definite demand for special creams for special purposes by female consumers. The women employees who conducted this innovative "toilet goods counter field work" concluded from their field experience that there was a distinct feeling in the Fifth Avenue (Lord & Taylor) store that Pond's lacked prestige and "smartness."

These findings by JWT indicated that it needed to devise new copy that addressed the enormous competition of good creams, the emergence of three or four leaders out of all these competitors, and the appearance of higher-priced beauty products such as Helena Rubenstein on the market. The Women's Editorial Department staff categorized these department stores according to class—with Saks Fifth Avenue (even though they did field work in Lord & Taylor) as the most prestigious. The comments they heard there were class-based, from class-consciousness customers. The Third Avenue store, Bloomingdale's, was even starting to bring in the more upscale cosmetics, which meant that Pond's would face new competition in even the mid- to lower-end stores.

From the findings that 86 percent of women were already using creams, and, of these, approximately 64 percent were using creams other than Pond's and its three leading competitors, JWT executives and Lansdowne and her team decided that it would be more profitable to convert the users of leading competitors and hundreds of smaller competitors to using Pond's creams rather than to cultivate new users of the creams. They deemed it essential to strike immediately at the higher-priced products selling on the prestige of their exclusiveness. Blind tests of Pond's creams and six other of the best-known creams were made among twenty-five women (from secretaries to the Women's Editorial Department staff) who worked at JWT. Since they showed little difference among the creams, JWT decided against ad copy appeal on product differentiation. Instead, it focused on the motive for using creams, that is, the results that women were promised in beautifying their skin. The women copywriters then had to determine how best to suggest that there was evidence of such results.

Although endorsements from actresses had been used at JWT from time to time in Pond's advertisements,[35] in this case, Lansdowne, Casseres, and her team did not feel that actresses had the social prestige the ads needed. They would secure endorsements from women of social prominence as well as beauty to lift Pond's beyond the class of its active competitors.

These were precisely the distinguished associations required to elevate an excellent but too-familiar product above all others in its field. The women ultimately chosen represented a certain class and a social prestige, and they exuded a "to the manor born" attitude. In a reminder of how different this is from today's frantic corralling of even "D-list" celebrities, it is important to underline that actresses were considered but thought too low in prestige to do the trick.[36]

In this particular case, this shift marked a move from celebrity and glitz (actresses) to status and respectability, represented by minor nobility of Europe and society women of the United States. This preference for using women such as Alva Belmont and Gloria Vanderbilt illustrates notions about women and respectability that lingered into the 1920s. Actresses took control of a dubious public space in their performances onstage, while Vanderbilt and Belmont came from solid families that, it was assumed, had brought their daughters up in a moral environment. Only one kind of woman could provide a prestige-based lift out of the ordinary.

Working with Lucille Platt in the Personality Department, Casseres and her team secured endorsements from distinguished women from various parts of the United States, and women of various interests, in addition to titled women from other countries. They wed local to international prestige, an important step in the internationalization of beauty that the overall argument of this book traces. Until 1928, when Platt joined JWT, these endorsements were secured through contracts established by JWT representatives in the United States and abroad and generally through personal contacts of the ad agency's employees. Thus, the first woman to appear in the Pond's testimonial advertisement was a woman of great wealth and social position who was equally noted as a leader of women throughout the United States for her wide interests in all women's causes and movements: Mrs. O. H. P. Alva Belmont.

In 1924, Belmont was a top name in society who had enjoyed the privileges of a wealthy family but who had turned away from the typical preoccupations of her class to win rights for her sex. She was a leader in the women's suffrage movement, and lobbied for better conditions for women in the workforce as well as the abolition of child labor. Embittered by the public reaction to her divorce from William Kissam Vanderbilt (grandson of Cornelius Vanderbilt) and her remarriage a year later to Oliver Hazard Perry Belmont (the son of the utilities and street-railway magnate August Belmont), Belmont readily embraced militant suffragism. Her story, like that of many great fortunes, held ironies, since the social position and wealth she enjoyed were based on the success of notoriously ruthless and corrupt Robber Barons.

Visits to her daughter Consuelo, the Duchess of Marlborough, brought her into contact with Mrs. Pankhurst and her "great army" of women. Belmont's admiration for the Pankhursts and her anger and outrage at the hypocritical public reaction to her personal life became catalysts that transformed her from an insulated society hostess into an ardent feminist.[37] Belmont led off the first endorsement for Pond's headlined, "An interview with Mrs. O. H. P. Belmont on the care of the skin."[38] Such an endorsement recalls the association of many of the key female employees at JWT with activism and social work. It also indicates that, as women now successful in their advertising careers, they had maintained and used their contacts from those organizations to attract women of Belmont's prominence. Alva Belmont was signed by Edith Lewis through Katherine Leckie, a former suffrage campaigner who worked with Lewis to secure Belmont's endorsement. Both Leckie and Belmont received $1,000 for their service. Belmont donated her $1,000 to the Women's Party.[39]

Another way of securing endorsements was through social contacts with the members of philanthropic boards. Helen Lansdowne submitted a list of the members of the Woman's Board of the Neurological Institute of New York (of which she was a board member) to the Women's Editorial Department staff, suggesting members' names that would be desirable for the Pond's campaign. A member of the Women's Editorial staff approached one Miss Blair, the board's secretary, and suggested that some of the members could raise money for the institute in this way. The arrangement was an early example of the mutual-benefit agreements that good-cause and corporations continue to strike today.

That (unidentified) employee was successful in obtaining the endorsement of Mrs. W. K. Vanderbilt, who insisted that JWT mention the Neurological Institute in Pond's copy in such a way that her friends would understand her reason for letting her name be used. Lansdowne, the JWT Research Department, and the Women's Editorial Department staff were fully conversant with the world of advanced medical and scientific research and the social circles that supported them. In that way, Lansdowne seemed to have a dual role. She was socially active in philanthropic organizations, where she mixed with the elite women of New York City, and she made her social contacts work for her (JWT) by passing along names of potential endorsers to her staff. In effect, Lansdowne used her social and cultural capital to secure endorsements. Surely there were a myriad of ways that these contacts manifested in new business and developing business relationships. The social networks must have functioned at a high level and have been strong because the Women's Editorial Department was able to sign up some of the wealthiest women in the United States to endorse Pond's.

Esther Eaton, a JWT copywriter, through personal friends in Washington, approached Mrs. Borah and Mrs. Nicholas Longworth (Figure 3.1) and signed them up to endorse Pond's. Eaton also approached Anne Morgan, who had been unapproachable until she became active in the plans for the new clubhouse for the American Women's Association. Morgan finally consented to endorse Pond's creams so that she could use her endorsement fee to increase her donation to the American Women's Association, and on the condition that the association be given publicity in the ads.[40]

Philanthropy of another kind was thus connected to the Pond's beauty campaign, enabling these ads to speak to several audiences—the general female consumer, the female consumer interested in social causes, and the elite associates of the women providing the endorsements. The endorsements from women connected to suffrage and other women's issues add another layer to the overlap between the commercial world of JWT's Women's Editorial Department and the social and political world of women's issues and suffrage. Suffragists were not only coming to work at JWT, they were being recruited by the Women's Editorial Department staff to endorse products for female consumers.

Petra Bjorkman, having seen the Pond's testimonial advertising, called on a JWT executive in 1925. There is no indication in the archival materials how Bjorkman connected with JWT; however, Frances Maule was married to a man named Edwin Bjorkman (a Swedish translator) and perhaps the connection was through Maule. Petra Bjorkman had signed up the titled European men whose names were being used in Melachrino advertising and suggested that she get their wives for Pond's. Even though JWT declined to use the same names that she had gotten for Melachrino, they accepted a list of highborn European women whose names were widely known and whose beauty was considered to reflect their social position, privilege, and wealth and to whom Bjorkman had access.

The fusing of beauty and wealth in advertising was (and is) so common that a reminder of all of its elements may be in order. By its logic, the fusion holds that wealth cannot possibly be unattractive, for wealth is synonymous with class standing and wealth seen in this light is one of the ultimate achievements—to strive for at all costs. The myth that wealth equals beauty is, after all, a part of the American dream and instills in workers the sense that they are not only working for money, but they are working for beauty—a beautiful home, beautiful gardens, beautiful children, beautiful places to travel to, a beautiful wife or husband, and so forth. The beautiful face of the wealthy woman who uses Pond's reinforces the myth of ideal beauty and also naturalizes the supremacy of wealth and power.

The Infanta Eulalia of Spain was a close friend of Bjorkman, and it was through her that Bjorkman was introduced to the following women who

Figure 3.1.   Pond's, "Mrs. Nicholas Longworth"

signed for Pond's: H. R. H. Henriette; Duchesse of Vendome; Princesse of Belgium; Her Highness Princess Eugene Murat; the Duchesse de Guise; the Duchesse de Gramont; the Duquesa de Alba; and the Duchess of Marlborough.[41] Thus, Britain and Continental Europe were represented by minor nobility—names that would have been somewhat exotic to the average female consumer, perhaps only adding to their allure for an American female reader and connecting the Pond's brand to an international clientele.

The stories of American beauties marrying into royalty were especially compelling. The Duchesse de Richelieu (with "hair of golden lights, shadowy blue eyes and a matchless cream-and-white complexion") was a Baltimore girl who married "the head of one of the most famous titular houses of France" (Figure 3.2). After marrying, the Duchesse is "oftenest seen in the smart circles of Paris and New York." This story is a recast version of the fairy tale; although, in this instance, the fairy tale serves the purposes of selling a product.

It is questionable as to whether or not the Women's Editorial Department staff would have had access to this group of nobility. That Petra Bjorkman approached a male executive (perhaps through Maule) at JWT, however, indicates that the agency was well known for its testimonial ads by this time. Indeed, since no definitive evidence exists, it is possible that the ads themselves, rather than a personal connection to JWT, brought Bjorkman forward.

Signed testimonials were displayed in the advertisements, and photographs of the women were reproduced. Interviews with the endorsers were reported in a narrative, with a careful style deemed appropriate to the particular woman who was being written up—gracious and dignified for one, vivacious for another. Detailed descriptions of their houses, their personality, and their social activities were a prominent and important part of the interviews. More than simply product ads, these endorsements were miniature ventures into "lifestyles of the rich and famous" and presented the creams as just one element in a whole way of life that the everyday consumer could ostensibly share.

This experience was highlighted by the other features in the magazine that reported on prominent women and by the film industry, which had sophisticated nationwide merchandising strategies. In many ways women's magazines and films complemented each other's goal in reaching out to as many female consumers as possible using beautiful women (society women and actresses) to appeal to the female consumer. In a sense, the placement of the ads in the overall atmosphere of publications gave the best of both worlds—dignity with glitz nearby.

JWT developed the argument in the endorsement copy that the society woman's active life taxed her skin to the utmost and therefore required the most perfect care to maintain its beauty. The actual use of Pond's two creams was presented with special interest in the method of applying them and when to apply them—the particular details that seem to be of eternal interest to women consumers. Such details conferred an additional feeling

"The woman whose life is given not only to Society but to concert-singing must always appear with a complexion fresh and radiant. Care of her skin is an obligation second only in importance to the care of her voice. This care can best be obtained by the daily use of Pond's Two Creams. They keep the skin exquisitely soft and lovely."

Duchesse de Richelieu

The DUCHESSE de RICHELIEU
Tells How to Have a Lovely Skin

HAIR full of golden lights, shadowy blue eyes and a matchless cream-and-white complexion which makes everybody turn to look, women with envy, men with delight. A smile of rare sweetness and the charm of a nature gay, generous and sincere. The graciousness of the true aristocrat.

These make the Duchesse de Richelieu a woman everybody loves to see—and know. And to hear, too, for she has another gift—a lovely voice, lyric soprano of limpid tone.

In the exclusive social set of Baltimore—always famous for its "Baltimore belles"—she spent her gay girlhood. But since her marriage to the head of one of the oldest, most famous titular houses of France, she is oftenest seen in the smart circles of Paris and New York.

Her home in New York, "The House on the River," is often the scene of delightful gatherings of the socially elect. Among its lovely old furniture, books and *objets d'art* from France—many of them handed straight down from the great Cardinal de Richelieu himself—she moves, a hostess full of grace and charm.

"The woman whose life is given not only to society but to concert-singing," says the Duchesse de Richelieu, "is compelled to be concerned about her looks." And it is this seriousness with which

she regards her art that makes her determined to keep her cream-and-white skin always as fresh and radiant as it is today.

When she learned—as so many of the beautiful women of society have learned—of the Two Creams that cleanse and protect the skin, the Duchesse declared: "They keep the skin exquisitely soft and lovely."

Try for yourself, today, this method which all the world's lovely women are pursuing. Begin using Pond's wonderful Two Creams. You will find for yourself that what the Duchesse de Richelieu says of them is true.

How to use them

First, Pond's Cold Cream for Cleansing. At least once a day, always after any exposure, smooth the cream liberally over your face and neck. Let it stay on a few

EVERY SKIN NEEDS THESE TWO CREAMS

moments, that its pure oils may bring to the surface the pores' accumulation of dust, dirt, powder and excess oil.

After wiping off all the cream with a soft cloth pat it on again and wipe it off once more. Just look at your skin now—as refreshed as rose-petals washed with dew!

Next, Pond's Vanishing Cream for a Delicate Finish and Protection. Before you powder and before going out smooth in a light fluff, only as much as your skin will absorb. Now see how soft and even the surface looks—transparently lovely. How your powder stays on too—long and evenly. And how well your delicate skin is protected from wind, cold and soot. The Pond's Extract Company.

THE PRINCESSE MARIE DE BOURBON
MRS. MARSHALL FIELD, SR.   MRS. CONDÉ NAST
THE LADY DIANA MANNERS
MRS. O. H. P. BELMONT
MRS. GLORIA GOULD BISHOP

are among the distinguished women who have expressed approval of Pond's Two Creams.

Free Offer—Mail this coupon and we will send you free tubes of these two famous creams and a little folder telling how to use them.

The Pond's Extract Company, Dept. 4
157 Hudson Street, New York.

Please send free tubes of Pond's Cold and Vanishing Creams, and

Name...

Street..

City................... State....

of insidership—and even a level of expertise and special knowledge that mirrors the perennial beauty "tips" article of the women's magazines in which they were featured. To carry on the story of Pond's creams between these endorsement advertisements, pieces of copy that were not primarily endorsements ran from time to time.

In such advertisements, endorsements were featured in a minor way, and the uses of the creams were given the greater prominence.[42] Women consumers were treated to the feeling of knowing about a very personal and private "regime" for the proper use of the product, given a topic for chatting with women friends, and, by association provided with the feeling of being up to date in a way similar to that of titled women of wealth. The endorsements offered a glimpse and inclusion—even if just in an enjoyable fantasy—into a privileged world.

The artwork for Pond's testimonial advertisements was planned to maintain this aura of dignity and distinction that did not preclude warmth and a personal interest. The portraits or photographs and the written names of the women were prominently displayed, the former with restraint in the use of borders, the latter with beautiful lettering. Actual photographs or reproductions of portraits were used in preference to sketches, JWT claimed, "for the sake of greater realism." The claim is interesting, for the realism intended was perhaps the "realism" of the old-fashioned world in which family portraits of titled ancestors, not snapshots, were signs of class status. Yet JWT did not hesitate to use the most modern and respected of contemporary photographers, such as Edward Steichen, hired by Helen Lansdowne, who was called in to make the portraits.[43] Old-world charm was one prong of attack, but so was atmospheric and tasteful modern photography by up-and-coming masters. Full-page space was used in the magazines, and full-page or large space in the newspapers, both for the dominance that space gives and for the opportunity it gave for editorial treatment of the text.[44]

The editorial treatment of the text also makes the ads look less like an advertisement and more like a magazine article, a precursor of the "infomercial" story. It probably was not uncommon for a reader to be halfway through the narrative before she realized she was reading an ad. The meanings generated by one text (the ad) are determined partly by the meanings of other texts to which it appears similar (the advice columns and stories in women's magazines). Since many ads took on an advice or editorial advertising copy style, the interplay between these ads and the rest of the women's magazine strengthened the meaning-making process. The seamlessness between ads and the rest of the magazine made it possible for female readers to approach ads as though they were produced by the editor. The interplay helped erase some of the commercial aspect of the ad. The magazine itself is a medium within a system of signs and the interplay reinforces the naturalness of consumption while at the same time erases commercialism. Buying and using the affordable Pond's gives access to feminine ideal beauty, which has a social meaning. To possess the product is to buy into the myth and to possess some of its social value for themselves.

Since women from the full spectrum of American, white-identified, social classes, living in cities and smaller towns throughout the country, constituted the market for Pond's creams, magazines reaching the greatest number of these women became the leading media choice for ad placement. The campaign was carefully planned, and the ads were placed in a selection of the largest circulation of women's magazines, in a half-dozen fiction and motion picture magazines, and in only one so-called class publication, *Vogue*. Therefore, the other women's magazines with the largest circulation were selected by Lansdowne and her staff to carry the Pond's ads: *Ladies' Home Journal*, *Women's Home Companion*, *McCall's*, *Pictorial Review*, *Good Housekeeping*, *Delineator*, and *Designer*. Lansdowne decided that the second logical group in the magazine field included those that ran fiction and motion picture magazines. A large number of women were among their readers—young women and a type Lansdowne and her staff thought highly responsive to the advertising of cosmetics. The leading magazines in this field were added: *Cosmopolitan*, *Motion Picture*, *Photoplay*, *Redbook*, *Motion Picture Classics*, and *Liberty*.[45]

An article in the June 1923 issue of the JWT News Bulletin nicely sums up the effect women's magazines had on creating desire for new products and therefore "educating" the modern female consumer. Titled "Mrs. Wilkins reads the *Ladies Home Journal*," author Dorothy Dwight Townsend describes Mrs. Wilkins's modern home: "There was a vacuum cleaner in the kitchen closet, and an electric iron; an electric grill on the tea wagon . . . and they were discussing a washing machine." Mrs. Wilkins savors the magazine and studies it with intensity—she recognizes a pair of curtains in the magazine that hang in her bedroom. She identifies with the readership. The magazine has taught her that using evaporated milk is acceptable, she now serves canned pineapple and Jell-O—products once thought too processed, too artificial, to belong in a traditional home, but are intended to go along with modern labor saving machinery. When Mrs. Wilkins reads the ad for a new product that softens hands, she sends in the coupon for a "beautiful miniature bottle for six cents," because she had always been "ashamed of her hands." As Townsend succinctly writes, "The magazine had done its work and another coupon was on its way."[46]

The internal JWT publication captures the unrepentant use of psychological shame to make the lotion appealing, the use of "discount" marketing techniques such as coupons and the process by which a reader recognizes herself as a part of a greater community of modern women in a domestic setting, Townsend educates the readers of the JWT News Bulletin enabling them to capitalize on these advertising concepts.

JWT research showed that certain front-rank society leaders who could readily afford the most expensive creams were actually using Pond's instead. Lansdowne, Casseres, and the Women's Editorial Department staff persuaded these women to endorse Pond's cream in advertising, extending the use of Pond's to other society women. This gave Pond's more convincing proof of status than any other maker of face creams could offer. Part of this strategy was JWT's belief that society news was the feature of most interest to women readers—on a par with the front page itself. This JWT basic strategy of mixing topical interest and endorsement by relevant social leaders has remained a constant; copy was continually updated to report on the liveliest news of the day.

The tactic was to seem current with new competitive conditions as well as keep a maximum number of women reading Pond's advertising. While keeping up to date, JWT's Women's Editorial Department staff still employed the tried-and-true formula of endorsement success. These copywriters were also operating from one element of their own ideology by supporting the dominant class as the arbiters of taste. They knew that philanthropic leaders had a dual social significance: rich but in some cases genuinely attuned to attempting to aid the poor, prominent in the public eye but often seen askance by quieter members of their social circle. From the one-time background that many of the women had in social work, their ad writing at JWT had brought them a long way in situating themselves in the complex interaction of social, cultural, and economic capital as it may be put in the service of not very rational consumption.

To sum up the Pond's social prestige campaign, JWT and Pond's executives identified a shifting market and adjusted their ads to meet it. During the testimonial ad campaign, sales of the creams jumped again, and they maintained their leading positions in a crowed marketplace of familiar products.[47]

The Success of the Pond's Prestige Testimonial Ad Campaign

How much were these ads really responsible for the success of Pond's Vanishing Cream and Pond's Cold Cream? At a Creative Staff meeting at JWT (no date, but probably in the 1930s), Ruth Waldo asked a Miss Taylor to talk about the test methods used on their advertising accounts. Taylor explained just how difficult it is to determine the results from any particular ad campaign: "You've got to step cautiously in analyzing results. There are so many catches."[48]

This certainly speaks to the analysis of the success of the Pond's campaign or the Woodbury, Cutex, Sun-Maid, or Lux campaigns—all of which the Women's Editorial Department developed. JWT consistently used two methods of testing—tests based on coupon returns or responses to an offer and other tests based on sales results in a given area. Though there is no data available to my knowledge regarding regional sales comparisons for Pond's, Taylor does discuss the use of coupon returns for the Pond's campaign.

The majority of Pond's ads had either a coupon for a free sample or an offer for a sample for a relatively small amount of money, four cents, for example. Taylor says that in 1927 the women working on the account could draw a few conclusions from coupon returns: the more glamorous or sentimental the photo, the better the returns. Also, in terms of the testimonial ads, younger endorsers brought in more coupons than older endorsers. The theory behind this type of test is "attention value." The copywriter's first concern is to get the ad read, to draw attention. While this does not necessarily mean that the consumer actually bought the product (as sales numbers would indicate), it does show that the consumer is reading the ad.[49] The sales increase figures in this chapter do indicate that as the years went on and the Pond's campaign was adjusted according to research reports, more and more women bought Pond's.

What did female consumers really think of the testimonial ads? According to unpublished marketing studies in the 1920s and 1930s, Pond's success seems to owe much to factors beyond print ads such as marketing strategies such as free or small sample sizes, retailers' recommendations, and saleswomen.[50] As Kathy Peiss points out, family and friends, class, and social background all came into play as women assessed the salience of an advertisement in their lives. One middle-class woman, for example, judged a Pond's testimonial advertisement "interesting in a way," but that she "would be more interested if my next door neighbor told me what good results she had had."[51] She continued, "Some of the wealthy women probably don't have as bad skins to care for as people who have come from large families with small incomes where doctors were too expensive to be called in always, and skins sometimes suffered because diseases were inadequately care for. So what Queen Marie does for her skin which is probably very smooth to begin with, would not help me as much as what my next-door neighbor uses."[52] The woman's interview makes clear that she was not a gullible copier of the habits of the rich and was well aware of the differences between her life and theirs. Some women praised the socialites' testimony—"it brings the story home to you to read about women whose names are known"—though others seemed aware that the endorsers were paid or had another agenda than beneficence.[53] In terms of the Pond's advertising campaign, however, sales show that despite some expressed skepticism, women bought the product in high numbers.

It is a misleading exercise merely to analyze the language and images in individual ads without contextualizing and historizing their production. The challenge is not only a matter of reconciling the creation of sexist, racist, and classist copy with the evolution of professional gains for women within the ad industry: we must also consider the coexistence in individual women of wildly contradictory expressed attitudes. Sometimes, such contradictions stemmed from the desire to promote women in the industry. And, as Simone Weil Davis points out, the self-contradictions that proliferate in all industry theorizing of the female consumer seem, in the work of women in the advertising industry, to stem from multiple identifications. These women "vacillate between manipulating the female consumer and serving as her advocate."[54]

The ideological paradoxes and the experience of "doubleness" that the women at JWT experienced are good examples of what Davis describes here. The women at JWT were in an interesting position in terms of when they entered the job market, the developing field of advertising they chose to enter, and the construction and manipulation of the female consumer, of which they were a part. On the one hand, they generally gained status by entering a male-dominated business world, they made more money than working as a social worker, for example, and they enjoyed an environment at JWT created by a powerful mentor (Helen Lansdowne Resor). On the other hand, they helped define a narrow concept of ideal beauty and feminine identity—something they argued against in their criticisms of stereotypes of women—and, even while they tried to reconcile the two, their focus was on the bottom line as opposed to the social good.

New Problem—New Approach

By 1934, research revealed vital facts that led to a new approach to the same basic Pond's Cold and Vanishing Creams endorsement story. The Depression during the 1930s made it more and more difficult to sell the two-cream method. New contenders such as Lady Esther Cream featured all-inclusive claims for one cream. In September 1934, campaigns for the separate use of Pond's Cold Cream and Vanishing Cream were launched for the first time. Although both creams continued to use society endorsers, the cold cream advertising dominated in stressing this theme. This strategy carried on into the Depression years, when Pond's society leaders showed how to save money—through beauty care at home.

JWT not only kept pace but also never lost sight of the smaller demographic audiences it might find within the broader category of female consumers who kept up with the times. Even with this nod to a larger category of appropriate endorsers, the look of and description of these young women remained true to past ad campaigns that featured fair-skinned, privileged beauties. In addition to the myth of ideal beauty, values such as patriotism, duty to family, and marriage are connected to a consumer product, which appealed to a particular moment in history and supported the political projects of the upper class.

The myth of ideal beauty is supported both in the images and the copy of advertisements and can be illustrated in most of the ads for Pond's. In one Pond's ad with the headline "What a man looks for in a girl,"[55] which uses actresses as endorsers, whiteness is highlighted in three ways: (1) through the images of the white models, (2) through the endorsement of one actress that Pond's is good for "softening and whitening my skin," and (3) in the ad copy itself that challenges the consumer to "make this test—see how one application makes your skin noticeably softer, whiter." In this case, race and class are inextricably linked. At the top of this ad appears a sketch of a white woman who daintily sits surrounded by four white men in evening attire. She is in a gown and pearls, striking a pose that indicates a nonchalant ease with being the center of attention. She stares off into space and fiddles with her string of pearls as the men compete for her attention. Since she is not engaged in conversation with her admirers, they must be drawn to the charm of her beautiful soft and white skin. The ideology of beauty relies on these emotive appeals to both a pure whiteness and smooth skin with the sole purpose of acquiring a "charm that has universal appeal" to catch a man.

Part of the myth of ideal beauty is that it is universal, that this particular beauty is the accepted as ideal all over the world, universally. Roland Barthes explores the ideology of universalism in a short essay called "The Great Family of Man." The title refers to an exhibition of photographs in Paris, which aimed to show how certain themes and practices occur in all the cultures of the world. Barthes analyzes the mythology at work in this exhibition as the conjuring of a universal human community out of examples of cultural diversity. He stresses that the sentimentality of the notion that we are all brothers and sisters under the skin disguises historical facts, not just of cultural differences, but also of domination and inequality. The claim that ideal beauty has a universal appeal suppresses history, whether the remark is made in reference to charm in particular, or to the universality of human experience.[56]

Of course there is a difference between saying that "people are the same in their actions and emotions the world over" and "people are the same in their desire for the same appearance the world over." Therefore, it is important to stress the psychological appeal of the Pond's campaign. The desire to be seen as "beautiful" is a desire to be accepted, to be a part of a community. Beauty standards vary by culture, but when one culture dominates a market segment and uses images and text to express an ideal beauty in advertising products to that market, a desire for beauty becomes a desire for an ideal beauty defined by another culture.

This same myth of ideal beauty supports other Pond's ads as well—both the domestic ads and international ads (discussed in Chapter 6). The "She's Engaged, She's Lovely, She Uses Pond's" campaign developed out of the original social prestige testimonial ads and ran during World War II. These ads feature young socialites or well-connected women who are engaged and contributing to the war efforts. One such ad ran in *Movie Story, Fawcett Women's Group, McFadden Women's Group, Modern Magazine, Cosmopolitan, True Story, Screenland Unit, Good Housekeeping*, and *Mademoiselle* in 1942. In the ad, a photograph of Marion Lynn, the "exquisite daughter of Mr. and Mrs. Claude E. Lynn of the prominent Chicago family" takes at least one-third of the page. Her engagement to Bertram L. Menne, Jr., of Louisville is announced in the ads, and a photo of her engagement ring is prominent with the description, "her ring is a beautiful brilliant cut blue-white solitaire, set fairly high and on each side a single round diamond set a little lower. The band is platinum." There's also another photo of Marion and Bertram strolling arm in arm just a few hours before he heads off to officer's training at Quantico, Virginia. The copy describes how Marion uses Pond's Cold Cream and Pond's Vanishing Cream to maintain her "soft-smooth" skin.

In the majority of ads in this campaign, the women describe the work they do for the war effort. Phylis Gray, whose "blue-green eyes are as changeable as the sea," has gone from "college to war industry."[57] Phylis "tests tensile strength of fabric for parachute bags, tents, summer uniforms for the armed forces. She is one of six college girls being trained in a big Textile Company, to replace young men called to the services." If the reader is not completely sold solely on the social merits of Phylis Gray, the ad copy reminds her that "you'll soon see why beauties like Mrs. Nicholas R. du Pont and Mrs. Elliott Roosevelt are Pond's users," employing the social status of these more recognizable names to reinforce the message. Not only are all these wartime second-tier endorsers white, they are also young, upper-middle-class, and college-educated. The photo of the engagement ring serves as a marker of desirability as well as class, and the description of her family firmly situates her social position.

The psychological, social prestige testimonial ad worked within the ideology of ideal beauty, which naturalizes whiteness and social class. That is, the depiction of all the women appearing in ads as white implies that this is just "the way it is." By the very subject matter of the ads, it also appears natural that beautiful women are college-educated and of a certain social class. To the millions of women reading the ad, including groups of African American, immigrants, and working-class women, this ad might appeal to their sense of social ambition, curiosity, or perhaps to their desire to look beautiful.

Pond's claimed that they could do so by spending as little as twenty-five cents on a jar of cream. In reality, the women who appeared in these ads were much closer socially and in terms of race and culture to the women at JWT who created the ads. The executives at Pond's and the copywriters at JWT had the power to use the sign system to serve the corporate interests of both the manufacturer and the advertising agency.

Inner Beauty: A Final New Appeal

JWT carefully noted in their research and campaigns many of the ways that women changed after World War II. According to JWT records, after the harsh inner conflicts brought about by war (the conflicting and new roles women played from icons like Rosie the Riveter to the war widow to the Women's Army Corps), women were searching not only for romance, for marriage and children, for beauty, but also for something deeper. To meet this end, Pond's in 1947 added a new appeal to its basic twenty-year theme of endorsements by leading society women. Through deeply personal advertising, Pond's told women that "experts of the mind" had proved: "It is not just vanity to develop the beauty of your own face. Beauty's self-discipline can make your whole personality grow. When you look lovely—you feel a happy confidence. It glows in your face. It sends a magic sparkle out from you that brings the real, warm, Inner You closer to others."[58]

This "new" approach built on the already established campaign that lifted a well-known and somewhat ordinary Pond's cream to a new height of social status through social prestige testimonials. What Anne McClintock calls a "semiotic space" surrounded Pond's creams, and this space had been filled with meaning by the women at JWT. The creams did not by themselves take on meaning; rather, it was an effort by the Women's Editorial Department that associated Pond's with titled Europeans and American high society. Through the manipulation of signs and text, meaning is transferred to the Pond's product. The signifiers (images of white, engaged, privileged women) were connected to the cream to reinforce the ideals being "sold."

Marriage, patriotism, whiteness, duty to family, and heterosexuality were all being extolled as virtues and institutions to uphold. JWT's women brought their own values and aesthetics to this product (as they did many others), and in this most recent effort to rebrand the product once again, they switched from shame (your face needs Pond's) to a promise of self-development (your internal beauty will surface with Pond's if you have the discipline). Beauty becomes a matter of self-discipline and "experts of the mind" verify that the product will give the consumer a "happy confidence" that will allow her to be closer to others. This adjustment in ad copy reflects the attempt to replace what could be perceived only as a frivolous desire for superficial beauty with a desire to "glow" from within. These ads assured women that it was not their vanity that propelled them to use beauty products—for there were other more important things for them to think about—but rather the self-discipline of their routine that would serve to bring out their inner, more true beauty.[59]

The processes described thus far are best understood as part of a larger system of values and beliefs—a function of ideology. Ideology is a complex and ongoing, all-inclusive set of practices in which all classes participate. This is the core strength of ideology; it has the ability to adapt and change. The power of a hegemonic ideology is that it works from within and is deeply inscribed in the practices of everyday life such as reading magazines filled with ads and shopping. The social experiences of subordinated groups constantly contradict the picture that the dominant ideology paints for them of themselves and their social relations. The dominant ideology, therefore, has to constantly overcome resistance in order to win people's consent to the social order that it is promoting; those resistances may be overcome but never eliminated.[60] An analysis of how ideology works in this particular business context provides a conceptual foundation for an examination of a privileged group of American women producing ads during the early decades of the twentieth century.

While the impulse to show how dominant ideology can blind consumers is useful (as in some New Left perspectives), my study is more particular: at times, consumers are fooled or misled by advertisers, but at other times they adopt or adapt products in ways that advertisers and marketers do not expect (like the door-to-door responses Lewis and Casseres encountered in suburban Connecticut). Yet there are no simple villains or heroines in my analysis; both the advertising world and the consumer often do not behave as theories of society and ideology predict.

Women have constantly strived to gain access to cultural meaning systems, as well as to exert control over the meanings such systems can produce. The advertisements produced by the women at JWT were a part of this cultural meaning system during the early part of the twentieth century.

Middle- and upper-class women and their various audiences attempted to exert control over the meanings in the developing system of women's magazines and advertising. These same women, though, experienced the difficulties of working within a male-dominated industry that limited them while at the same time they also belonged to a social group that was privileged by the system—hence the paradoxes for women who strove to build their own market share.

Lansdowne and her staff in the Women's Editorial Department had a feminist consciousness, but the hypermasculine corporate culture in which they worked created a sense of doubleness. While they struggled for the right to vote and for entry into the business world by marketing their feminine intuition, these women also manipulated the emotions of the female consumer. By looking closely at how Pond's advertising was created, we can see the psychological strategies and techniques based on the myth of ideal beauty. These women's own class position enabled them to work at JWT, but in creating the type of ads geared toward women, they became part of the dominant class's political project to create myths that sold more products and served the goals of corporate America. If we did not examine the JWT agency as class-based, gendered, and racialized, however, we would fail to understand the processes of making meaning—we would fail to see how attaching meaning to products perpetuates certain myths such as ideal beauty.

Placed in historical context, the newly ascendant advertising industry marks and contributes to a society increasingly dominated by consumerism, as well as the emergence of the pervasive gendering, classing, and racialization of American consumerism. The Pond's campaign was a complex interaction between marketing research, shrewd development of copy and upscale product positioning, an intelligent modification of the campaign to current events and current trends (the rise of psychology and sociology in explaining to consumers what products promise them), and a brilliantly planned testimonial ad campaign. All of the pieces of this puzzle were carefully crafted by a unique group of women working at JWT—women who were comfortable assessing the role of political and social change and who also bestowed an aura of class and their expertise in beauty on the female consumer.

4

Selling Sex and Science

Woodbury's Facial Soap Case Study

> The Woodbury's business and the Jergens business . . . is what physicians
> would call a perfect case: it touches almost every problem of an advertiser.
>
> —Stanley Resor, in a speech to a JWT class, April 12, 1920,
> JWT Archives, Woodbury's Account Files

> Soap Is Civilization.
>
> —Unilever Company slogan

Helen Lansdowne was instrumental in the creation of the Woodbury's Facial Soap advertising campaign; she spent months on
research and product analysis prior to the initial educational/scientific
campaign in 1910.[1] Lansdowne is also credited with the provocative campaign slogan "A Skin You Love To Touch," which debuted in 1914 and was
accompanied by a sensual and romantic image and supporting ad copy.
The ad captured the imagination of the American public and educated
women on various skin problems.[2] Lansdowne's Woodbury's ad campaign is listed as one of the top ten achievements of J. Walter Thompson (JWT) in one of its company histories. And the Woodbury's slogan
"A Skin You Love To Touch" came to be the "descriptive trademark" of
the Woodbury products, which embody "beauty, and the love, envy and
admiration beauty engenders."[3]

What the Women's Editorial Department undertook with the Woodbury's Soap campaign was an approach to educate women about the
nature and working of their skin, the cause of skin problems, and the ways

in which these defects could be overcome by the right cleansing method with the advertised product. A scientific and educational approach to dealing with skin problems was reinforced by a strong emotional appeal to women's desire to be beautiful and charming, to have clear, smooth, and attractive skin—"A Skin You Love To Touch." Edith Lewis, a member of the Women's Editorial Department, and a graduate of Smith College, was the Group Head on the Woodbury's account. Lewis worked closely with Lansdowne and was responsible for the writers working on the account and was the liaison to the account representative who dealt directly with the client.

Lansdowne, Lewis, and their group of women copywriters perfected the use of commercial sex appeal, couched in the myth of romance, in the Woodbury's campaign. It was an unheard of advertising approach during the early part of the twentieth century. Earlier ads had exploited sex and attractive women, but none with the effectiveness and persistence of the Woodbury's campaign. The combined approach positions the woman as consumer in such a way that she would think she was a modern woman who used the facts, the authority, and the latest advances in science. The use of scientific claims in service of a romantic sex appeal makes the Woodbury's Soap campaign truly modern.

Lansdowne had an insightful understanding of the appeal to American women and men of those things stereotypically feminine, whether it was the marketing of a Women's Editorial Department to gain new household and cosmetic product accounts for JWT or the use of romantic sex appeal to boost sales of a flagging soap product. In addition, Lansdowne understood why women bought "women's goods" such as soap, cold cream, and shortening, so she presented provocative arguments for improving oneself and aspiring to the lifestyle of wealthier people, something she had achieved herself.

As a result of the various ad campaigns that Lansdowne and the Women's Editorial Department staff created, the myths of ideal beauty, romance, civilization, and class mobility became deeply entrenched in the American collective consciousness. Their ads tapped into the rise of science and an increasing public explicitness about sex and beauty. And this process was only bolstered by similar changes and messages reflected in fashion, film, and theater.

Recent scholarly analyses of soap advertisements claim that soap carries a special inherent meaning. Soap is a cleaning agent, therefore associated with purity, and serves as a magnet for social messages of anxiety and desire; ideas about race, class, and nationality; and ideas about femininity and masculinity. Anne McClintock's revealing study of soap advertisements—in particular, the Pear's Soap campaign—during mid-nineteenth-century Victorian England shows how the cult of domesticity and the popular justification for imperialism found in soap an exemplary mediating form. Soap, she claims, came to symbolize middle-class values: "monogamy ('clean' sex, which has value), industrial capital ('clean' money, which has value), Christianity ('being washed in the blood of the lamb'), class control ('cleansing the great unwashed'), and the imperial civilizing mission ('washing and clothing the savage')."[4]

All of these values found representation in soap ads while the British were experiencing the waning of their empire as well as the threat of uncertain boundaries of class, gender, and race identity. And in the images of the Pear's campaign, McClintock exposes a paradox: these ads took intimate images of domesticity (scenes of bathing, shaving, various stages of dress, bedrooms) into the public realm (walls, buses, shops, billboards). The Pear's advertising images, coupled with scenes of empire and racial difference, were mass-marketed as an organized system of images and attitudes.[5]

In her cultural history of advertising personal hygiene in the United States, Juliann Sivulka describes similar messages concerning unstable social differences and unequal power illustrated through the subtext of soap ads. She proposes four specific mechanisms of knowledge and power centered on personal cleanliness that reinforced an ideology of American, white-identified, middle-class values and beliefs: (1) women's clubs from the Civil War to 1920; (2) the reformist, urban, settlement movement from 1890 to 1920; (3) advice literature, ranging from etiquette books to popular magazines; and (4) the advertising industry.[6]

Though she does not provide a gendered analysis, all four of Sivulka's points can be shown to be connected to achievements of white, American women or are processes directed toward the gendering of consumers in the United States, especially women's magazines and the advertising industry. Sivulka claims that these cultural mechanisms of knowledge and power focused attention on middle-class standards of cleanliness and sent a powerful message: "Keeping clean was not only healthy, but it was important to the country's standard of living, social welfare, and economy. In the new industrial America, personal cleanliness rituals ensured order and advancement; these rituals also disciplined, built character, and created new customers for an emerging consumer society."[7]

As with other analyses in the structuralist style, the relation of cause and effect is only indicative, not definitive. Such signs of values did not necessarily cause anything in and of themselves, but the complex social forces indicated by real-world organizations such as women's clubs, the settlement house movement, and ad agencies were certainly in interplay with these signs.

The images and text of soap ads supported a significant sign system associated with ideologies of gender, class, race, and imperialism. The mythologies that were formed through these ideologies helped naturalize the unequal distribution of power in the United States, a formula that was used to justify American imperialist expansion as well as a domestic colonization of those who needed to be "cleansed." There were, of course, more concrete economic and political reasons such ambitions were made, yet not-withstanding, the cult of cleanliness, with its deep religious roots, was a powerful force.

The images and messages crafted by JWT's Women's Editorial Department for the Woodbury's Facial Soap ads support this claim and tie such analyses to forceful, creative, and palpable business institutions. The messages and images in these soap ads, as well as in other product ads, reflected a distinct ideology that had real implications, to varying degrees, for all Americans.

Sivulka's and McClintock's analyses reflect one aspect of the cultural process of advertising—that is, the reading and meaning-making of advertisements. Their analyses are important in understanding how ads can reflect and perpetuate societal anxieties, desires, and ambitions. My aim in the Woodbury's case study is to build on and add to this type of work by including the actual process of creating an ad campaign—a "behind the scenes" look into the motivations of manufacturers and advertisers and the creative process of putting together a campaign that advertisers think will appeal to consumers. This chapter also explores where and when women worked behind the scenes and how that matters in creating the type of campaign that was ultimately produced for Woodbury's Soap.

As mentioned earlier, the two outstanding features of the Woodbury's Soap advertising campaign strategy was the JWT decision to combine sex appeal (referred to as "sentimental" in JWT records) and science (in both the ads claims and in the use of systematic market research). Lansdowne, Lewis, and the women copywriters who created the Woodbury's campaign were influenced by both of these concepts, although they seem to exist on the opposite ends of the "logic/emotion" spectrum. Perhaps it seems somewhat contradictory to use these concepts together. So what does the JWT's women copywriters' decision to use sentimental and scientific claims tell us about the early twentieth century and about modernity? What does it tell us about the romance myth and how the image of science was marketed at this time?

Peggy Kreshel suggests, in an article about the culture of JWT, that Stanley Resor[8] redefined the work of the agency in terms of "scientific research" and marketing. He attempted to provide an environment within the agency and the industry that fostered the development of that scientific approach and to market JWT competency in scientific investigation to a business community now routinely pursuing commercially useful science.[9] Resor intended to rationalize the process of advertising, and, at the same time, he reinforced the importance of science as the appropriate basis for decision making. Over time at JWT, the pursuit of science took on a life of its own, achieving symbolic proportions.

It became difficult to distinguish the rhetorical from the real, the utility from the symbol. Resor set an agenda for an attitude toward the profession of advertising as a science-based enterprise—research became institutionalized at JWT. It is worth repeating that the appeal of science held sway within the masculine business community; science had wrought technological advances and striking advances in productivity. Resor strove to connect the appeal of science in advertising to a business community that valued science in its more concrete applications, hence legitimizing his profession and agency.

The story of Woodbury's Facial Soap shares some of the same elements of social anxiety and desire that McClintock untangles in her analysis of Victorian soap advertisements, while it also sheds further light on gender and some aspects of Sivulka's analyses. The Pear's campaign further blurred the demarcation of private from public with its intimate images of bathing and states of undress, just as Woodbury's later campaign reveals the new and rising association of science and sex that is routine today: sex appeal backed by scientific claims in ads aimed toward mainstream America.

Exploring the tensions in the Woodbury's Soap campaign and the positioning of the company and JWT's efforts in a larger cultural discourse will reveal the intersections of nationality, gender, sexuality, class, and race. It will also situate the perpetuation of ideologies in the meeting rooms of the Jergens Company (owners of Woodbury's) and through the corporate culture of JWT, and come to know some of the actual people who talked about, made decisions, wrote copy for, and selected the images for this symbolically freighted product.

Advertising and Marketing Soap in the United States

Mr. Otley of Colgate told me about buying a prescription for a shoe polish, and after much effort, got the product successfully on the market. He put the formula deep in his safe and could hardly sleep for fear someone would get it. But sales continued to be good and he had offers to buy the business. Finally, he realized that the success of the business was not the formula, but the way the product was made and marketed. From then on he opened the safe and breathed easier.

—Stanley Resor, in a speech to a JWT class, April 12, 1920, Woodbury's Account
    Files, JWT Archives, Duke University Library, Durham, North Carolina

In a way similar to that of patent medicine manufacturers, early soap makers pioneered the merchandising and packaging of brand-name goods. To differentiate their soap from other soaps on the market, the manufacturers experimented with packaging and what would come to be known as branding their product. The goal was to infuse the product with many positive meanings. Manufacturers worked with advertisers to bestow meaning that transcended everyday use on the product and the act of using it. Working with codes that indicated what was considered properly feminine and masculine, they attempted to get American consumers to more fully associate products and genders than they already did. Beyond gendering their soap, manufacturers and advertisers tried to infuse soaps with a particular nationality—English, French, or American—all suggested by the soap's packaging (pink wrapper for women), the name of the soap ("Yardley from England"), and the scent (stronger for men and delicate for women).[10]

In the United States, until the nineteenth century, most commercially sold soaps looked identical. In the typical local general store, the clerk would cut off a chunk of soap from a larger slab, weigh it, and wrap it in paper. As more people stopped making their own soap and started buying it from the local merchant, and made distinctions between varieties of soap, manufacturers recognized consumer desire and increasingly began to brand their products so the customer would remember a particular quality. At about this time, manufacturers also realized that they could charge more for a product that consumers recognized thanks to the attractive packaging and branding. With higher profits as a motivating factor, manufacturers began to spend time actually thinking about bestowing their products with meaning and inspiring consumer confidence and loyalty.

Dr. John H. Woodbury—a druggist—decided that in order to inspire consumer confidence in his soap, he would use his name and portrait on his packages. Other early American commercial soap makers such as

Colgate, Procter & Gamble, Babbitt, Dobbins, and Larkin, among others, did this as well.[11] The message was clear—using one's professional name and face to advertise a product illustrated a superior confidence in the product. These manufacturers could be seen as staking their reputations on the quality of their products. They separated themselves from name-less, faceless manufacturers who pumped out vats of inferior product with no clear lineage.

In addition to the motivation of making more money with an identifi-able product, manufacturers were also interested in getting their products known on the national market—nationally advertised products could be sold for more (and of course had to be in order to recoup ad and market-ing costs). So to distinguish their products, manufacturers used a graphic image or symbol for visual identification, which was in effect one of the early trademarks.

Dr. Woodbury never put out an advertisement for Woodbury's Facial Soap unless it included his name and face; he also used the authority of his title "Dr.," establishing his expertise in the field of dermatology. The advertising and packaging promoted the soap as a cure for skin diseases, as well as part of a family of specially formulated remedies for the skin, hair, and scalp. Woodbury claimed in his extensive ad copy that his soap was made "by one who has had over 20 years' successful experience in studying and curing all the ailments peculiar to the skin."[12] He presents himself as the authority on skin and at the bottom of the ad under John H. Wood-bury's name appears "Dermatological Institute," further establishing his credentials in the field of skin care. Woodbury's trademarked face came to be associated with assumptions about curative powers and identified and drew consumers to the product.

Dr. Woodbury's belief that a purely scientific advertising approach based on the authority of medical doctors and the reputation of a scientific institute would continue to appeal to female consumers was off base. His masculine image and scientific appeal alone could not maintain consumer interest and did not spark the imaginations of thousands of female con-sumers across the country who were purchasing the majority of goods for the home. Dr. Woodbury's Soap had to undergo a complete regendering if it was to compete on the market with hundred of other soaps undergoing modern, specialized branding.

History of Woodbury's Facial Soap

The story of Woodbury's includes a dramatic narrative of a product reaching new heights in sales after steadily dropping for a number of years. For twelve years after its first appearance on the market in 1885, Woodbury's Facial Soap enjoyed a growing demand. Then, in 1896, it had apparently saturated its market. Sales became flat; they lessened under the pressure of competition and finally dropped so low that in 1900 the Woodbury name, the associated goodwill, and trademark were sold to the Andrew Jergens Company for $250,000.[13]

By 1907, however, Jergens managed to revive sales for Woodbury's Soap, reaching a sales income of nearly $150,000.[14] But that success did not last. In 1910, Woodbury's sales fell again to not much more than $100,000, with the revival effect perhaps attributable to the bounce in sales that can occur with any more or less successful restyling or reintroduction.

With declining sales, Jergens decided that radical measures were necessary, and, accordingly, Jergens executives decided to appropriate huge sums for advertising. They spent them in almost every conceivable form of sales promotion, featuring a variety of appeals. Jergens experimented with three principle methods of handling the account: first, through an agency; second, through media owners; and third, through in-house advertising managers. The media owners were the Street Railways Advertising Company, to whom the account was given in 1906; not surprisingly, they put the entire Woodbury's Soap appropriation into streetcar advertising. After this proved unsuccessful at raising Woodbury's Soap sales, Jergens placed the account with an advertising manager from 1907 to 1910. The advertising agency is not named in the account files.[15] Woodbury's sales fell from $148,860 in 1907 to $108,286 in 1910 (Table 4.1). As sales began to decline, Woodbury's advertising appropriation got smaller and smaller.

Table 4.1.   Sales and Advertising for Woodbury's Facial Soap (cost incurred by Jergens), 1901–10[16]

Year	Sales ($)	Advertising ($)
1901	72,900	70,673
1902	106,498	95,154
1903	114,498	78,464
1904	120,779	91,266
1905	128,647	72,592
1906	133,025	109,167
1907	148,860	85,936
1908	130,027	68,890
1909	108,331	48,423
1910	108,286	44,383

While it is not clear which happened first, the sagging sales or the cut in advertising appropriation, the mistaken reliance on streetcar ads instead of placements in powerful magazines or newspapers certainly contributed to the decline in sales. Bringing in another firm also suggests that part of the problem may have been that Woodbury's was not marketed and advertised consistently and with a progressive or long-term strategy.

In 1910, Jergens executives awarded the Woodbury's account to Stanley Resor, who was then the Cincinnati manager for JWT. The advertising budget was set at $25,000 for the next year, as compared with Jergens's $44,383 appropriation, the sum that had been spent with poor results during the previous year. Jergens executives had been prepared to abandon advertising entirely at this point, which accounts for the extremely small amount of money they were willing to invest in advertising the soap. Their expectations were low, to say the least.

With the new advertising campaign designed by Lansdowne and later managed by group head Edith Lewis, sales of Woodbury's Facial Soap increased every year from 1910 through 1921, reaching more than twenty times the 1910 sales figures. In the Woodbury Account History, JWT (not attributed) says that it gladly accepted the small initial appropriation because it saw a "sure, though possibly, distant, future for the account."[17] After the first year of developing the Woodbury's campaign, Lansdowne stopped the falling sales curve for the first time in fourteen years. For four years, sales grew steadily, and each year's advertising appropriation was based on the previous year's sales. Sales gained momentum and swept steadily upward, until the advertising appropriation for 1926 was seven times as large as the total sales when JWT took the account ($25,000 to $175,000). Salesmen's commissions of 10 percent were reduced to 1 percent due to the tremendous increase in volume. Distribution of Woodbury's became absolute: 50,000 retailers and 350 wholesaler druggists in the United States alone carried the soap. Stanley Resor claimed that Woodbury's was by far the largest-selling soap in its field.[18]

JWT seems to have made an almost magically successful bet on science. Taking the last-ditch appropriation of only $25,000, Resor and Lansdowne undertook to bring Woodbury's back into the market by spending every dollar on insuring what they considered a sure-fire tactic focused on scientific accuracy and the prestige of science. This strategy, with its focus on science, had already been a winner in the past, since it was created and used by Lansdowne on her handling of the Crisco account. Recall that Lansdowne wrote headlines for Crisco that read, "A Scientific Discovery Which Will Affect Every Kitchen in America."

Science: The Skin Treatment

JWT's inclination toward scientific strategies—both in their internal research methods and in their advertising copy—created the context for Lansdowne's development of a new template for Woodbury's based on treatments of the skin for each specific skin trouble: oily skin, shiny nose, conspicuous pores, sallow skin, and sensitive skin. Note, too, that the strategy of product differentiation was also applied to consumer differentiation, a brilliant move and a harbinger of ad strategies still viable today. The consumer was set apart from peers, given a possibly partly invented but definitely distinctive need, and then sold on precisely the scientifically valid serum that would cure the partially invented "ailment."

In July 1910, the first advertisements for Woodbury's appeared as a series of treatments in the *Saturday Evening Post* and the *Ladies' Home Journal*.[19] The first copy that appeared read, "We Are Making Our Twenty-Fourth Million Cake" and showed a number of soap cakes at the top of the page to give the illusion that Woodbury's was a big seller. This introductory piece was followed by a series of small advertisements devoted to the special treatments of Woodbury's on facial skin and also to the use of Woodbury's on hair and for children. These two latter uses were dropped in 1915 because of lack of response in comparison to the skin treatment copy. Hair and kids did not, apparently, warrant special treatment in the domain of soap.

The new advertising strategy and campaign were successful in boosting Woodbury's sales, and the following year (1911) the appropriation was increased from $25,000 to $58,900, $53,000 of which was spent in magazines and $5,600 in newspapers—a testament to the effectiveness of advertising in women's magazines in particular. In 1920, while discussing the Woodbury's account with a group of newly hired JWT employees, Stanley Resor said, "Women's magazines are the backbone of our media schedule. Unquestionably the most economical single medium, they will reach more homes per thousand dollars invested in any other . . . their total circulation for Woodbury is 13 million."[20]

Resor and Lansdowne had also made it clear during the development of this campaign that local advertising was out of the question because of the overcrowded soap market (Woodbury's main, same-price competitors were Cuticura, Cashmere Bouquet, and Resinol). They were emphatic about a comprehensive national campaign. Nineteen magazines and eleven newspapers were used, and the sales for 1911 increased to $162,000.[21] The bet on women readers, on newspapers, and on national branding succeeded.

Lansdowne and her female staff of copywriters were instrumental in developing the hands-on elements of a scientific research strategy for Woodbury's Soap; the entire department spent over six months in laboratories, going house to house, in medical libraries, and among dermatological experts, behind retail counters, and distributing trade and consumer questionnaires in person and by mail.[22] In addition, the department examined "over 100 books and articles on the care and treatment of the skin."[23] The department conducted a retail survey that showed that retail distribution of Woodbury's Facial Soap was good, but consumer demand poor.

Woodbury's was far outsold by Cuticura, the leading twenty-five-cent toilet soap. At this time most toilet soaps, such as Palmolive, were priced at ten or fifteen cents and Ivory, produced by Procter & Gamble, cost just five cents. The Women's Editorial Department survey showed that Woodbury's Facial Soap was stocked by a majority of the druggists in the United States—so distribution was extensive but thin: "Nearly every backwoods druggist had at least one cake of Woodbury's on his shelves, where it had probably lain for some time"[24]

Good distribution but poor sales supports the evidence that the Street Railway Advertising Company and the firm that Jergens hired before JWT had entirely missed the mark when advertising Woodbury's Soap. They had not considered the female consumer nor had they considered the power and reach of women's magazines and advertising in newspapers. The efforts of both firms pale in comparison to Lansdowne, Lewis, and the Women's Editorial Department's emotional appeal, which was supported by scientific "facts" about women's skin for Woodbury's Soap and a shrewd understanding of the media that were then on the rise.

Laboratory analysis of the soap and its competitors, opinions from the medical profession, and interviews with housewives revealed how people washed and cared for their skin and what distinct service Woodbury's soap could be said to perform. By 1910, JWT had built a reputation among consumer product manufacturers for using scientific methods in general both for its own market research as well as for using the expertise of the scientific community. The Woodbury's Soap investigation was a good example of its desire to show its client and the consumer that it had done its research and had the backing of a medical expert. Lansdowne received permission from the Jergens Company to retain the former head of the New York Skin and Cancer Hospital, Dr. Broemer, to make sure that the Woodbury's ads made no claims that could not be substantiated. Broemer remained there for ten years in his capacity as medical expert.[25]

Consumer confidence responded and grew in accord with this tactic. In turn, that success factored into the creation of a new campaign that, by 1914, used a combination of two approaches: (1) specific cleansing treatments based on the practice of leading skin specialists; and (2) an emotional appeal, based on romance and sex, as expressed in the previously noted phrase "A Skin You Love To Touch." The copy was scientific, restrained, and conservative—emulating the authoritative tone of the scientific research and medical profession—and at the same time, personal, human, and oriented toward women. A booklet of instructions for the treatments was wrapped around each cake of soap, and the packaging itself improved.

It was not only because of the promise of this comprehensive research and repackaging, however, that JWT decided to take the scientific route. The competitor—Cuticura's success had already been attributed to its medicinal appeal while Woodbury's had been sold on a general beauty appeal.[26] Lansdowne and Lewis sought to combine the two appeals, which was a shrewd and elaborate development of Dr. Woodbury's original tactic of using his medical and clinical authority to promote his soap. The good doctor had just not been as ingenious in combining the allure of science and sex.

The "face" of the product itself was also enhanced. In 1914, the Woodbury's Facial Soap wrapper was redesigned. For legal reasons, Dr. Woodbury's head remained as part of the design, though his depiction and the lettering were improved. Lansdowne and Lewis suggested to Jergens clients that they package Woodbury's Soap in a way that was hermetically sealed to keep the soap free of "dirt, dust and human touch," at that time a very modern approach to packaging that also carried overtones of a medicinal and clinic-grade purity in the product.[27] The JWT "Woodbury Treatment Booklet," noted above, that was wrapped around each cake of soap, contained twenty full pages of skin-care advice. Interestingly, the booklet was originally produced in four languages: English, Spanish, French, and German.[28]

Lansdowne's slogan "A Skin You Love To Touch" was copyrighted by JWT, and the overall ad copy was described as being "thirty percent sentimental and seventy percent treatment." In 1921, the copy had shifted slightly and was described as 40 percent sentimental and 60 percent treatment, perhaps because of success of the emotional appeal of smooth, touchable skin had proved irresistible.[29] It seems that the sentimental approach worked better once the treatment copy boosted the sales of the soap.

By 1920, the JWT strategy was more decidedly to take on product differentiation in an overcrowded U.S. market of soap, in which many of the advertisers of best-selling soaps used medicinal claims. When Stanley Resor talked about hiring Dr. Broemer to ensure that JWT made no claims that could not be backed-up, he recalled,

Cuticura was a tremendous success, known everywhere through consistent and frequent claims which the Jergens Company and ourselves would never think of making. They claim to cure eczema, a very acute skin trouble which even the best specialists find hard to cure. It is a positive evil even to intimate that you can cure eczema by any soap on earth. I do not believe they did it intentionally. It is just one of those business problems that begin when people do not think enough. So for Woodbury's the danger of exaggeration had to be shunned, yet previous advertising, by merely calling it a beauty soap had failed. Therefore, Woodbury's soap would have to do something real for the reader yet make no claim, which could not be substantiated.[30]

From this speech it appears that Resor showed considerable restraint in deciding which scientific claims he was willing to make—he does not want to make a claim that is false, yet he knows that without a scientific claim, his client cannot compete against other manufacturers. What is also interesting about this scientific approach just tallied is the belief that an ad's effect could be divided up by percentage: 30 percent sentimental and 70 percent treatment. This kind of "science" permeated JWT's general approach to creating ads and is a direct result of a culture that developed theories and practices to embrace a more scientific basis for advertising.

Lansdowne, starting with the Crisco ad campaign, had used the rhetoric of science but with a "slant": she incorporated scientific claims in an editorial style in her Crisco ad text that made the science appear as if it were a natural element in an advice or beauty column. Women's magazines served as a distinctive medium within the advertising and beauty sign system. By using images of women and writing in an editorial style familiar to those in other parts of the magazine, Lansdowne borrows the legitimacy of those images and text, the assumption that as "editorial" copy they are not solely motivated by profit.

Flipping through the pages of her new magazine, a reader of such copy may not even be aware that the ad for Crisco is an ad selling a product. This was the era before many editorial departments at news venues established the practice of prominently heading such copy: "This is a paid advertising supplement" or using similar language. These types of ads were common in women's magazines during this period; they blended in so smoothly with the rest of the magazine content that the readers' skepticism normally provoked by an ad was not activated. The educational or instructional focus of the ad also contributed to an article-like tone, reminiscent of other articles in the magazine.

Scientific copy was appropriated by Lansdowne and Lewis and given a light and intimate tone with exhaustive facts and details about skin care (treatment ad copy). Though it was based on "scientific" research on the skin, the women copywriters took an approach that appealed to women's possible motivation toward self-improvement. It was as if the woman copywriter had taken aside the reader to tell her in confidence that her nose pores were too large but not to worry because she had the solution to her skin problems.

In the case of the Woodbury's Soap campaign, for example, treatment ad copy was occasionally mixed with the sentimental ad copy. Sometimes "A Skin You Love To Touch" was a minor part of the treatment copy (appearing on a visual reproduction of the Woodbury booklet that was wrapped around the cake of soap). Similarly, sentimental ads often included skin treatment advice, though JWT was able to identify the ads and categorize them into two types for the purposes of marketing and to compete with the leading soaps that used treatment copy exclusively. Although the exact measure of sentiment versus treatment might seem impossible to quantify, JWT kept to the policy of making such distinctions.

Sex Appeal and Science: Woodbury's Sentimental and Treatment Ads

Promoting "A Skin You Love To Touch" kicked off the first Woodbury's Soap window display, a three-paneled design that included the slogan. This display made the message graphic and visual. Consumers would gain beautiful, smooth skin that a distinguished white man would love to touch. Stanley Resor claims that the slogan took three years to really take off, but once it did, it was heard "on the stage and elsewhere."[31]

Although Lansdowne's slogan is tame by today's standards, at the time it claimed for its potential female soap consumer a sensuality and sexuality not often used in advertising until then. Even so, creating this sensual sentimental appeal did not require images that were vastly different from the scientific treatment ad. Both ads typically show a white man and woman in a romantic embrace or in an intimate social setting gazing into each other's eyes. Most often the couple is in evening clothes in a beautifully furnished home or hotel.

In partial contrast, Woodbury's treatment ads sometimes show a close-up sketch of a woman's face (especially when the ad discusses the problem of large facial pores), but the ad inevitably portrays, in a small third or fourth image, a romantic encounter between a man and a woman. To emphasize "A Skin You Love To Touch," the man is touching the woman in the ad images. The differences are more ones of emphasis and top billing for sensual appeal or treatment appeal, not true redesign of the images and symbols.

Occasionally, JWT copywriters altered the slogan to read, "A Skin He Loves To Touch." With the exception of that slogan, it would seem, oddly, that "A Skin You Love To Touch" was actually aimed at a male audience. Surely, the slogan is not aimed directly at women or meant to be taken literally; otherwise, the images would support the message with women touching their own or another woman's skin. While there may be something akin to modern fashion apparel advertising—in which ad makers recognize that women are dressing for other women more than for men and women's *perception* of feeling beautiful is as important as the supposed "sexiness" to men of a garment—clearly there are layers of appeal to both genders in this tactic.

In reality, Lansdowne and her female copywriters meant for the slogan to be read by a female reader who is most likely looking at a women's magazine. She, in turn, is being encouraged to imagine a "secondary reader," the man who will, thanks to Woodbury's Soap, be enticed to touch her skin. The slogan is a message of male desire for a woman with skin he loves to touch. Perhaps this slogan was so well received because it was not about female sexuality as much as it was about male desire. Perhaps the ad tapped into the desires of the women who looked at and read it—her desire to be desired.

The well-established theoretical concept of the male gaze and desire, illustrated by the Woodbury's Soap slogan seemingly meant for a male reader, has perhaps its best known expression in Laura Mulvey's article "Visual Pleasure and Narrative Cinema." Even though Mulvey focuses in her article on the medium of film, the concept of the "male gaze" (popularized by Mulvey) is useful in understanding why this print ad slogan had so much power.

Mulvey's psychoanalytically inspired studies of spectatorship focus on how the position of subjects—the place of the reader or viewer—is constructed by media texts. She argues for doing such analysis rather than investigating the viewing practices of individuals in specific social contexts to make a broader point about societal habits of vision. Mulvey notes Freud's famous article on the extension of infantile scopophilia into adult neurosis, when an adult takes an obsessive interest in the pleasure of watching bodies and receives an erotic charge akin to voyeurism. Mulvey argues that various features of cinema viewing conditions facilitate for the viewer both the voyeuristic process of *objectification* of female characters and also the narcissistic process of *identification* with an "ideal ego" seen on the screen. One can think of "ideal ego" as the film stars that we invest with almost godlike sexual power and appeal. Mulvey declares that in patriarchal society "pleasure in looking has been split between active/male and passive/female."[32]

By the early twentieth century, many women experienced greater leisure time than their earlier generations and devoted a good deal of it to reading about and identifying with the women written about and illustrated in the magazines, taking a great deal of pleasure in an identification with the women in those magazines. The male gaze, however, was an everyday experience for the twentieth-century reader: men do the looking and women are looked at. Women ad readers were, of course, adept at viewing and being viewed, but had to face a reality in which their own gaze was rarely allowed to take an aggressive form in the real world to the extent that the male gaze was so authorized.

It is much more likely, however, that these particular women were reading the ads in a number of ways and positioning themselves (and their own desire) in relation to the images and text in the ads. For example, Teresa de Lauretis argues that the female spectator does not simply adopt a masculine reading position but is always involved in a "double-identification" with both the passive and active subject positions.[33] This could certainly be the case with the Woodbury's soap ads, which followed an advertising strategy that brought significant signs from the ideological code of masculinity (male gaze, the privilege of looking and desiring) into relationship with the product and into women's homes. The ads let the male gaze into the female private and domestic realm.

Examining three other Woodbury's Soap ad campaigns reveals the number of possible subject positions that a reader could take in relation to the images and text in the ads. These ad campaigns also reveal much about the artistic training and the "eye" of a male photographer and the ability of the women copywriters at JWT to revitalize ad strategies used in previous successful campaigns.

During 1936, Lansdowne and her team worked with the photographer Edward Steichen on a series of female nudes to be used in Woodbury's Soap ads, in addition to other cosmetic and food accounts. Steichen was recruited by Lansdowne for a retainer of $100,000 a year, and she persuaded clients to use him. This was part of a larger agency effort that, in 1925, started to promote photography as a means of bringing greater realism into advertising. Well-known photographers, such as Edward Steichen, were enticed to enter the commercial world and their talents were offered to clients for the first time.[34]

In 1936, the *Ladies' Home Journal* ran a series of Woodbury's Soap ads that used Steichen photography. These particular ads featured photographs of nude women, which makes one wonder, for whom were the ads created? One ad shows a photo of a lithe young woman with her back to the viewer. She reclines on a stairwell wearing only a pair of chic espadrilles. The model has one arm bent up with her hand on the nape of her neck allowing the viewer to see the curve of her breast. She has a mop of short curly blond hair. The headline reads, "Science enriches Woodbury formula with Benefits of 'Filtered Sunshine,' Nature's source of beauty for the skin." The focus is on the woman's body; the photograph takes up approximately two-thirds of the page. In another ad, a nude woman looks directly into the camera; she is lying on her back with one arm strategically draped over her chest. Again, the claim of the science of filtered sunshine is made in the headline. It is science, but it is also "nature's source of beauty for the skin." So, through science, Woodbury's Soap promises that it has captured the benefits of nature for the purposes of beautiful skin.

In a third ad, the photograph shows a young woman lying on her stomach next to a reflecting pool or fountain. One arm is under her head and the other dangles gracefully down to the water, tips of fingers grazing the surface of the pool. It seems to be a time of peaceful contemplation. This ad too promises the benefits of filtered sunshine through scientific advancements. And the images imply that those benefits are a beautiful, desirable body with blemish-free, fair skin.

The reflection pool in this ad is an interesting element with its reference to Narcissus, the god who fell in love with his own image in a reflecting pool. Within the context of cosmetic ads during this time, what could it mean? Is it Steichen's training in art that sparked the idea of such a photograph and does the story of Narcissus have particular meaning for a woman reader in the 1930s? The images of nude women seem to be created for male viewers, yet they appear in the *Ladies' Home Journal*. They are amazingly similar to contemporary ads for cosmetics in which women are shown as objects of desire—as opposed to other images of women in Woodbury's and Pond's ads that are dated through clothing, furniture, and the trappings of the period.

Women are viewing these ads, but are they viewing the ads through the lens of male desire? Perhaps readers are caught in what de Lauretis calls a "double-identification" in which they are both passive and active: passive in identifying with the object of beauty in the photo and active in the desire to be beautiful, the desire to be desired by men, the desire for pleasure.

The concepts of the male gaze and double-identification and the processes by which meaning is made through advertising images are particularly important in understanding how ideal beauty is constructed and perpetuated. By looking at the "distinguished white men" testimonial ads in the next section through this perspective, the system of meaning that supports and perpetuates an ideology of ideal beauty is revealed. Just as in the Steichen/Woodbury's ads, the Woodbury's testimonial ads reflect a manifestation of the male gaze. In this series, the ads are fashioned for women readers using a much more visible male "beauty" authority—the actual judges of the beauty contest. These ads reveal a more obvious male gaze and desire positioned to entice women to buy a product that taps into women's desire for acceptance and love and a desire to be desired by men.

Vanderbilt, Fitzgerald, and Barrymore: Woodbury's Testimonial Ad Campaign

As shown in the chapter on Pond's, the Women's Editorial Department and Helen Lansdowne, in particular, developed a thoroughly modern testimonial ad. That is, they developed the testimonial from its former role as regional advice advertising (e.g., Lydia Pinkham's) to a sophisticated and national series of ads showing beautiful, young actresses, socialites, and royalty testifying to the effectiveness of a product. Under Lansdowne's direction, the successful strategies the Women's Editorial Department employed for the Pond's account were modified and transferred to other accounts for beauty products, both in domestic ad campaigns and eventually in international ad campaigns. This was certainly the case with Woodbury's Facial Soap—only this time with a twist.

In the fall of 1928, with an advertising appropriation from Jergens of $646,000, JWT presented a plan to Jergens for advertising that contemplated a national beauty contest. The plan was to invite women to send in their photographs to be judged by a selected group of prominent men in order that Lansdowne, Lewis, and their copywriters might publish the names and testimonial of the winners in Woodbury's ads. After much debate the competition idea was rejected on the basis that it "was cheapening to Woodbury, and that it was devoting too much interest to the contest and not enough to the product."[35]

Weeks later, Lansdowne, Lewis, and their copywriters presented a modified form of this plan, which it termed a "National Beauty Survey." This plan was to hire investigators to look up prominent people in various sections of the country and to find out if they were Woodbury's users. If so, and if they were of "striking appearance," JWT would request that they submit their photographs to a committee composed of John Barrymore, F. Scott Fitzgerald, and Cornelius Vanderbilt, Jr. Lansdowne argued that this method removed the onus of public competition. It was also arranged that the testimonials of each winner would be featured prominently and that the product would get as much attention as the personalities themselves.

There was no reason for the agency and client to not use this advertising approach. After all, JWT had had great success with this testimonial or "personality" advertising, as it was sometimes called, on other products. The Women's Editorial Department put the plan into effect and divided the contestants into twelve groups: The Loveliest Debutante, The Loveliest Sportswoman, The Loveliest Mother, The Loveliest Coed, and so forth. The first announcement for the "survey" appeared in the February 1929 magazines and the campaign proceeded according to plan.

Just like JWT's Pond's ads, its Woodbury's ads reflect much about the advertisers' attitudes and assumptions concerning gender, race, and class. The people depicted are white, they are placed in an upper-middle-class setting, and women who look beautiful are judged by men. The images and text support the world of the advertisers and beyond that—a fantasy world where women achieve more than just beauty through a product. The women who use Pond's and Woodbury's products are shown as "lovely" and "engaged," and winning the approval of distinguished men. In this system of meaning, value is placed on female beauty ("fair," "pink," and "white"), middle- or upper-middle-class accoutrements (clothing, education, leisure), and male approval (via the judges, the fiancés, the men who love to touch soft skin, etc.). At least in these ads, the reader is told directly who the authority on beauty is: men. And women are encouraged to look closely at their own face, to judge it through the gaze of an ostensibly objective judge.

In an ad announcing the contest, F. Scott Fitzgerald, John Barrymore, and Cornelius Vanderbilt, Jr., are identified as judges and their qualifications for judging such a contest are spelled out in the short bios under their photos. The ad introduces them as three "distinguished American men, known for their appreciation and knowledge of beauty." F. Scott Fitzgerald was chosen "because, as the most brilliant of America's younger novelists, he was the first to discover and portray an enchanting new type of America[n] girl. Because at the age of 23, he woke up to find himself famous as the author of *This Side of Paradise*. Because no other man of his time writes so sympathetically, skillfully, and fascinatingly about women."

John Barrymore was chosen "because, being a member of the most distinguished theatrical family in America, he has been associated with the most beautiful women in the arts. Because in his choice of motion picture heroines he has set a new—and different—standard of feminine loveliness. Because he is himself the most romantic figure on the stage today." And Cornelius Vanderbilt, Jr., was chosen "because, he is the fourth Cornelius Vanderbilt in one of America's oldest and most distinguished families. Because he has struck out for himself and achieved an independent career, and as a journalist is familiar with people everywhere. Because he has driven across America twenty-three times and his hobby is remote places and interesting types."[36] JWT and Jergens turned to these three white, "distinguished" men from "distinguished" families in letters, the theater, and business because they could not bring themselves to choose from "literally heaps of the charming portraits. . . . [They] were bewildered."[37]

More than likely, these well-known "distinguished" men were chosen because of their appeal to the Women's Editorial Department and the senior male executives at JWT. To the Women's Editorial Department staff, these men may have represented the type of man most appealing to them (some of them, at least) for their wealth, good looks, presence, intelligence, and charm. The male executives admired the men for all those same qualities as well. Whiteness and social status, were, however, the most outstanding criteria for these judges, which reflected the values and beliefs of the male executives and women copywriters at JWT. The male as authority on beauty (male gaze) is reinforced in this testimonial ad campaign, with the female reader reading about men looking at photos of women and choosing the most beautiful. And, without a doubt, the addition of these men to the campaign lent it a certain flair and drama that gained attention for the product.

The text of the ads, in which the winners are announced, shown, and described, tells the reader exactly what makes a woman beautiful. In the ad announcing the most attractive high school girl (photographed by Edward Steichen), Miss Thelma Harris of Sausalito, California, is described as having a "slim, straight little figure, a mop of curly brown hair twisting into babyish gold tendrils, deep blue eyes fringed with black lashes, and a skin like the pinkest and whitest apple blossoms." The ad says that "she has used Woodbury's Facial Soap on her lovely pink and white skin all her life."[38]

In another ad announcing the twins who won the "prettiest of co-eds," Helen and L—— Ladd, students at the University of Chicago where they studied psychology, math, and biology, were described in much the same way. They grew up in Chicago on "the shores of Lake Michigan," where they "swam, canoed, sailed, sunned themselves on the sand, from the time they were babies."[39] And, in case there was any doubt as to the color of their skin, the ad reads that these coeds turn heads when they walk down the street or through the theater: "Perhaps it is their wonderful Northern fairness, their cheeks the color of roses and carnations, their starry grey eyes; or perhaps it is just that they seem to have a warmer, more effervescent sparkle of life in them than most people . . . [t]hey both have dazzling pink and white skin, and they have been brought up on Woodbury's Facial Soap."[40]

The language and images, crafted and chosen for these ads by Lansdowne and her female copywriters, point to the desirability of female whiteness—fair skin and pinkish tones were appropriate for a healthy glow. A "Northern" fairness has multiple meanings: the coed twins are from Chicago, a northern U.S. city, but "Northern" could also allude to a Northern European racial background. A nation of immigrants would likely take notice of such a reference. That these young women are students at University of Chicago and grew up on the shore of Lake Michigan pursuing such activities as sailing and sunning also points to a privileged class position. They live in comfort, are judged beautiful by three distinguished American men, and seem to have a bright future. These are common themes in the Woodbury's Facial Soap testimonial ads just as they were in the Pond's ads, most notably in the case of the "She's Young, She's Lovely, She's Engaged" ad campaign.

The ideologies that emerge from the series of Woodbury's ads support the values and beliefs of a privileged class. The words used to describe the female objects of the ads such as "fair" and "pink," and the description of middle- and upper-middle-class leisure time and education, reinforce the images showing white women and men in grand hotels and beautifully elegant homes. The combination of image and text forms a foundation for an ideology of gender, race, and social status in the United States. The emerging field of advertising, the construction of a female consumer, and the system of communication and transportation that enabled the nation to view these messages were all influenced by and helped to perpetuate an ideology that placed value on whiteness, male authority and desire, and the upper class. For the Jergens products, the emphasis on whiteness and sentimental advertising continued.

Fern Johnson coined the term "discourse imaging" to explain how verbal and visual elements in advertising draw on each other to create meaning through an interpretation of the reader. Johnson says, "Consumers make sense of advertising by the interplay of verbal and visual representation within a meaningful cultural context to form some type of meaningful expression."[41] The slogan "A Skin You Love To Touch" is reinforced with the image of the man touching a woman's skin in a romantic setting; meaning is created by the reader within a particular cultural context already imbued with beliefs and values concerning gender roles, race, and social status. The 1936 Woodbury's campaign focuses on women's bodies, laid bare, through the lens of a male photographer. And the beauty contest follows century-old scripts of power relations, with male judges who determine what is beautiful at any particular time.

The Jergens Lotion advertising campaign, developed in 1922 by Ruth Waldo, Edith Lewis, Gladys Phelan, Elizabeth Devree, Mrs. —— Smith (Women's Editorial Department staff), and Stanley Resor and Helen Lansdowne, had much of the same language of whiteness. In the notes from a meeting about Jergens Lotion, with Ruth Waldo presiding, headlines for the cream ads are presented: "White Loveliness For Your Hands," "Your Hands Can Have This White Loveliness," and "For The New Styles—Backs Must Be Dazzling White." [42] Edith Lewis was credited with giving this campaign copy an "unusually human, moving quality," and, that, beginning in January 1931, the illustrations for Jergens Lotion "were made more emotional, in line with the current trend in movies, newspapers and magazines." [43]

Helen Lansdowne, Edith Lewis, and the women who managed the Woodbury's Facial Soap campaign are credited by JWT company historian Sidney Berstein with having created some of the most successful modern advertising and marketing innovations: the sexual sell, testimonial advertising, and, especially in the case of Woodbury's, the fusing of science and sex. They made the sexual sell acceptable by combining it with the authority and rationale of science. Not only did they use the language of science in the ads they created, they used new marketing science in product research and analysis. To understand the effects of their ads—beyond the incredible increase in the sale of Woodbury's Facial Soap to the more ideological messages contained in the ads—is to understand the existing and emerging system of meaning in place at the turn of the century in the United States.

This chapter identifies important mechanisms of knowledge and power that hint at why particular ad campaigns are created and why they have such an impact. Established systems of meaning, informed by religion, class control, race, gender, industrial capitalism, reform movements, popular magazines, and the advertising and film industries, adjust to subtle changes and movements in the making for decades.

An understanding of these mechanisms of knowledge and power, and how changes occur over time, helps account for changing concepts of gender, race, and social status in the United States. Sometimes the shifts appear as contradictory messages (what is personal and female becomes public), and sometimes the shifts are more clearly illustrated (the modern woman must buy these modern products, thus creating a gendered modern consumer). It is not just that a woman must be modern—she must be a modern woman.

Looking closely at the Woodbury's Facial Soap advertising campaign as part of a system of meaning enables an understanding of how ideology, or a system of meaning, adapts, reinforces, and perpetuates ideologies of gender, class, and race. Understanding the privileged class backgrounds and educational experiences of the women who created these ads also contributes to a more comprehensive view of the total process of cultural production. For the women at JWT, that also meant creating a place for themselves in a newly emerging industry. Their place within that industry and the innovative work they contributed was part of the advancement of women in the business world as well as in contributing to the creation of the gendered modern subject—the modern woman that they strove to be themselves. They were creating images of women in the ads that they strove to be, while their own race, class background, and educational experiences propelled their choices of those depictions.

J. Walter Thompson's International Expansion and the Ideology of Civilization

America has invaded Europe not with armed men, but with manufactured products.

—F. A. McKenzie, *The American Invaders*, 1902

... the sun never sets on JWT.

—*Fortune*, November 1947

It would be a mistake to imagine that the globalization of American advertising imagery dates from the 1960s or 1970s. In fact, it began *at least* sixty years earlier. Moreover, women were at least as important as men in spreading the U.S. ideal of feminine beauty around the world. Taking seriously the ideas and professional work of those pioneering women of JWT's Women's Editorial Department produces a much more complex—and, I think, realistic—understanding of how and why American advertising globalization was affected by and perpetuated ideas about gender, status, and racism in the late nineteenth and early twentieth centuries.

This chapter tells a forgotten story of how women were kept in the back office despite generating a great deal of revenue and creating many ad techniques that worked in global markets as well as in the United States. The surprise in the narrative is that some women did, at least briefly, venture abroad and make their impact. Yet, then, as now, the most status and power in ad agencies comes to those who do direct client work—the deal and rainmakers. Interwoven with this story is the familiar tale of how companies from the industrialized world look on less industrialized countries and their cultures as inferior even while they were eager to sell to them, a point of view that, perhaps, has been more reformed than eliminated. JWT's bid to become a global tastemaker through the opening of foreign offices ties those two narratives together.

The Women's Editorial Department contributed to the internationalization of the J. Walter Thompson Company (JWT) during the late 1920s in four crucial ways: (1) the revenue its work generated in the United States was used by senior male executives to build the infrastructure that enabled the agency to establish a solid domestic base and expand internationally; (2) the advertising innovations developed by the Women's Editorial Department in New York City were used in international ad campaigns—for both masculine-coded ads (automobiles) and feminine-coded ads (beauty, food, and household products), most notable was their development of the social prestige testimonial ad; (3) some of the Women's Editorial Department went to work in JWT's new international offices, continuing to develop and maintain advertising campaigns for large accounts such as Pond's, Lux, Cutex, and Sun Maid; and (4) Helen Lansdowne and the Women's Editorial Department were credited by JWT senior executives with helping to establish an international JWT corporate structure, emulating and putting into practice the policies and procedures of the New York City office (world headquarters). Moreover, having been convinced of the value of hiring women as professional copywriters and once international offices were established, local women and men in those countries were hired by male managers to lend their insight into the minds and hearts of the "native" consumers, female and male.

Client accounts for beauty products by the late 1920s had become a substantial proportion of JWT's entire business. As noted previously, between 1909 and 1929, the number of American perfume and cosmetics manufacturers nearly doubled, and the factory value of their products rose tenfold—from $14.2 million to nearly $141 million.[1] Key to revealing how JWT's internationalization was a gendered process is paying attention to the revenue generated by the Women's Editorial Department. Its work contributed greatly to the economic base of JWT—the largest and most powerful ad agency well into the 1970s. In 1918, for example, the billings for copy written in the Women's Editorial Department totaled $2,264,759 out of the total $3,902,601, or 58 percent of the total revenue for the company.[2] Women and women's work were integral as they provided the financial base for the expansion of JWT beyond the mainland United States.

The power invested in a hypermasculinist JWT corporate culture also has implications for how American cultural patterns and habits of consumption were exported internationally. After mastering the mainland United States, the JWT agency created campaigns for Latin American, Asian,

African, and European markets. In just six years (1929–35), JWT opened offices and established commercial business partnerships in: London, England; Berlin, Germany; Buenos Aires, Argentina; Sydney and Melbourne, Australia; Vienna, Austria; Antwerp and Brussels, Belgium; São Paulo and Rio de Janeiro, Brazil; Montreal and Toronto, Canada; Santiago, Chile; Copenhagen, Denmark; Paris, France; Bombay, New Delhi, and Calcutta, India; Jakarta, Indonesia; Osaka, Japan; Wellington, New Zealand; Mexico City, Mexico; Lisbon, Portugal; Cape Town and Johannesburg/Sandton, South Africa; Barcelona and Madrid, Spain; and Stockholm, Sweden.[3] JWT had begun to serve an emerging multinational arm of an economy it had helped to develop in the United States. Many of these multinational corporations were the relatively new, modern business enterprises that evolved around 1850, which had implications for the gendered managerial force so crucial to these expansions into new markets.

Starting during the late 1920s, a cadre of high-ranking women from the Women's Editorial Department in New York City traveled mainly to the London office, where they maintained large accounts and "supervised" the creation of the office—though there was always a male director. And a few of the women traveled around the globe conducting marketing and consumer research. The New York City office was the central headquarters for the Central, South, and North American offices.[4]

In the London and New York City offices, the Women's Editorial Department created their most outstanding and valuable work. This included creating the modern testimonial ad, introducing a feminine sex appeal in advertising, and combining a feminine sex appeal with "scientific" copy. A study of JWT's international ads illustrates that the testimonial ad was used again and again. And the company used research methods developed in the New York City office to try to understand female (and male) consumers internationally.

Scientific methods of understanding the female consumer were used in each country into which JWT expanded. Some of these research methods applied internationally were developed and carried out by women in the Women's Editorial Department who routinely spent weeks in department stores behind the counters as saleswomen to better understand the female consumer. They also participated in more expansive market research including surveying women door to door, adding coupons to ads and analyzing the results, and direct mail surveys to female consumers. Women at JWT adapted and applied these research projects for new markets abroad.

Strategies that JWT's trade magazine ads employed to market the Women's Editorial Department to U.S. manufacturers were also used to sell their expertise in international markets. JWT's trade ads claimed that the agency had scientific data relevant to manufacturers who were interested in expanding their market internationally, and fueled a subsidiary business selling research reports written by the JWT research office staff. JWT, in effect, was advertising a world wide open to new trade possibilities; they had done their research and took full advantage of the offices initially established exclusively for one of their biggest international clients: General Motors (GM).[5]

In the United States and across the world, the women at JWT made an impact on the spread of American ideas concerning class, race, nationality, ethnicity, and, ultimately, an ideal beauty. A close examination of the ads created for beauty products, in particular, shows that the values and beliefs of certain middle- and upper-middle-class American advertisers were widely circulated. These representations of "America" and "Americans" were the fantasy of a few; the representations reflect a distinct ideology that drew from a metanarrative of "civilization." The ideology of corporate imperialism is the force behind the spread of these advertisements, and the ads themselves reflect an ideology of a dominant group of Americans. Corporate imperialism and a desire to dominate coupled with messages about a feminine ideal beauty, modern femininity, and good feminine taste created a system of communication like no other in existence during this time.

JWT Wins General Motors Account

The story of JWT's international expansion beyond the London office begins with winning a contract from, and thus gaining as a major client, the multinational GM.[6] GM's expansion to international markets was swift and comprehensive; as it opened plants and offices in Europe, Africa, South and North America, and Asia, it sometimes acquired local car companies and plants in those countries. GM expanded significantly during the 1920s, and an agreement between GM and JWT stipulated that JWT would open an office in every country where GM had a manufacturing plant.

Yet, even prior to the acquisition of the GM account in 1927, JWT had been placing advertisements in international markets. For example, after the Spanish-American War, a Spanish department was organized in JWT's New York City office for the preparation of advertising to be placed in Latin American countries and the Philippines.[7] JWT senior executives wasted no time in moving in on a "virgin land" where they could take a dominant market share. GM had its own internal advertising department, but its male executives wanted the expertise of a larger advertising company to help handle its new international markets. JWT and GM's advertising department worked together on the ad campaigns—though

JWT's distinctive advertising style and strategy are evident in most of the GM ads.

Despite the myriad of scientific studies conducted by JWT for its international markets, the bulk of ads produced for consumers in new international markets were similar in image and language to the ads produced for the American market. The science ethos so strongly embedded in JWT corporate culture carried over to its international expansion and JWT used its "expertise" in scientific methods to attract new clients for international markets. In fact, GM finally hired JWT to handle its international business after John Watson, a JWT executive and prominent behavioral psychologist (formerly at Johns Hopkins University), unexpectedly met GM export head James Mooney on a ship bound for Europe. JWT had been trying to acquire the GM business for some time, but Mooney was evidently swayed by Watson's knowledge of scientific advertising. Shortly after their meeting, JWT signed an agreement to represent all of GM's international business accounts.[8]

The professional copywriters in JWT's Women's Editorial Department never dealt directly with GM executives, although some of the women did work on the GM account—for example, Aminta Casseres while she was stationed in the London office. This was not unique to GM, but rather the "natural" way of dealing with clients at JWT. While the women copywriters' work was used on GM accounts, the corporate culture excluded their presence at account representative meetings with the client. GM and JWT executives exported distinctly American dominant ideologies that included a hypermasculine corporate culture. The practice of excluding women in client meetings and in the boardroom helped solidify this exclusion as a business standard. Even with Helen Lansdowne as a mentor, and the extraordinary opportunities they had at JWT, the women at JWT faced their own "glass ceiling"—a ceiling that still exists and is especially apparent in multinational *Fortune* 500 companies.[9]

The Women's Editorial Department and International Offices

Despite corporate sexism, some of the women at JWT should be given equal credit to the men so often mentioned in the JWT histories of expansion. Archival records show glimpses of the significant roles these women played in the company's domestic and international expansion. Yet fully documented or attributed references to the women who wrote ad copy and headed copy groups are few and far between.

On the surface, the evidence points to a masculine, in-house decision-making process, which, by the late 1920s, became the international commercial process. But the actual process by which American consumer goods were being made, appealing to potential buyers from London to Argentina to the Philippines, was far from being an all-male affair. When JWT went international, male executives convinced many American manufacturers to expand their business to new markets. Many manufacturers had already expanded to international markets and JWT worked on acquiring those accounts as well. What happened to the roles of the women in the Women's Editorial Department, within the agency, as the agency expanded outside American borders? What influence did their innovative advertising campaigns have on international markets?

The London office reopened in 1919 after the war and its first big client was Libby, McNeil and Libby, an account that was valued at $100,000. Other American food companies such as Heinz had expanded internationally decades before Libby's. Both Stanley Resor and James Webb Young saw this as an opportunity for international expansion. And, by 1931, the London office grew to 200 staff members with new American clients including GM, Kraft, Chesebrough, and Pond's.[10]

JWT also set out to gain the advertising accounts of British companies and was successful in earning the business of Horlick's and Rowntree. One of the most significant additions to the client roster was probably Lever. Lever Brothers, Lever's U.S. subsidiary, introduced a new bar of soap called "Lux" ("light" in Latin) in 1925. JWT's New York City office got the account and when, two years later, Lux Toilet Soap was introduced to the British market, JWT's London office won the account there. Ultimately, according to a JWT executive, the "Unilever business was as important, or even more so, than the massive GM assignment because Unilever was one of the Worlds [sic] largest international advertisers."[11] The Lever account ad campaigns were handled by the Women's Editorial Department and Helen Lansdowne.

Most women who were sent overseas from the New York office went to the London office—with a few exceptions. Ruth Waldo's assignment there was to "survey and supervise,"[12] to research surveys and supervise the copywriters in a seven-person office that included Margaret McKendrick. McKendrick worked as a copywriter for at least two years during the time Waldo was there. It was she who reported on Stanley Resor and Helen Lansdowne's visit to the London office in 1924, writing that Helen Lansdowne "made history by getting titled women from the topmost layer of society to give their names to Pond's Creams."[13] Waldo and McKendrick worked on the Sun-Maid Raisin account, an account whose ads were placed all throughout Europe and was considered one of the biggest accounts alongside Lever Brothers. Those big accounts (cosmetics and food) enabled the office to move to a bigger office space (Bush House) and hire additional staff. Also there at the time was Therese Olzendam, who most likely worked with them on the Sun-Maid Raisin account. For four years, Olzendam supervised women's copy written in London on twenty-two accounts as well as copy written in Belgium, France, Holland, Denmark, and Germany.[14] Other JWT overseas accounts handled through the London office (and not exclusively for the British consumer) included Elizabeth Arden, Cutex, and Royal Baking Powder.

This level of involvement by women copywriters in London significantly increased the influence of the outlooks and strategies of the New York office's Women's Editorial Department. To the extent that Lansdowne and her team of women copywriters influenced the ad campaigns of JWT's London office (food, household, and beauty product accounts), they were influencing JWT's messages in all the areas for which the London office was responsible: Europe, Africa, and Asia.

London was the training ground among JWT's international offices. Not only was it the first international office, but it also served as a jump-off point for ideas and people who went on to more far-flung offices or went to start up new offices. JWT London office art director George Butler (there from 1925–28) recalled,

> The education and development which a few of us in London had received was somehow transmitted from New York, and from London to people in other countries. It resulted in a standard practice, which, though revolutionary at the time, has spread with little change to the advertising industry all over the world. The credit for this is entirely due to the influence of the Resors [Stanley Resor and Helen Lansdowne] and Jim Young. Three brilliant people making quite a different and separate impact on all of us with the common factor of 'find out the facts about the performance of a product in relation to peoples' needs and wants, then, in order to communicate with them, bring into play all the skill and understanding you can muster.[15]

Waldo, Casseres, and Olzendam all played an important role in the development of the London office and undoubtedly influenced those who were working there on European, African, and Asian advertising accounts. Their experience and knowledge would have been passed on to the staff they supervised as well as to those in international offices who would have relied on them for advice on market research and campaign development and design. Researching potential consumers and gathering continental media information in London was given a high priority by JWT executives.

Some of the London-based employees were surprised at how their efforts were received by the Europeans. Douglas M. Saunders, an Englishman, became manager of the London office in 1933 (he retired from JWT in 1959). About one of the market research techniques pioneered by the American women of the Women's Editorial Department, he said that "this 'American' idea of house-to-house interviews was received variously. Ellen Krough, previously a young London insurance secretary hired by JWT in 1927, was sent to Denmark to research Sun-Maid Raisins. She recalls that while some were surprised and pleasant, others slammed the door in her face saying 'What Cheek!' and one man threw her down a flight of stairs."[16] Since door-to-door surveying was also undertaken by the women in the United States, the London office manager must have felt comfortable sending Krough out to knock on doors even though it was apparent that it could be physically dangerous work.

Despite some rather rigid gendered work roles, some women at JWT traveled extensively, performing cultural analysis geared toward business, and for extended periods. During 1923, Helen Martin traveled to England, France, the Rivera, Italy, Switzerland, and Algiers. That same year, Martin also spent three months in the London office from which she made trips to Holland and Scotland. Alice Boughton and Margaret King "traveled together through Japan and made an investigation on the toilet goods market in China after which Miss. King sailed from Shanghai, leaving Miss. Boughton to take a 1,600 mile trip up the Yang-tse River. Miss Boughton then traveled through Egypt, India, and Burma [Myanmar], returning home by way of London. She remained in the London Office five weeks to make a study of the grocery and drug fields."[17] The far-reaching significance of women's work at JWT is apparent through announcements such as this in the company newsletter.

Freda Davidson, an American, also worked in the London office during the 1920s and 1930s. It is unclear exactly when she started there, but she lived and worked in London for ten years. Before starting at JWT London, she did advertising work in the United States for Condé Nast and Crowell. In London, Davidson worked as a copywriter on JWT's Lux account and "other larger accounts."[18] Her New York superiors sought her observations on advertising to British consumers. In a 1932 presentation to the New York office on particular accounts and British work culture at JWT London, Davidson talked about market research, echoing the stories of Saunders and Krough: "This Lux investigation . . . was probably the first to be conducted on such a scale and with such thoroughness in Britain," Davidson told her New York colleagues referring specifically to an effort to apply to British women a survey approach first crafted with American women in mind: "One thousand housewives were interviewed and the questionnaire was elaborate. There had always been the conviction before this was done that house-to-house question-asking would not be possible in England.

The English housewife would resent the intrusion, it was said. Servants would block the way was another objection. However, the Lux investigation, and many others since then, have been carried out with no more difficulty than you have here [in New York]."[19]

Even though JWT's expansion was carefully contrived and narrowly controlled by male executives back in New York City, women found jobs—and used the expertise they had developed appealing to the American market—in the London office and even in Berlin and Paris. Some women at the JWT London office were put in the position to help the male executives in New York recreate its masculine corporate culture even while their valued female insight was transposed to new cultures.

But women's contributions were not just confined to supposedly feminine realms. They also forged the prototypes for logistics. Augusta Nicolls, who worked in the JWT London office, is credited by JWT male executives with the systemization and standardization of JWT practice and procedure there. Since the London office was the European headquarters, Nicolls had influence over and responsibility for communicating the JWT procedures and policies, by extension, in many parts of the world. Perhaps Nicolls was just following in the footsteps of her mentor. Helen Lansdowne was part of a three-member committee that approved and passed on all policies at JWT, including payroll and personnel from 1916 to 1918, an important time of growth.[20] In a fast-growing international expansion, branding the JWT method (market research and specific, identifiable advertising strategies) was extremely important in maintaining corporate identity, continuity, and agency cohesion. How ironic that Nicolls would be responsible for guiding the replication of a masculine multinational corporation that limited her own role. Yet, on the other hand, it must have been flattering that JWT would entrust her with the responsibility and gratifying to see her work create a pattern that would be widely used abroad.

Aminta Casseres was another major influence on the London office; she was sent there in February 1931 to work on the Lux, Rinso, Gem, Meters, Lloyd's Bank, Cutex, and Kraft mayonnaise accounts, as well as on the Pond's account. In a February 18, 1931, cable from Stanley Resor to Casseres, he writes, "Do see that Pond's has the benefit of everything we have learned here [New York] . . . I am convinced that one of our biggest sources of less in time, money and nerves is wrong starting. The asking of writers to start work immediately results in wasted time . . . work should begin with a thorough digestion of facts and an agreement as to where the thing should be headed."[21] In another cable a few days later, Resor wrote to Sam Meek (European Director) in London: "Have you considered Casseres for the Berlin Pond's job?"[22] Stanley Resor had a great deal of confidence in and respect for Casseres; he was familiar with her work from the New York City office and trusted her to expand the New York accounts in Europe as well as to introduce JWT methods and practices of market research and innovative advertising copy. Just as the international office managers needed the assistance of "native" staff to navigate their particular commercial and social landscape, the male executives needed JWT women copywriters to travel to and work in the London office to ensure that JWT policy and procedure was standardized, implemented, and carried out by all European JWT offices. These women also continued work on the Pond's testimonial ad campaign, giving the ideology that accompanied that ideal of beauty an international sway and power.

Through an examination of archival materials, it becomes clear that Casseres was sorely missed back in the New York City office; only ten days after she started working in the London office, Howard Kohl sent a cable to Sam Meek that said "Suggest Casseres returns at once unless you have special assignments." Meek responded to Kohl's cable by replying directly to Stanley Resor and makes his case to Resor in a February 17, 1931, letter: "Miss. Casseres completed her review of Pond's materials . . . [s]he recently completed her review of Lux Flakes and has already started work on Rinso and McVitie and Price. As soon as these are out of the way, she is planning to review GM [General Motors], Lloyd's Bank, Cutex and Kraft Mayonnaise. She is also working on the solicitation of Gillette."[23] According to Kohl, Resor asked Casseres to return to New York but then changed his mind, asking her to stay in London to work on the accounts mentioned above and to develop the Pond's accounts, as evidenced in Resor's cable to her and to Meek about developing copy and handling the Berlin Pond's account.

Another JWT copywriter, Gladys Phelan, worked in the Berlin office in 1931.[24] But it was Casseres, Nicolls, Olzendam, and Waldo who were instrumental in developing European accounts—through the London office—and who were also seen by Stanley Resor and Helen Lansdowne as a crucial part of the New York City office. At the same time, the four women did not go on to open JWT offices in South America, Africa, or Asia as some of the men who worked in the London office did. Instead, they returned to New York where they continued to have a great deal of influence on the beauty, food, and household product accounts that they had introduced to a nation—and now a world—of consumers.

These women copywriters were experiencing a kind of double-edged sword, a weird paradox: while they were highly regarded and valued as experienced advertisers in the New York office, one of the reasons they probably did not stay longer in the international offices was that they were needed in New York. One might speculate that the senior male executives in New York held the belief that these JWT women were so good at what they did there, they could not be spared for any length of time. The other reason they did not take management positions in international offices no doubt had to do with the fact that women did not interact directly with clients. In addition, during the late 1920s to 1945, no record exists of a person native to the host country being promoted to manage an international JWT office despite their contributions to the understanding of local customs, traditions, and language(s).

What is it that we come to understand about the gendering of the influential JWT ad agency in an emergent American expansionist industry? Despite the contributions of the Women's Editorial Department in New York and London, as JWT expanded internationally, talented, professional, female copywriters were not promoted to direct an international office. Nor was the Women's Editorial Department staff explicitly credited for its work in crafting successful ad campaigns that were used in overseas markets. Nor were they ever credited with helping to build a solid base in the United States through their successful campaigns for women's products that enabled JWT to expand internationally. As JWT male executives became more efficient in acquiring market share around the world, JWT hypermasculine, corporate culture became even more embedded in the institutional character of the company.

New Frontier: The Buenos Aires Office

In South America, one of JWT's most successful offices was in Buenos Aires, Argentina. By the late 1920s, Argentina had a large middle-class population with a relatively high literacy rate—the country was seen by JWT as ripe for a new commercial market. In addition, GM had a manufacturing plant in Argentina and sold cars to this market. Russell Pierce wrote a memoir based on his experiences opening the Buenos Aires office in 1929 mainly to service the GM account but also to cultivate more customers for its Pond's account there and to cultivate local business.[25] During the first two years, the billings in the Buenos Aires office almost doubled, reaching approximately $300,000 in 1930. As the business grew, Pierce had to hire more staff, which became, according to Pierce, a cross-section of the Argentine "urban middle class." In addition, "the number of women . . . increased from five at the end of [the] first year to nine at the end of the second year."

The first woman hired was Anita Tibaldi, an Argentine with "Italian blood." Pierce describes her as "plump but energetic"; she was hired as a secretary but became indispensable because of her guidance on issues regarding local customs and attitudes and her fluency in Spanish. One of the copywriters in the Buenos Aires office was a woman by the name of Countess Franca Paganini de Castano, an Italian noblewomen married to an Argentine. Pierce says that "judging from the French designer clothes she wore to work, I guessed that she had some sort of inheritance." The Countess wrote the advertising copy for Modess (a Johnson & Johnson feminine hygiene product) and Scott Toilet Tissue. Though the Modess ads met with some resistance, the JWT Buenos Aires office was the first to run ads for feminine hygiene products in Argentina. It is likely that the Countess also wrote or translated the copy for the Buenos Aires Pond's ad campaign as well. There is perhaps special interest in the Countess's role, given that Helen Lansdowne and her group at JWT were the principal creators of the aristocracy testimonial endorsement—and now the Buenos Aires office hired a genuine aristocrat to put these products across.

Another fascinating hire was Maria Victoria Candia, a woman from Paraguay who worked as a copywriter. Pierce tells of their first meeting and of learning about Candia's involvement in the war between Paraguay and Bolivia. "A friend of our family, General Estigarribia, the head of our armed forces, was desperate for medical help. I had studied nursing, so I enlisted as a nurse. I was the only woman in the armed forces," recalled Candia.[26] The Buenos Aires staff may have been more ethnically diverse than the U.S. offices, but the common thread—that transcended even national boundaries—was that of class position. The men hired to work in the Buenos Aires office ranged from "one that was from an elite family related to a historic Argentine political leader; another was Austrian; three were Jewish in religious faith but Argentine citizens; four were Anglo-Argentines with British-Irish and Italian-Spanish-British ancestry."[27] An urban middle class staff (with a few aristocrats) meant a particular privileged perspective— they were part of the new professional managerial elite while at the same time could make a case for their descent from older elites.[28]

Women from the New York office who traveled to work in international offices continued working on international accounts once they returned to the United States, thus influencing the look and message of American advertising worldwide. By 1945, both the New York and Chicago offices contributed to advertising campaigns placed by the international department in New York City:

In addition to the large amount of advertising placed through JWT's six-teen international offices, a growing amount of advertising is placed by the international department in New York in international magazines published in the United States and distributed abroad. A compilation of advertising placed in the leading international magazines shows that JWT led all other agencies in the amount of advertising placed during 1945 with a billing total of $292,682.... JWT's international personnel outside the United States now numbered approximately 1,000. In addition, a count reveals that about 100 people in the New York and Chicago offices worked on international adver-tising campaigns during 1945. The international department in New York during 1945 placed campaigns in 35 countries in addition to that placed by JWT's international offices.[29]

In short, though women worked as copywriters in other U.S. JWT offices and in the London office, the only formally organized Women's Editorial Department was in the New York City office. Lansdowne lived in Green-wich, Connecticut; New York was her home base even though she traveled to international offices with Stanley Resor. Because of JWT's corporate cul-ture, it would have been difficult to establish another Women's Editorial Department outside of New York without Lansdowne's presence.

Conquering International Markets and the Ideology of Civilization

We are perfectly confident that this business of establishing an office there [Port Elizabeth, South Africa] and of creating a J. Walter Thompson Com-pany world empire is a very sound one.

—F. J. McArdle, Port Elizabeth Office Manager, speaking to JWT representatives in New York City, Representative Staff Meeting Minutes, May 26, 1931, JWT Archives, Duke University Library, Durham, North Carolina

In 1928, the *J. Walter Thompson News Bulletin* put out a "foreign issue" with articles titled "Markets Are People—Not Places," "When Carmen Goes Shopping," "What Does South America Offer the American Adver-tiser," and "Major Difficulties in Asia Minor." Each article reflected the masculine, and imperialist, corporate culture of the agency in terms of its approach to international expansion and the possibilities of understanding and managing international markets. At the time the foreign issue was dis-tributed, JWT had offices in Paris, Berlin, Madrid, Stockholm, Copenha-gen, Antwerp, Alexandria, and Port Elizabeth, and, in 1929, JWT opened an office in Buenos Aires, Argentina. At the same time, JWT executives knew that American manufacturers were willing to explore the possibilities of expanding their markets overseas. In the introduction to the foreign issue, Stanley Resor alluded to a report by the Foreign Commerce Department of the Chamber of Commerce of the United States that showed the growing interest of American manufacturers in seeking outlets for their merchandise abroad and showed that there was a marked increase in American exports during the first quarter of 1928.[30] JWT executives positioned the agency so that it would be ready to serve the needs of these particular manufacturers.

Throughout the early 1920s, American growth into international markets boomed. JWT was already realizing this potential in part through its relationship with GM. However, JWT did not waste any time cultivating new clients for international markets and, once it set up shop, cultivating local accounts. Resor went on to explain that each JWT international office was supervised by an American manager but staffed largely by what he called "native" personnel. Just as the male executives at JWT realized the importance of a Women's Editorial Department in reaching the growing numbers of female consumers in the United States, they realized the importance of a local connection that hopefully brought insight into new international markets. JWT executives saw the value in the Women's Editorial Department for domestic markets because they believed a distinct feminine intuition could help them expand their business. The same approach was applied to international markets but this time with a "native" as the guide to what the "natives" wanted.

Both JWT executives and the women copywriters claimed a special feminine insight into the minds and hearts of the American female consumer. The male executives claimed this to gain business and the women copywriters and Lansdowne claimed this to gain a foothold, for herself and for her copywriters, in the industry. The sign of the JWT woman copywriter in the United States, then, was transposed to the feminized sign of "native" in the international offices. As support to the JWT corporate culture, women copywriters in New York, and, eventually, London, and the native were indispensable, yet, in the sign system of this corporate culture, interchangeable when it served the dominant ideology of the agency. For example, a "native" in an international office had distinct insight into his or her peer and could provide translations of copy text, insight into the local business practices, and could even give advice concerning which social clubs the manager should join. Each international office was equipped to make field surveys and carry out organized advertising research—which would make the "native" staff even more valuable as JWT American managers attempted to study a new group of male and female consumers.

Regardless of the native's expertise, JWT generally followed the status quo, the practices and policies already in place at JWT in the United States. For example, according to Julio Moreno, the first five years JWT spent in Mexico were a failure largely due to misunderstandings brought on by the ignorance of JWT executives there of Mexican culture and customs. Evidently, JWT managers hired two of the best advertising men in Mexico but did not use them wisely. JWT had difficulty making connections and contacts in Mexico because the local business people did not trust JWT's general manager. JWT blamed this failure on Mexican "nationalism." That the JWT account representatives and general manager in Mexico did not fully understand the concept of *abrazo* (an embrace followed by a firm handshake among business men) did not help matters. It appears that the American JWT ad men consistently used this handshake inappropriately further alienating themselves from Mexican businessmen.[31]

Long before JWT established itself in Mexico, it had been recruiting a certain type of man and woman to work in its international offices. Starting as early as 1927, Sam Meek drew on the waves of youth coming out of Cambridge and Oxford, including Rhodes Scholars such as James Hamilton Russell, who was hired by JWT and went on to direct the JWT office in South Africa. Rhodes Scholars were often chosen to work in JWT offices in their home country and helped in the expansion of JWT internationally. Meek was able to attract leading British academicians, journalists, and occasionally members of the nobility. Basil Nicholson, one of the founders of the London *Daily Mirror*, worked at JWT as did Lady Elizabeth Pelham, daughter of the Earl of Chichester. Pelham worked on the Lux account in London where she also spent time in a department store demonstrating the product by washing and ironing clothes and talking to customers.[32] Meek felt that JWT was a company of "scholars," "adventurers," and "voyagers." Though what seems apparent is that these scholars, adventurers, and voyagers had to have a common experience regarding class position and race. Pulling recruits from the Rhodes Scholar program and elite institutions ensured this commonality. As a result, even by 1959, American and British men continued to hold the leading roles for JWT internationally.[33]

A kind of "universalism," apparent in some of JWT's beauty product ads (described in previous chapters), becomes even more pronounced as JWT expands into international markets. The history of American expansionism supported the attitudes of these JWT male executives: beginning in 1898, the United States emerged as an imperial power when it annexed Hawaii and went to war in Cuba and seized the Philippines from Spain.

As the United States expanded as an imperial power, American businesses followed suit in greater numbers. By 1914, American multinational companies that had two or more plants abroad numbered forty-one. Many of these multinational companies are still familiar brands such as Coca-Cola, Du Pont, Quaker Oats, Sherwin-Williams, Standard Oil, Alcoa, Gillette, Kodak, International Harvester, Ford, General Electric, Otis Elevator, U.S. Rubber, and Parke Davis, just to name a few.[34]

At one of the representatives meetings, William Resor (Stanley's brother) introduced a Mr. Ferguson from the Buenos Aires office. Ferguson had been one of the managing directors of one of the largest advertising agencies in South America, the McCall Agency, which had previously handled the GM account. Now working for JWT, Ferguson made a presentation to the all-male account representatives in the New York City office on JWT's work in Argentina. He started out by saying that "the little I could say about advertising agency methods in the Argentine would be similar to someone talking to a group of leading doctors here in New York about witch doctors in Africa. Advertising agency methods are terrible, and do not compare at all to anything here in New York."[35]

Ferguson's remarks reflect an American dominant ideology of civilization. He carefully chose an example that was both "scientific" (medical) and practical (the practice that arises from medical science) and demeaned Argentina on both accounts as uncivilized. Ferguson's description codes the United States as civilized and Argentina as savage and superstitious. The double-coding evoked the long-time prejudice toward the Latin American world as inefficient and lazy, consumed with religious-inspired superstitious magical thinking. The male executives at JWT were invited to see themselves not just as modern professionals, scientific, rational, and practical men of business, but as the sort of leaders who could truly "cure" what ailed the deluded consumers of folk medicine south of the border. The approach is perfect for a company selling modern cosmetics, beauty, and automobiles. The code of "civilized" vs. "bewitched" was compactly articulated.

Ferguson worked with William Ricketts, the author of the article "What Does South America Offer the American Advertiser," which appeared in the *J. Walter Thompson News Bulletin* foreign issue of 1928.[36] Ricketts's commentary on advertising conditions in Argentina is not as crude as Ferguson's (perhaps because it was expressed in an article for publication as opposed to in an oral presentation at an in-house representative meeting), but he nonetheless echoes Ferguson's arrogant sentiments toward Argentina. Ricketts claims in his article that "the greatest deficiency in the advertising as used at the present time is the poor quality of the advertisements themselves. Most of these are poor in design and execution. Very little effort has been made to appeal to the consumer from his own point of view or to use a consistent selling idea."[37] Ricketts explains that in Argentina the common advertising style was to use a "novel" appeal, that the ads used clever tricks and unusual effects to catch the consumer's attention. He says that "one sees it everywhere—revolving globes in the subways, illuminated signs underfoot, moving signs in the street cars, reversed plates, sensational 'teaser' advertisements, etc."[38]

Interestingly, what Ricketts demeans is what one is exposed to at every turn in twenty-first century New York City: "revolving globes in the subway" are now flat-screen monitors at subway entrances flashing the latest ads, "moving signs in the street cars" are now television monitors in taxi cabs. "Illuminated signs underfoot" are actually a great idea. Perhaps some cutting-edge agency will discover that idea, or maybe that particular strategy is already being used somewhere.

Even though Ricketts describes Argentina's advertising methods as being far superior to other South American countries, as far as he was concerned, these methods had not reached the highly sophisticated standards of American advertising. The executives at JWT had an express interest in consolidating their advertising strategies and style making it thus possible to export their own distinctive product to the international marketplace. Their JWT-branded product included intensive market research, the reputation of a large and powerful advertising company with the most experienced and talented staff, gendered testimonial advertisements, the use of feminine sex appeal, and images of a privileged American lifestyle.

Clearly, Ricketts does not appreciate the Argentinean way of advertising. He demeans the strategies as almost circus-like in their childlike simplicity. Ricketts and the male executives at JWT are not interested in adapting Argentine advertising strategy, and why should they be? They want to export not just a product but a whole new way of seeing and a new way of understanding one's relationship to things and oneself. Since perception and understanding of reality are constructed by the words and other signs that we use in a social context, the importation of JWT's American advertising would be altering—to some degree—the consciousness and experience of those Argentines who are reading the ads. New or at least altered codes were introduced into Argentine culture through JWT advertisements—codes that organized ideas about femininity and masculinity, codes of dress, and even codes of behavior. Though consciousness and experience do not change overnight, the infiltration of JWT's ads in Argentine newspapers and magazines must have had some effect over time even if the intended effect was appropriated by the consumer. For the male executives at JWT and other businessmen,

the commercial colonization of Argentina and other countries was justified through American expansionism and ideologies of civilization. The
privilege of their position and their arrogance bolstered the assumption
that new markets were theirs for the taking and that by taking those markets, they were both educating a new group of consumers and introducing a better way of life.

Yet while all of his observations have a self-serving and convenient bias
to them, Ferguson had a unique insight into JWT's move to Buenos Aires
since he had been working for a competitor when JWT established an
office there. Evidently, the process for establishing an advertising company
in Argentina was relatively easy—one only had to pay a $40 annual fee.
Others costs were kept at a minimum, Ferguson claimed, because "[adver-
tising companies] take most of their ideas from the *Saturday Evening Post*
and *Ladies' Home Journal.*" Ferguson also claimed that newspapers were
afraid of JWT because they felt that JWT would impose conditions they
did not want to accept and would "change all they had been accustomed to
and take their living away from them."[39]

The newspaper advertising executives indeed had reason to worry. The
executives and office managers at JWT eventually were able to convince
the newspapers to work with them, but the concerns expressed by local
businesses show that they were aware of the far reach and power of a globally ambitious JWT. They were concerned with the disruption JWT would
cause to their ways of conducting business and creating advertisements
that used "revolving globes in the subways, illuminated signs underfoot,
moving signs in the street cars, reversed plates, sensational 'teaser' advertisements." This was a legitimate concern since the goal of JWT was clear:
JWT wanted to dominate advertising worldwide and expand into any market that held promise for its clients.

Nevertheless, the male executives and office managers at JWT did see
their expansion into the international market as a kind of imperial conquest and the language they used expressed that goal quite clearly. Writing
to Stanley Resor, Berlin office manager Clement E. Watson says, "I understand from Sam that you and Mrs. Resor are expecting to sail in July, and I
hope that you will find it possible to include Berlin in your itinerary, so that
you can see at first hand what Henry Miner [manager of JWT Alexandria,
Egypt] chooses to term 'the thin red line of outposts on the frontiers of
our far flung empire.'"[40] It seems that JWT had already outlined its empire,
and JWT male managers posted in this territory were eager for Stanley
Resor and Helen Lansdowne to see how far and wide they had staked claim.
These types of colonial- or missionary-style letters were not that unusual at
JWT; they were read at representative staff meetings with the senior male

executives present as if they were gathering the officers to give a report on the "troops'" progress.

This militaristic language seems to be rather common practice during this period of expansion at JWT. William Day, an executive at JWT, led a representatives meeting (at which Waldo, Casseres, and Nicoll were in attendance) on June 4, 1930, by recounting the battle of Arbela—Alexander the Great versus Darius. Day explained that even though Alexander the Great was outnumbered, he won the battle. He also recounts the battle of Marengo at which Napoleon was outnumbered by an Austrian army—again, the so-called outnumbered but brilliant strategist wins. JWT may have been outnumbered by new consumers, but the ad men saw themselves as brilliant strategists with the technology and connections to make their mark on new markets and, therefore, winning the battle.

James Webb Young, a young JWT executive introduced earlier, traveled extensively and shared some of his observations of international operations and of the countries in which they operated. Other JWT representatives sometimes traveled with Young and together were referred to as "Mr. Young's expeditionary forces.'"[41] Young began a presentation to the all-male representative meeting group by defining the borders of the JWT empire: "I think perhaps you might be most interested in hearing a little about the places that are beyond our present company frontier." He details the vast population of India, identifies a literate market (important for print ads), and then disparages that market:

> There is a country, half the area of the United States, with 325,000,000 people. Those people are of as many different kinds and as many different languages, religions, social conditions and backgrounds, as the nations of Europe. Ninety percent of the people live in villages and depend upon agriculture of a primitive kind for their existence. They have an income of perhaps thirty rupees per capita per month, or about ten dollars. Only 250,000,000 out of the 325,000,000 can possibly be reached by any form of the printed word. It requires about eight or nine languages to do that . . . [t]he dominating people of India, of course, are the Hindus, of whom there are about 200,000,000. They are a peculiarly literary people, that is, they have a passion for reading, a passion for education. A Hindu might appear on the street without his pants but never without his fountain pen. The fountain pen is the badge of learning in India and there is a tremendous sale of fountain pens all through the Country.[42]

Young's dismissal—and his urging of his JWT male colleagues' dismissal—of the Hindus' passion for reading and education reflects a certain degree of knowledge about the values of that culture. Yet Young undermines the notion that these qualities, valued in a "civilized" society, with the derogatory comment about forgetting to wear pants in public. Though highly literate, Hindus are fit subjects to colonize because of their attitude toward material goods such as trousers—as opposed to material good such as pens. Young tells his male audience the significance of a pen to Hindus, as that may be foreign to them, but he does not tell the audience what trousers signify, for the audience knows already. Young emasculates the Hindu man in this story by presenting trousers as a sign of masculinity and bourgeois civilized restraint and removing it or making it absent from the Hindu man's body.

One should also keep in mind Young's audience for this presentation: the most powerful men at JWT, precisely those advertising professionals who no doubt perpetuated this disdain—especially in the early days of JWT's internationalization—for the consumers they were "colonizing" into American consumer culture. The male executives at JWT, along with attempting to convince international manufacturing company executives that American advertising methods were the most civilized and advanced, seem to have been trying to convince themselves. In a sense, Young's remarks attempt to justify JWT's presence in international markets as well as to ease the minds of the executives in New York that no "real" competition exists on the international advertising scene.

As in most colonizing efforts, there was the issue of language that the colonizers and, in this case, the ad men had to address. Since JWT was covering such a wide territory ("virgin land"), it too had to deal with translations, hiring and training a "native" staff, and its ad men were confronted with their own inadequacies with the new language and the cultural nuances so familiar to them in the United States. Rather than colonize through brute force, JWT ad men had to learn about the potential consumers in their territory and ostensibly created ads that appealed to that new market. Finesse, rather than the fist, was the order of the day.

Translations of advertisements did present a consistent problem for those who worked in countries in which English was not going to get the message across to a large number of people. Again, JWT relied on the feminized "native" staff at those offices to interpret the nuances and subtleties of the language not easily accessible to a nonspeaker of that language. Concerning JWT's international expansion and the language issue, Lubertus Smilde, who was the manager of the JWT Hague office from 1932 to 1934 and marketing research and account executive for the Antwerp office from 1929 to 1932, told Sam Meek, JWT's vice president, that

> there was a big difference between pre-war and post-war [World War II] managers. Pre-war, the idea was that it wasn't necessary for a manager to learn that language at all. Deke Colman [manager of Antwerp Office and

in 1946 the Sydney, Australia, office] married a Belgian girl, so he could at least say "oui" and "merci." But generally managers were one-hundred percent English speaking and this annoyed many people—prospective clients—because our top man couldn't speak the language. . . . Now there is a change. Don Johnston, manager of the Amsterdam Office, which has only been there two years, was learning the language before he went there and he can speak quite passably now.[43]

It was not as if the male executives at JWT in the 1920s knew nothing about their new consumers—they completed detailed research analysis of the regions into which they expanded. Prior to World War II, however, managers relied on "native" staff to translate the local language in day-to-day operations as well as to translate copy text that came from either the New York City or London office. Sam Meek, in fact, claimed that language facility was not one of the criteria for heading an international office: "If there's anything we *don't* need in a foreign country, it's the language . . . we can get plenty of people there who speak the language." Although, Meek contradicts this claim later in this same interview when he says, "if he's the man we think he is, he'll learn the language."[44] Taken in all, however, the point is consistent: the managerial style and the technical procedures in developing and promoting advertisements were the valued items—the culture and language were not.

In order to dominate these markets completely and exert their power, JWT male executives positioned themselves and the agency as the authority on taste, design, style, business acumen, and culture in general. The distinction Smilde makes between the emphasis put on language acquisition pre- and postwar in the passage above is interesting. As multinational corporations expanded and globalization took a greater hold after World War II, there would seem to be less reason to learn the local language, and yet there was actually perceived to be more reason. Perhaps prolonged interaction with international markets had the effect of broadening perceptions about the value of knowing a language other than English. This insight hints that through exposure to cultures beyond their own, JWT's ad men and ad women were undoubtedly influenced and changed—the act of going into a market beyond the United States affected their view of the world too.

A young JWT executive in 1929, Russell Pierce was certainly changed by his experience establishing an office in Buenos Aires and working and living there until 1936. Pierce writes about his adventures with Henry Flower and Arthur Farlow, procuring and servicing clients in South America. Henry Flower was a vice president at JWT and the director of the new Buenos Aires office; he came from a wealthy family in Kansas and had been a successful businessman as the president of Durham Hosiery Mills in North Carolina. Farlow also had a privileged upbringing—his father had been the private secretary to Cornelius Vanderbilt. Pierce had a more modest upbringing in Chicago, and, comparing himself to Flower and Farlow, felt at least some initial sense of social inadequacy. Though as an American in Buenos Aires, this feeling seems to dissipate somewhat as he makes a name for himself as a successful ad man and finds common ground with the U.S. and Argentine sales representatives, local newspapermen, and local ad men.

Before leaving New York, Pierce describes a meeting with Stanley Resor and Helen Lansdowne at which time Helen said, "We had a meeting yesterday with Pond's. They are so eager to widen their distribution of beauty creams in South America, particularly in Argentina. They say that upper-class women in that country are very beauty conscious. They regard Paris as the inspiration for everything from clothes to manner and cosmetics. What an opportunity for testimonials from Argentine and French beauties!" Stanley added that GM and Pond's were to be their first clients in Buenos Aires: "I'll wager there will be a lot more coming."[45] Helen and Stanley were right about the testimonial ads and about the success of that office.

Once in Argentina, Pierce is fascinated by and ultimately identifies with the Argentine "gaucho," evident in both naming his memoir *Gringo-Gaucho* and by creating a successful ad campaign for the Swift Meat Processing Company in Argentina that featured the gaucho. Perhaps not surprisingly, the ad campaign was a variation of the testimonial ad—Pierce interviewed gauchos and included their stories and their photographs for the Swift ad campaign. Just as the North American cowboy and his horse ventured into the vast new territory of the western United States, the gaucho roamed the Argentine pampas on horseback, "took Indian women as their mates, captured wild horses and slaughtered wild cattle, which were roaming the pampas after the Spanish conquest."[46]

The mythology of the American cowboy and Argentine gaucho glorifies and perpetuates the concepts of freedom, independence, ruggedness, and a hypermasculinity. It certainly did take a sense of adventure to go into "wild" territory as young ad men setting up new offices in far-flung places. Some JWT ad men took their family—as Flowers did in Argentina. Some admen who traveled to international offices were bachelors—as were Pierce and Farlow. And others married women they met while "stationed" at an international office. International offices marked the next frontier for these men—virgin territory for market share—and, on a more personal level, a chance for adventure. George Butler, the head of the art department in London, noted that the young men who appeared in London before going off to international offices were young and enthusiastic; they were, he said, "very raw-looking young men."[47]

If we think of JWT's international expansion in terms of Kolodny's metanarrative of virgin land, it becomes clear that not only was the new territory feminized, but the "uncivilized" occupants of those territories were also feminized. Perhaps this is why JWT executives (the cowboys and gauchos) would not consider hiring a "native" director at any of the international offices during this time. Even experienced ad men in the "host" countries were not regarded as appropriate leaders for JWT's masculine business culture. JWT's expansion into international markets expanded on the basic gendered division of labor already in existence at the company so that male "natives" were excluded from leadership roles, though the male consumer in the new market was highly valued. These new consumers, however, still needed to be educated to desire new products and taught how to use those new products.

In an excerpt of a letter read at a representative staff meeting, F. J. McArdle, manager of JWT Port Elizabeth, wrote that "in many ways South Africa is a virgin field for other American manufacturers, for this excellent middle-class market has not been educated to its needs."[48] Thus JWT's male executives in the United States and overseas in the 1920s developed a masculine in-house culture that was unabashed, even proud of their imperial aspirations: moving into "virgin" lands, which were coded female,[49] and connecting them by a "red line of outposts." In this, JWT's senior men were in step with American culture in the 1920s, a masculinist culture that generated pride in U.S. control of Hawaii, Puerto Rico, and the Philippines.

In addition, the idea that the occupants of any new frontier needed to be educated regarding American consumer products—and the superiority of those products—echoes assimilation projects of the Progressive Era in the United States during which time immigrants were instructed on how to be a "good" American. Nineteenth- and twentieth-century advertising certainly played a role in this instruction, especially ad campaigns focusing on feminine beauty, cleanliness, and modernity. This interconnection between an internal colonization and an international commercial expansion reflects the position of the United States as both colonized and as an empire, constituting a particular American identity informed by interactions on the domestic and international front.

American influence, exerted abroad, was taken by many American women and men to be proof of a distinctively potent form of American manly vitality. With their empire of potential markets mapped out, the male executives at JWT formed a group of capitalist missionaries whose goal it was to educate middle-class consumers in a myriad of ways to desire the products of their clients. Where desire did not exist for unnecessary products, they worked hard to create it using techniques such as psychological appeals and the testimonial ads developed at the New York City office by the Helen Lansdowne and the Women's Editorial Department.

JWT ad men and women tried to position commercially colonized subjects as consumers who had a need or desire not just for certain products but also for the social meanings these products imbued. Most often, people did not have the need for the new products; therefore, what JWT really exported was desire—a distinctive brand of consumer desire. The myth of a consumer culture claims that one can be a civilized, sophisticated, attractive, and a smart man or woman if he or she buys and uses the products that carry those promises. In the United States, women who wanted to be the modern housewife bought Crisco and threw out their chicken fat or olive oil.

Women who wanted white, feminine skin and bought into the American dream of class mobility slathered on Pond's Cold Cream. And women who were invested in the desire of a man, used Woodbury's Soap for skin men would love to touch. This sign system with all its inherent meanings was transferred to international markets through images and text that reflected ideologies of civilization. Advertisers in the United States during the late nineteenth century were confronted with this task of educating an entire nation to desire products. The appeal used time and time again in the United States by JWT was exported to markets beyond its borders.

Considering the masculine corporate culture of JWT and its clients, it is somewhat surprising that women had anything at all to do with the internationalization of the agency. In an atmosphere where imperialist language and a discourse of conquering international markets prevailed, women had a role confined to developing ad campaigns and supporting the existing agency policy and procedure. Women copywriters rarely dealt directly with JWT's clients in the United States, nor were they promoted to account representative positions. This exclusion of the Women's Editorial Department professionals from direct contact with the agency's highly prized clients, the manufacturing sales executives, continued when JWT's senior men decided to expand overseas. There were a few exceptions. In 1911, Helen Lansdowne was invited by Procter & Gamble into its boardroom to pitch her ideas for the Crisco ad campaign, and she also dealt directly with Pond's and Woodbury's executives. The only other places women appeared in the JWT empire, however, were in agency market research reports (as the subject or consumer) and in the advertisements themselves (as object).

Paying attention to the gendering of institutions and the power relations in the constitution of difference, such as patriarchal forms of domination and subordination, helps us understand how sexism and racism are justified on an international scale and domestically. JWT's masculine corporate imperialism, which was couched in an ideology of civilization, set out to conquer new markets, echoing the American expansionist model both as it played out in the American West and internationally. In understanding the values and beliefs that reside in the hearts and minds of individuals and, as an extension, powerful institutions, we come to understand how those ideologies become globalized through American corporate expansionism.

J. Walter Thompson's International Advertisements

The Universal Appeal to Beauty

The problems of advertising Pond's products overseas are multifold and must always be considered on an individual market basis. There are variations in climate, differences in women's makeup habits, varied preferences for color and fragrances, uniqueness in skin problems, and oftimes [*sic*] a greater resistance to change. However, there still remains the universal appeal to beauty, those qualities of femininity which provide the basic common denominator for our advertising and sales.

—William M. Peniche, "Beauty From Bangor to Bangkok: A Brief Review of Chesebrough-Pond's World-Wide Advertising," a presentation before an International Seminar, April 18, 1961, Sam Meek Papers, JWT Archives

What are those basic qualities of femininity and the universal desire for beauty of which Peniche speaks? To answer that question, one just has to look at and read the many successful ad campaigns created by Helen Lansdowne and her team of copywriters. Whether women accept those qualities of femininity or not, women do know what those qualities are. "Feminine qualities" are, after all, just another way to describe ideal beauty, the "common denominator" in "advertising and sales." The advertising strategies developed by Lansdowne and her team, such as the "modern" testimonial ad, and its appeal to class mobility, fashion, and taste, were also used to reach international markets. These strategies were based on a "universal appeal to beauty" that had already saturated U.S. media. The universal appeal in the United States perpetuated a denial of differences among consumers and a focus on middle-class, white women. J. Walter Thompson's (JWT) approach was that all women are fundamentally the same in their desire for beauty, and this concept spread to their international advertising campaigns.

Some executives at JWT claimed to have adapted advertisements created in the New York office to suit specific overseas markets, especially when discussing the value and effectiveness of market research. An examination of international ads during the 1920s, 1930s, and a few from the early 1940s, however, shows a different story for some of the cosmetics accounts, most remarkably, the Pond's account. A 1922 Woodbury's British market study concludes that "experience has shown that an appeal which has been successful here [the United States] will, with a little editing, be successful there. Examples of this are Cutex, Pepsodent, Cuticura, and Palmolive Soap which have built up large volumes of business by using the same copy appeal and the same advertising they use in America." In his presentation to a JWT international seminar, William Peniche says that "even though . . . [Pond's] ads were produced by our offices abroad, their appearance except for the language, varies little from the successful U.S campaign. Apparently, their appeal and message were universal."[1]

For the most part, the same images of ideal beauty, created for the U.S. market, were recycled for international beauty campaigns. Furthermore, the images of women and the language used to describe them in the Pond's campaign is similar to the language analyzed in the Woodbury's Soap, Lux Flakes, and Cutex ad campaigns, among other ad campaigns originally created by Helen Lansdowne and her team of women copywriters. Once this approach proved successful, these advertising techniques and strategies were used again and again. As a result, the language and images of ideal beauty that reinforced particular ideas of race and class in the U.S. market were exported to international audiences.

The Global Expansion of Pond's

As was discussed in earlier chapters and here, corporate America is not itself undifferentiated. Rather, one must explore which firms in each U.S.-based industrial sector came to wield disproportionate influence. One must consider what were the exact racialized, classed, and gendered dynamics inside those U.S. corporations that were disproportionately influential and globally expansionist. If, as conventionally still happens in the literature on corporate America's overseas influence, one goes about trying to explain how and why U.S.-based capitalist commerce has had the effects it has without being interested in (a) particular firms and (b) the gendered and racial dynamics inside those firms, one is not likely to shed much light.

American manufacturers were expanding globally, and their presence at the turn of the nineteenth century created an opportunity for advertisers such as JWT to expand their market as well. Out of all the clients that JWT served, Pond's had the biggest presence in its international offices.[2] The Pond's account went to just about every JWT international office, and by 1950, the Pond's testimonial ad circulated in forty-six countries and appeared in eighteen languages.[3] JWT worked with Pond's "in a multitude of world markets ranging in size and population from England, Germany, India to tiny Ceylon and the Windward and Leeward Islands." [4] Pond's domestic sales for its two creams increased from $307,000 in 1916 to $1.6 million in 1923, passing all its competitors.[5] And Pond's international business was just as impressive. From 1923 to 1948, Pond's total world sales increased 8.8 times as compared with 7.6 times for domestic sales. International sales of Pond's during this time increased 12.7 times. Table 6.1 shows percentages of total sales and advertising.[6]

Table 6.1.   Pond's International Sales

Net sales	1923	1937	1941	1948
U.S. only	69%	63%	70%	60%
UK and Europe	21	25	12	16
Other countries	10	12	18	24
Total in millions	$2.5	$9.5	$9.8	$22.0
Advertising				
U.S. only	—	59%	83%	67%
UK and Europe	—	31	2	11
Other countries	—	10	15	22
Total in millions	—	$2.8	$2.1	$3.2

Net sales and advertising numbers show that "other countries" started to outsell the United Kingdom and Europe by 1941, which is not surprising considering the effects of the war. To reach those "other countries," JWT used a variety of media and strategies to advertise Pond's in those markets. In Central Africa, JWT employed African drums to deliver a Pond's ad throughout the center of the region. One snag, however, was the inability to translate the name of the product into African drum language. JWT also devised creative ad campaigns in the Philippines and Haiti by using trucks with large speakers and portable film projectors. These trucks traveled the length and breadth of the islands selling Pond's products.[7]

Women in villages and towns not reached through conventional media and normal distribution were able to purchase Pond's products, which they did, further enforcing the idea in the minds of ad men and ad women that the desire for beauty was universal. Yet, just how that beauty would be portrayed fell into the hands of those who controlled the media and created the ad campaigns. An examination of some of JWT's international ads reveals how images and languages—discourses on race, class, and nationality often couched in the rhetoric of the "modern"—reached these potential international consumers.

Overall, JWT gained prominence through its international offices through serving large clients such as Pond's. JWT's new multinational clients powered JWT's growth and its international operation gathered strength rather quickly so that even during the Great Depression in the United States, overseas operations still managed to show a modest profit. In 1932, there were 248 accounts being handled by fifteen international offices and billings increased to $6 million. JWT's domestic billings were $24 million and its world total was $30 million. The total shows a decrease from 1930 of almost $8 million, yet it was not as serious a loss as other agencies experienced during this time. By 1940, domestic billings had recovered almost to their 1929, pre-Depression level of $31 million and international billings reached $10 million accounting for approximately one-quarter of the company's total $41 million for that year. Shortly after World War II, in 1950, international billings reached $25 million and from that point on moved toward parity with JWT's domestic earnings. In 1973, international surpassed domestic billings and represented approximately 56 percent of the total world business by 1980.[8]

International Exposure: The *Ladies' Home Journal* and *Saturday Evening Post*

The ad campaigns created by the Women's Editorial Department that reached international audiences appeared in local newspapers and magazines as well as in American magazines that circulated in those countries. Jennifer Scanlon notes the importance of the relationship between JWT's Women's Editorial Department and the *Ladies' Home Journal* in her history of the magazine, *Inarticulate Longings*. And indeed, JWT placed record-breaking volumes of advertising in the *Ladies' Home Journal*. During 1924 and 1925, JWT consistently broke its own records for the volume of advertising placed in the magazine: the record achieved in March 1925 was $230,640 and exceeded by $19,380 the previous record made in April, 1924.[9] The majority of those cosmetic, food, and household accounts that the ad women worked on appeared in the *Ladies' Home Journal*, many appeared in the *Saturday Evening Post* as well, which was considered second only to the *Ladies' Home Journal* in advertising soap products and toiletries.[10]

In terms of an international appeal, displaying an issue of *Vogue* or *Ladies' Home Journal* on one's coffee table seemed to connote a cosmopolitan flair. Arthur Hartzell, director of JWT Spain, pointed out the influence of these two magazines in Spanish homes: "It is an interesting thing to note in Spain that the foreign magazines are popular; the *Saturday Evening Post*, the *Ladies' Home Journal*, *Vogue*, *Femina* of Paris and *English Illustrated* weeklies are sold in the principal cities and one finds them in a great many homes of the upper class. It is considered smart and up-to-date to have a foreign magazine on your library table, whether you can read it or not."[11] The international (beyond U.S. borders) circulation numbers for these two magazines are revealing and give insight into just how widespread one medium for American advertising images and messages were—as early as 1913.

The *Ladies' Home Journal* and *Saturday Evening Post* were both published by the Curtis Publishing Company. Data from the company archives show that in 1913, the *Ladies' Home Journal* circulated in at least eighty-six countries for a total circulation of 139,656. Those countries and continents with the highest circulation numbers (100 or more) included Africa (1,009), Australia (7,367), Canada (115,385), China (442), France (101), Germany (350), Great Britain (10,770), India (365), Italy (112), Japan (208), Mexico (803), New South Wales (100), New Zealand (637), Argentina (131), Brazil (170), Switzerland (119), and the West Indies (166).[12] Numbers were not available for Cuba and Puerto Rico, which may have also been significant in light of available numbers from subsequent years.[13] As Hartzell points out in his comments about the Spanish market for the *Ladies' Home Journal* and *Saturday Evening Post*, these magazines were found mainly in upper-class homes. If this was the case, they most likely found their way into the homes of the media elite, the most visible and influential taste-makers and trendsetters in those countries. Many subscribers, then, were similar socially and economically (middle and upper-middle class) to the ad men and ad women who worked at JWT.

Overall, by 1920, the *Ladies' Home Journal* international circulation numbers had increased slightly (a little over 1 percent). Subscriptions increased dramatically, however, in Africa (3,444, countries not identified), Asia (2,337, countries not identified), Europe (3,464, countries not identified), Cuba (522), Hawaii (1,350), the Philippines (990), Puerto Rico (567), and Oceania[14] (6,934, countries not identified). Though these numbers may not appear to be that impressive at first glance, the Curtis Publishing Company estimated through customer surveys that each magazine was viewed by more than one person. In fact, one survey found that the average number of readers per magazine was 3.84.[15] This makes sense if one thinks about how magazines are passed from family to family and from friend to friend. If a magazine is placed in a public place of business such as a beauty salon or a doctor's office, it is read by even more than three or four people. Since it is known that Lansdowne and her team of copywriters placed record-breaking number of ads in the *Ladies' Home Journal*, the presence and impact of their work become apparent through international circulation numbers as well as the international sales numbers for Pond's Cold and Vanishing Creams.

Pond's International Testimonial Advertisements

What follows is an analysis of Pond's advertisements in various countries. The organization of ads in this manner shows the worldwide spread of Pond's advertising. It also shows that as a Pond's ad went from one country to another, from one culture to another, and from one language to another, the basic look of the ad stayed the same. Furthermore, these ads went to the JWT London office or the JWT New York office for layout or design or copywriting work. At least for Pond's, the JWT New York office was a "control center," a place were all the Pond's ads were reviewed regardless of whether they were created in the United States or in an international office.[16] This consistency resulted in dominant U.S. ideologies of civilization, modernity, and a particular ideal beauty infiltrating sign systems, which were not built on American values and beliefs. Though we can only speculate as to how those markets absorbed or adapted American messages about ideal beauty, sales figures show that Pond's was well-received globally. The fact is that these images did appear in international markets, sometimes in local newspapers and magazines and sometimes in American magazines such as the *Ladies' Home Journal* and the *Saturday Evening Post*.

Pond's in England, Australia, Ceylon (Sri Lanka), Malaya (Malaysia), and Rangoon (Yangon, Myanmar)

At JWT, it was an agency-wide belief that people, no matter where they lived, were more alike than different. An approach based on universal desires and beliefs certainly made it easier to dominate a new market; market research wouldn't have to extend beyond the categories of occupation and class. Or, in other words, who could afford to buy this product? In terms of the Pond's account, an aspirational appeal embedded in the testimonial ad was universally successful. A testimonial Pond's ad that ran in England in 1931 illustrates many of these points. The headline reads, "Society's Loveliest Women Entrust Their Flower-Like Skin to These Two Creams," and the text reads, "A peach bloom skin—velvety soft—invitingly smooth and clear . . . the loveliest, most distinguished women in the world have found this to be true . . . 'The surest protection I have ever found for my skin' declares the charming Countess of Galloway."[17] This ad appeals to the consumer's desire to identify with a higher socioeconomic class, and a "peach bloom skin" refers to a light skin that these society women no doubt possess. The images in this ad reinforce the good taste of the upper class with photos of the two jars of Pond's (Cold Cream and Vanishing Cream) and an elegant single strand of pearls—the mark of any well-bred young woman.

The Countess of Galloway also appears in a Sydney, Australia, ad for Pond's prior to 1934.[18] The countess is photographed wearing a single strand of pearls—that marker of class and sophistication—surrounded by delicate flowers. She is described as slim with "flawless olive skin," which, interestingly, is not consistent with the description of her skin in the British ad that calls her skin "peach-bloom skin." Nevertheless, in this particular ad, a photo of her country home, Cumloden (the country seat of the Earl and Countess of Galloway), appears and reinforces her status as upper-class, beautiful, and, hopefully for JWT and Pond's, imitable.[19]

These testimonial ads are practically identical to the ones that appeared in the United States, for two main reasons: the Pond's domestic testimonial ads were successful and all Pond's ads had to be approved prior to printing by the New York City office. Yet, while these ads were similar to the ones circulated in the United States, they had never before appeared in newspapers and magazines internationally. They were new to the international market. Furthermore, in testament to the success of the modern testimonial ad created by Helen Lansdowne for Pond's, other domestic and international testimonial ad campaigns were created for clients such as General Motors (GM) and Swift meat products.

The power of beauty products and their sign systems (the language and images that give particular meaning to the products) lies in their role in generating and maintaining shared expectations and shared interpretive frameworks. The Pond's ads did not force readers to have certain interpretations as much as they created a context for interpretation. If certain messages about female beauty or the status of women within England, Australia, Ceylon, Malaya, and Rangoon share any of the same codes of femininity (or feminine "qualities" that Watson refers to at the beginning of the chapter) that are represented in the Pond's ads, the potential consumer may be drawn to that ad. Even if the ad has messages and images that do not share similar codes of femininity, the ad might draw attention for that reason alone—it would seem unusual and out of place. These feminine codes would include representations, selected by the JWT's Women's Editorial Department, of beauty (fair skin, regular features, youth) and behavior (gentle, docile, passive, nurturing). Also part of the narrative of the ads is the beautiful woman as engaged in modern, stylish, and entirely civilized pursuits. As a consumer, she is free to pursue her desires, to climb the class ladder, to aspire to ideal beauty, and to take advantage of scientific breakthroughs to achieve ideal beauty. The modern woman who exists in the world of advertising is nonthreatening; she may golf and drive a car, but only insomuch as she supports the "common denominator" of sales and advertising.

Lady Georgiana Curzon endorses Pond's in another testimonial ad that appeared in England in 1931. A photo of an elegantly turned-out lady in profile appears at the top of the ad, and the headline reads, "This Charming Debutante Lady Georgiana Curzon Guards Her Youthful Loveliness With Pond's Two Creams," and the text below describes Curzon: "Lady Georgiana is dark, slender, enchanting . . . You notice her exquisite complexion the moment you look at her . . . its ivory texture and delicate colouring."[20] She is fair-skinned, slender, and a "lady," just like the women in the United States who endorsed Pond's. The darkness attributed to Curzon most likely refers to her dark hair and eyes, for the text later goes on to call her skin "ivory," in line with what is considered beautiful in U.S. mass media. The women copywriters of the New York JWT Women's Editorial Department, so seemingly in their own personal pursuits of women's autonomy, women's political franchise, and women's commercial professionalism, were still entirely enamored with women of inherited upper-class privilege. They promoted this confirmation of classist feminine criteria of beauty (ideal beauty) internationally with the testimonial ad.

Pond's is not the only client for whom Lansdowne and her copywriters produced testimonial ads. In England, both Cutex and Sun-Maid Raisins had endorsers—from the beauty editor of *Modern Woman*, Mansel Beaufort, who endorsed Cutex, to Lady Cayzer, who endorsed Sun-Maid Raisins.[21] Considering the women who worked in the London office at this time (many of whom worked in the Women's Editorial Department in New York), it is not surprising that these advertising campaigns used testimonials. The modern testimonial ad was a successful strategy that appealed to consumers' sense of style and class and a desire to be desired like those portrayed in the testimonial ads. But again, both messages in the Cutex and Sun-Maid Raisin ads reinforced and perpetuated discourses on race and class by describing the most desirable women as fair, upper-class, and slender. Fair skin, privilege, and a fashionable body that could show off the latest styles were most desirable.

In her presentation on the Lux account to the creative staff in New York City, Elizabeth Devree, who had worked in the Paris office,[22] talked about developing the strategy of connecting a product to the upper class, to good taste, and fashion: "Anticipating a swarm of competitors, J. Walter Thompson built up an added appeal for Lux. They exploited it as something magical, mysterious and in some way synonymous with fashion. Fashion and style, always belonging to the upper class, especially of the unemployed women of those privileged classes, were becoming the prerogatives of the middle classes. And Thompson tied up with fashion and rode it through years of success."[23] What is the appeal of this strategy? And how do ads take on "magical" and "mysterious" qualities? Here Devree describes the production of meaning for a product based on a connection with the desired quality—in this case, fashion. The idea of being fashionable fits into the system of meaning already established through advertising. The reader knows what a fashionable woman looks like through reading women's magazines.

This intertextuality—when the meanings generated by any one text are determined partly by the meanings of other texts to which it appears familiar—reinforces the ideological message of modern feminine fashion and ideal beauty. What is being described as magical and mysterious by Devree is the possibility of the middle-class woman attaining the style and sophistication of the upper-class woman's fashion through the magical process of attaching a variety of meanings to a product. Lower- and middle-class women do not have access to the resources by which upper-class women attain their goods. But this ad promises that through some magical and mysterious process the ordinary consumer can have access to that luxurious world.

Pond's reach extended far beyond England and Australia. For example, a Pond's ad appeared in Ceylon (Sri Lanka), Malaya (Malaysia), and Rangoon (Yangon, Myanmar) in 1941 in English (Figure 6.1). This ad appeared in local newspapers and seems to be targeting British women who perhaps had moved with their husband or worked for the British government in these colonies. The headline reads, "Be Fair To Your Skin," a play on the word "fair," which can mean both light-colored and unblemished and just and honest. Both meanings are useful for the purposes of an advertisement circulating in these (former) British colonies. The woman in the ad appears in different scenes: looking dreamily to the side while holding a letter with a well-jeweled hand and wrist and perfect bee-stung lips. In other scenes she is sunbathing, motoring through a landscape with a palm tree in the background, and in her home applying Pond's cream to her face. Finally, she is in a scene reading a warning sign that reinforces the denotative message of the ad: "BEWARE of Scorching Sun, Dust & Grime, Hot Dry Air."[24] The connotative message in this ad is don't lose your whiteness while you are away from home—keep your skin youthful and "fair." The indication that this woman is a visitor (besides her Anglo appearance) is revealed in the first paragraph of text: "Have you, since you arrived in the tropics, given real thought to your skin? Now, even more than ever, it needs your constant care to keep it soft and fresh looking . . . Use Pond's Creams regularly and, in spite of the trying conditions, your skin will be youthfully soft and glowing, with that petal-like texture you have envied so much at Home."[25]

The circulation of this particular ad in these three British colonies shows just how an ideology of "civilization" is reinforced and perpetuated. Anglo

Figure 6.1. Pond's, "Be Fair To Your Skin"

beauty, prestige, class, and style come to represent the "civilized," the thoroughly modern woman who had the time and luxury to focus such attention on her skin. The conditions in these colonies are described as especially harsh on petal-soft, fresh, glowing peach skin, and it takes the protection of Pond's cream to maintain the beauty of these visitors. The phrase "trying conditions" is similar to the headline "Be Fair To Your Skin" in its double message: the change in weather can be trying, but the implication is that living in these tropical colonies was "trying" for the modern woman who was used to living in a civilized country with every convenience.

Pond's in Buenos Aires, Argentina: "S.A.R. the Princess
Eulalia of Spain talks of the beauty in the courts of Europe"

A Pond's testimonial ad also appeared in Buenos Aires, Argentina, endorsed by the Su Alteza Real (S.A.R., the equivalent of "Her Royal Highness"), the Princess Eulalia of Spain. In this ad, circulated in 1930, Princess Eulalia is photographed in profile, in a regal pose complete with tiara and a single strand of pearls. Princess Eulalia seems to possess qualities similar to Alva Belmont, the first woman to endorse Pond's in the United States—an American royal. An authoritative figure, Princess Eulalia is middle-aged and accomplished in her own right; she wrote a book titled *Courts and Cities After the War*. The Pond's ad copy reads, "Her book . . . is a subtle and penetrating commentary, filled with profound observations." Furthermore, the princess is presented as "an intellectual woman of the greater world, the Princess has the authority to talk about the importance that a woman should give to the care of her beauty and to instruct us in the method for maintaining the beauty of our complexion."[26]

The princess, who was the aunt of King Alfonso XII, established herself as an authority on the life of a royal and explained how Pond's helped her cope with the pressures: "The social life in the courts of Europe . . . demands much of us; the self assurance and confidence that high birth and social status gives us must be considered along with personal charm, and the daily use of Pond's creams give us the security of having it."[27] In addition to emulating the testimonial style, this ad also has a coupon offer for a sample of Pond's, a strategy used in the United States for market research purposes.

In this ad, Princess Eulalia speaks of the responsibilities of being a woman in the Spanish royal court. In addition to the self-assurance and confidence that is expected of a woman in her position, she explains that she is also expected to be charming. Her endorsement of Pond's cream, then, includes the assertion that this cream gives one the confidence, charm, and the self-assurance to endure even the most rigorous of social schedules.

The connotation is that if a princess—with all her available resources—chooses Pond's cream to boost her self-image (thus making her seem more human and more accessible), then the average Argentine woman has access to at least some of the same resources of a princess through consuming a beauty product. If this accomplished princess chose a distinctly American product, which was reasonably priced, then why shouldn't the average female consumer?

This aspirational appeal is the very essence of the Pond's testimonial ads. The Pond's ads in the United States used American royalty (e.g., Belmont and Vanderbilt) as well as European royalty. For the Argentinean female consumer, JWT capitalized on this emotional appeal of prestige by securing the endorsement of a princess—something Helen Lansdowne had imagined before the opening of the JWT Buenos Aires office. Just before Russell Pierce headed off to Buenos Aires to start a JWT office, Lansdowne brought up the Pond's account during their meeting in New York: "They say that the upper-class women in (Argentina) are very beauty conscious . . . what an opportunity for testimonials."[28] To Lansdowne, the Argentine woman's desire to be beautiful (or stylish, both of which necessitates buying new products) fits perfectly with the aspirational tone of Pond's modern testimonials that featured beautiful, accomplished women.

Pond's in Bucharest, Romania: "Why Does Every Complexion Need Two Face Creams?"

In response to the headline of one of the Pond's ads from Romania (placed in Hungarian newspapers), the copy explains that "as a result of the hurried life, which women lead nowadays, the sensitive tissues of the complexion are much more exposed to harmful effects than before"[29] (Figure 6.2). It appears as though the ad targeted to a Romanian audience takes on the plight of the "modern" woman: she is busy and perhaps stressed, which affects her skin. This ad is not claiming that women have always had a hurried life but, rather, women lead this life "nowadays," implying that the routine of women had changed in some way. Instead of a photograph, this ad uses a sketch of a woman in a modern art deco design, stressing the modern quality of the product and its association with the intended consumer—the modern woman. To further enforce its message, this ad combines the scientific approach (the endorsement of the medical field of dermatology and the two-step system of skin care technology) and the endorsement of two successful European actresses, Lil Dagover (1894–1980), whose Dutch family worked in Romania, and German actress Olga Tschechowa (1897–1980): "Pond's two creams are produced by the finest dermatological

Figure 6.2.   Pond's, "Why Does Every Complexion Need Two Face Creams?"

experts so that the fine tissues of your skin are protected. This is why the most beautiful women in the artistic world, such as *Lil Dagover* and *Olga Tschechowa* and many others use the *two Pond's creams*."[30] Instead of using a royal society endorser, this ad uses the allure of actresses.

Another Pond's ad distributed in Romania (using Romanian copy) appeals to a more modern, and perhaps younger, Romanian woman. This ad shows a photo of an attractive young woman using the product. The copy explains how women could have beautiful skin even if they didn't have what seemed to be the perfect face: "Beautiful skin is as important as a beautiful face ... Women who know how to take care of their skin and keep it clean, velvety and soft, enjoy their lives. Damaged skin makes even the most perfect face ugly. A face that is not so perfect seems beautiful if the skin is smooth and soft. Beautiful skin brightens the face making it look young and pleasant to the eye. The two Pond's creams, manufactured in the U.S., are ideal for skin care."[31] The ad is similar to many other Pond's ads in its claim that women with good skin can enjoy their life. And even if the reader of this ad is not the perfect beauty, she can still enjoy the beautiful skin possible with Pond's. This ad includes detailed instructions for cleaning and moisturizing the skin so the consumer of this product can enjoy a complexion that brightens her face and makes her look younger. As in most other Pond's ads, in the United States and abroad, this particular Pond's ad also includes a coupon that offers a sample of Pond's for a small fee.

Pond's did not enjoy the same level of success in every country in which it was advertised. Occasionally, it seems that political matters may have cast a shadow on the modern Pond's woman. In these cases, the feedback from account representatives and office directors abroad reveal how some consumers reacted to American beauty product ads. Some of the explanations given for the lower sales numbers reflect a reluctance on the part of JWT executives to consider obvious political tensions and a tendency to explain away resistance to American beauty products as disinterest in "beauty." Germany is a case in point.

Pond's in Frankfurt, Germany: "A Wonderful Cream For Taking Care Of Your Skin"

Pond's is yielding very slowly in the German market, for some strange reason. Maybe I haven't been able to get under the surface enough. The mass of the population of German women are not beauty-mad the way they are here—virtues of the mind seem to be still a premium in Germany—so it is a little hard to get an angle on them.

> —Dr. Watson, Representatives' Meeting Minutes,
> December 9, 1930, JWT Archives

Dr. Watson says that there is a "younger element" in Berlin and this group is "thin, (which [he] admires very much); they use rouge and powder and lip sticks."[32] JWT had an office in Berlin to manage ad campaigns directed toward this younger group of women and apparently even the older generation who seemed to appreciate "virtues of the mind" over beauty. Aminta

Casseres worked on the Berlin Pond's account and was in attendance at this particular meeting. Unfortunately, she did not speak about her experiences working for a German market. Watson had concerns about German consumers and attempted to make a connection between a perceived general apathy women had toward living up to an ideal beauty and the Germans' resistant mood, as he described at this meeting: "I tried to send out and get quite a few individuals to come in and talk over the various types of campaigns, as to whether authority, for example, would lead them to try a thing. It is very curious about that. They have been in a very resistant mood for the last ten years on any question of authority at all. Germany is the only country that I really feel bad about at the present."[33] This resistance to American products may not be so surprising considering the shattered German economy and its weak infrastructure, post-World War I. In addition, the heavy war reparations that were imposed after the war may not have left German businessmen predisposed to wholeheartedly embracing American products. Considering the political situation, Watson's comment about reluctant consumers as "curious" seems disingenuous.

The "authority" that Watson is referring to is the ubiquitous endorser that appeared in testimonial ads—a figure of style and grace who might influence German women to buy Pond's just as endorsers had done in many other countries. Watson concluded, however, that Germans won't listen to "authority" and that testimonial ads would not be effective for that market. In response, JWT created ads that temper the beauty appeal (referring only to "leading women") and instead focused more heavily on a scientific approach. But the ads still appealed to beauty, youth, and fashion: " . . . leading women [illegible] . . . The secret of new beauty lies in both of these skin creams. With regular use, minor fatigue lines will vanish, pores will open, and skin that was previously neglected will be restored. Your color will become more youthful and more radiant each day."[34]

Another German ad for Pond's also uses a scientific appeal, with a mention of "modern dermatology" at the beginning of the ad and placing a mention of the beauty, Elisabeth Pinajeff, at the end of detailed instructions on how to use Pond's: "The basic principles of modern dermatology require that the skin breathe—just like the lungs—so that its natural freshness can be protected. The pores must be free of dirt and powder residue so that the skin can take in oxygen. The skin, however, must also be protected."[35] JWT adjusted the German ads to fit the market preference, it seems, though the ads don't appear much different from other Pond's ads. The German ads focused just a bit more on scientific copy, but that adjustment had been made in other Pond's ads.

Personal biases also seemed to play a part in the adjustments made in the Pond's ad campaign in Germany. The perceived reluctance on the part of German women to reject claims based on beauty alone—they were not "beauty mad" like other women—seemed to have been puzzling to Watson. But why? Was Watson so entrenched in the belief of a universal desire for beauty (through consumption) that when he stumbled on a group of women who valued virtue of the mind he thought it strange? And why didn't Watson put more emphasis on the political and economic climate of Germany during that period? Perhaps Watson put his faith solely in the strength of Pond's international sales figures and expected markets to be essentially the same, despite the political climate. But all was not lost in the quest for German consumers. The younger market of German women interested in cosmetics, to whom Watson alludes, were more aligned with the modern female consumer JWT had helped to shape.

Ultimately, JWT copywriters put together ads that used both a scientific approach and a subtle authority appeal through endorsers for a German audience. Both appeals had proven successful in the United States and many other countries for the Pond's account. That ability to adjust the standard beauty appeal and scientific appeal in the Pond's testimonial was actually the campaign's strength. Helen Lansdowne and her team of copywriters had created a brilliant campaign for Pond's; the concept of the modern testimonial ad had just enough flexibility both in image and content to tweak on occasion, when necessary.

Other International Ads Created by JWT

Even though most of the ads used here to explore JWT's international ads are for the Pond's account, other international ads are relevant to understanding the reach and influence JWT exerted across the globe. In addition to all the testimonial ads mentioned in this section, most for the Pond's campaign, the influence of the testimonial extended to the GM account. In one particular GM ad, produced by JWT's Warsaw office and approved by the international department in New York City, there is a familiar face— that of Lady Curzon, who also appeared as an endorser in Pond's ads. A familiar appeal to a consumer's taste, class, and fashion are exemplified in this GM ad: "One of many Cadillac owners among the aristocratic spheres . . . Lady Curzon, much like numerous ladies of the world's high society, owns a Cadillac automobile. As a matter of fact, owing to harmonious lines and beautiful bodywork, this automobile undisputedly appeals to people whose fancy and good taste are beyond doubt."[36] And, if there was any doubt about other aristocracy (that included men), the ads points out that: "*Cadillac owners include such members of royalty and aristocracy as*: Emperor of Japan, Shah of Persia, Countess Maria Esterhazy, Countess du Bourg de Bozas, Prince of Bedford, Prince de Vallombrosa."[37]

Jeff Merron points out that the women in GM international ads resemble the "Fisher Body" girl who appeared in U.S. ads for the motor carriage company of the same name.[38] The Fisher Body girl is the epitome of modern beauty: young, slim, and sophisticated. She has the "regular" features of the Steel-Engraving Lady described in Chapter 2—bee-stung mouth, heart-shaped face, fair skin—images of ideal beauty that seem to easily transfer from ad to ad, from magazine to magazine, and from country to country. Malcolm Thomson, who worked for Arthur Hartzel at JWT's Spain office, illustrates this point when he says, "We prepared a campaign; I don't know if for Buick or Chevrolet. We drew on the *Ladies' Home Journal* and *Saturday Evening Post* to see what was done in America and to have something to refer to."[39] It would seem plausible then that other JWT outposts were also borrowing from ads in American magazines—even if they were not entirely appropriate for the audience. An ad for baby powder illustrates this point.

In a 1933 advertisement for Johnson's Toilet and Baby Powder, produced in the JWT Bombay and Calcutta offices for an Indian and British market, a seductive sketch of what appears to be an Anglo woman in her bathroom appears at the top of the ad.[40] The woman only wears a pair of slippers and a precariously draped towel seemingly held up by her right breast. Her other breast is covered by a well-placed arm, which extends to her knee to smooth in the powder. Besides its sex appeal, the ad copy describes Johnson's Toilet and Baby Powder as "white magic." "Whiteness," in this ad, is closely aligned with "fineness," another word used to describe the powder. Though there is no way to tell why this image was chosen (besides convenience), it seems chosen exclusively for a British audience.

The denotation of this copy is that the powder is indeed fine—in its weight and texture. And the white magic is the refreshing feeling one experiences when using the white powder. However, the connotation is that white is associated with fineness: the white skin of the Anglo (represented in this ad and all others discussed here) is fine, it is upper class, it is privileged and in good taste. After all, does not everyone look like this? The JWT advertisement connotes that it is better to be white: those are the only people in ads who look happy, who are beautiful, powerful, and modern. And white magic, the special ingredient in the Johnson's Toilet and Baby

Powder, will make you white. Just a few decades prior to this particular baby powder ad, some soap ads in the United States and Great Britain implied through images that the product had the power to make consumers white.[41]

By 1962, JWT had created Pond's Cold Cream ads for an Indian audience that showed an illustration of a woman in a sari with a bindi (Figure 6.3). The facial features of this Indian woman look amazingly close to the features of the Steel-Engraving Lady described in Chapter 2: heart-shaped face, bee-stung lips, fair skin, and delicate features. A man smiles approvingly behind her. This woman is straight out of a *Ladies' Home Journal* ad but with the appropriate cultural markers for a new demographic.

The social construction of race, gender, and class would not be possible without a well-established system of signification, which makes meaning and the institutions that perpetuate meaning. Early ad women and ad men drew on established binary oppositions to create a system of meaning useful for advertising their clients' products—a kind of shorthand for understanding the value of a product: white/black, civilized/uncivilized, high-class/low-class, modern/primitive. For example, we already know that the male account executives at JWT who managed the agency's ad campaigns believed that the United States was the epitome of civilization. They were well educated, cosmopolitan, and they were out to gain their share of the market. It is not surprising, then, that they focused on the superior quality of their clients' products to gain a foothold in new territories using the language of the colonizer.

These attitudes shaped a corporate culture that was standardized and replicated throughout each international office. Those same attitudes were also reflected in ads such as one for GM that circulated throughout Egypt, in which a modern automobile passes by a primitive mode of transportation—the camel.[42] The juxtaposition of the car and the camel highlight the contrast between the civilized and the primitive, and particular meanings are produced in the choice and arrangement of images and text. This results in a particular ideology that values modernity above old-fashioned and even today serves businesses built on creating new consumers who continually consume, consumers who consistently desire better models, and consumers who are forever searching for the next scientific breakthrough.

An effect of the signs, in the advertisements discussed in this chapter, is the assumption that the values represented are so basic, so widely shared, and so natural that they do not need to be stated directly. For example, the copy in the GM ad does not need to spell out that a GM car is superior to the camel, and Pond's or Johnson's Toilet and Baby Powder copy does not need to spell out that whiteness is preferred, that it is beautiful and tasteful—the images and connotation work that subtle magic. Though copy

How lovely you look
TOMORROW
depends on how well
you clean your face
TONIGHT !

Beauty begins with a clean, clean skin
POND'S COLD CREAM cleanses deeply, completely

TONIGHT—Smooth Pond's Cold Cream generously over your face and throat. Massage with gentle, upward movements, giving special attention to areas around eyes, nose and lips. After two minutes tissue off excess cream. Pond's Cold Cream penetrates deeply into pores to lift out the 'hidden dirt' and make-up that often cause blemishes...works all night to clean and smooth your skin.

removes
the hidden dirt
and make-up that
soap and water
cannot reach

TOMORROW—You wake up with a complexion that looks and feels beautifully refreshed—smooth, soft and truly clean. Pond's moisture-rich Cold Cream has nourished your skin, replaced natural oils, and smoothed away dryness and wrinkles. Every day, let Pond's Cold Cream protect your complexion. *Remember,* How lovely you look tomorrow depends on how well you clean your face tonight.

CHESEBROUGH-POND'S INC. (Incorporated in the U.S.A. with Limited Liability)

This advertisement will appear in the GENERAL PRESS in INDIA

ADVT. No. P. 3324
Space: 8" x 3 cols.
April 1962

Prepared by :
J. WALTER THOMPSON COMPANY
PRIVATE LIMITED

Figure 6.3. Pond's, "How Lovely You Look Tomorrow Depends on How Well You Clean Your Face Tonight"

often does say that "white is fine" through connotation, the overwhelming presence of whiteness in ads during this period ensures its connection to an ideal beauty. Through an examination of the JWT archives, which include voices from the highest level of the agency (representatives' meeting minutes, market research reports), and the voices of copywriters (creative meeting minutes, personal letters), one can start to understand how systems of meaning are created within a particular context. Through the voices of JWT's male executives, we read about their desire to conquer new territory and come to understand that those desires were put into action through establishing international offices on every continent. And by analyzing the Pond's ads—created by the Women's Editorial Department and used internationally—we understand that the messages in these ads drew from those same myths of ideal beauty, civilization, and modernity that informed the account representatives' thinking and actions.

Ideology is not a magical process—it only appears to be when the processes and people who maintain certain ideologies are not revealed. Even though it can appear mysterious and out of the control of mere mortals, it is, in fact, shaped by humans who are making decisions every day about what they communicate, just as JWT decided what images and text to use in advertising campaigns. In the case of the women who worked at JWT, however, it is a more complicated story. The women in the Women's Editorial Department created images and copy they drew, in part, directly from their experience as privileged Anglo-American women. They also crafted images of beauty derived from an upper-class strata of women whose lives they seemed to deliberately challenge, while, at the same time, they desired the lives of those wealthy women. In an effort to gain some market share of their own in the nascent advertising industry, these ad women tapped into some of the very stereotypes of women that they had worked against in former careers. They did not have the option to directly challenge those stereotypes or those images of ideal beauty in advertising since the appeal to those feminine qualities was a tremendously successful advertising strategy and partially responsible for their success at JWT.

Were the male executives and female copywriters at JWT attempting to alter systems of meaning throughout their new global corporate empire or were they just using advertising campaigns that had worked for a domestic market internationally as good business strategy? And, did using those ad campaigns coincidently result in shifting ideas about ideal beauty and modernity? Rather than exploring how JWT might work within already existing cultural systems of meaning in the countries in which they set up offices, they chose to impose a new way of seeing on new audiences. In fact, JWT male executives were working from an ideology of civilization, which, to them, justified their approach of domination. Ad men and ad women used images and texts based on Western notions of beauty and modernity that were similar to the ads that circulated throughout the United States. Helen Lansdowne and the Women's Editorial Department crafted these images and messages and developed new advertising strategies that made their ads aimed at the female consumer particularly effective. While the Women's Editorial Department staff positions within the agency remained fairly static, their work was used to capture the imaginations and to create new ways of seeing for new consumer markets around the world.

Notes

Introduction

1. I use her maiden name, Lansdowne, throughout.
2. Cynthia Swank, "Not Just Another Pretty Face: Advertising Women in the 1920s," presentation to the Philadelphia Club of Advertising Women, March 9, 1982. JWT Archives, Duke University, Durham, NC.
3. Ibid.
4. Gaye Tuchman, Arlene Kaplan Daniels, and James Benet, eds., *Hearth and Home: Images of Women in the Mass Media* (New York: Oxford University Press, 1978). Roland Marchand, in *Advertising the American Dream*, also made the argument that advertisements themselves do not reflect society at large, but rather the beliefs and values of the creators of the ads.
5. Stuart Hall, "Encoding/Decoding." In *Culture, Media and Language*, ed. Stuart Hall (London: Hutchinson, 1980), 128–38.
6. Roland Marchand, *Advertising the American Dream: Making Way for Modernity, 1920–1940* (Berkeley: University of California Press, 1985); Victoria de Grazia and Ellen Furlough, eds., *The Sex of Things: Gender and Consumption in Historical Perspective* (Berkeley: University of California Press, 1996): Fern Johnson, *Imaging in Advertising: Verbal and Visual Codes of Commerce* (New York: Routledge, 2008).
7. Judith Williamson, *Decoding Advertisements: Ideology and Meaning in Advertising* (London: Marion Boyars, 1978), 99.
8. See Martha Banta, *Imaging American Women: Idea and Ideals in Cultural History* (New York: Columbia University Press, 1987); Lois W. Banner, *American Beauty: A Social History . . . Through Two Centuries of the American Idea, Ideal, and Image of the Beautiful Woman* (Los Angeles: Figueroa Press, 2005).
9. Alys Eve Weinbaum et al., *The Modern Girl Around the World: Consumption, Modernity, and Globalization* (Durham, NC: Duke University Press, 2008).
10. Jennifer Scanlon, *Inarticulate Longings: "The Ladies' Home Journal," Gender and the Promise of Consumer Culture* (New York: Routledge, 1995).
11. William Leach, *Land of Desire: Merchants, Power, and the Rise of a New American Culture* (New York: Vintage Books, 1993), 72–75.
12. Frank Presby, *History and Development of Advertising* (New York: Doubleday, Doran, 1929), 339–41.

13. Jean Kilbourne, "Killing Us Softly 3," DVD (Northampton, MA: Media Education Foundation, 2000).
14. Fern Johnson, *Imaging in Advertising*, 110.
15. Ibid., 110.
16. Donald Pease and Amy Kaplan, *Cultures of United States Imperialism* (Durham, NC: Duke University Press, 1993); Emily Rosenberg, *Spreading the American Dream: American Economic and Cultural Expansion, 1890–1945* (New York: Hill and Wang, 1982); Cynthia Enloe, *Bananas, Beaches and Bases: Making Feminist Sense of International Politics* (Berkeley: University of California Press, 1989); Laura Wexler, *Tender Violence: Domestic Visions in an Age of U.S. Imperialism* (Chapel Hill: University of North Carolina Press, 2000); Kristin Hoganson, *Consumers' Imperium: The Global Production of American Domesticity, 1865–1920* (Chapel Hill: University of North Carolina Press, 2007); Robert Rydell, *All the World's a Fair: Visions of Empire at American International Expositions, 1876–1916* (Chicago: University of Chicago Press, 1984).
17. Mona Domosh, *American Commodities in the Age of Empire* (New York: Routledge, 2006).
18. In *Spreading the American Dream*, Emily Rosenberg says that "products that sold well overseas were also often scientifically advanced . . . American Bell, Edison Electric, Western Electric . . . General Electric (1892), Westinghouse (1886). . . . Other path breaking American exports included National Cash Register, Otis Elevators, Columbia Gramophones, Kodak cameras, Heinz ketchup, Colgate tooth powder, Borden condensed milk, Ford and General Motors cars" (21).
19. Alfred Chandler, *The Visible Hand: The Managerial Revolution in American Business* (Cambridge: Harvard University Press, 1977).
20. Other relevant studies on American imperialism and empire include Walter LeFever, *The New Empire: An Interpretation of American Expansion, 1860–1898* (Ithaca, NY: Cornell University Press, 1998); William Appleman Williams, *The Roots of the Modern American Empire: A Study of the Growth and Shaping of Social Consciousness in a Marketplace Society* (New York: Random House, 1969); Klaus Schwabe, "The Global Role of the United States and Its Imperial Consequences, 1898–1973," in *Imperialism and After: Continuities and Discontinuities*, ed. Wolfgang Mommsen and Jurgen Osterhammel (London: Allen and Unwin, 1986); Gail Bederman, *Manliness and Civilization: A Cultural History of Gender and Race in the United States* (Chicago: University of Chicago Press, 1995).
21. Karen Ordahl Kupperman, "International at the Creation: Early Modern American History," in *Rethinking American History in a Global Age*, ed. Thomas Bender (Berkeley: University of California Press, 2002), and Kristin Hoganson, *Consumers' Imperium: The Global Production of American Domesticity, 1865–1920* (Chapel Hill: University of North Carolina Press, 2007).
22. Alys Eve Weinbaum et al., *The Modern Girl Around the World.*

23. Laurie Mintz, Emily A. Hamilton, and Susan Kashubeck-West, "Predictors of Media Effects on Body Dissatisfaction in European American Women," *Sex Roles: A Journal of Research* 56, nos. 5–6 (March 2007): 397–402. Also see William O'Barr, *Culture and the Ad*; Angela McRobbie, *Feminism and Youth Culture*; Jean Kilbourne, *Killing Us Softly 3, Can't Buy My Love*; Fern Johnson, *Imaging in Advertising*; C. Frisby, "Does Race Matter?: Effects of Idealized Images on African American Women," *Journal of Black Studies* 34 (2004): 324–47.

24. Roland Barthes, *Mythologies* (1964; repr., New York: Noonday Press, 1990).

25. Diana Fuss, *Essentially Speaking: Feminism, Nature and Difference* (New York: Routledge, 1989), xii.

26. Judy Temes, "Advertising's top women are sending a strong message, but making it on the creative side is a hard sell," *Crain's New York Business*, November 3, 2003 (Special Report on Women in Business).

27. Peter Carlson, "The U.S.A. Account: Ad Woman Charlotte Beer's New Campaign: Getting the World to Buy American," *Washington Post*, December 31, 2001.

28. Ibid.

29. Ibid.

Chapter 1

1. Stephen Fox, *Mirror Makers: A History of American Advertising and Its Creators* (Chicago: University of Illinois Press, 1997), 94.

2. Ibid., 81.

3. Jennifer Scanlon, *Inarticulate Longings: "The Ladies' Home Journal," Gender and the Promise of Consumer Culture* (New York: Routledge, 1995), 205.

4. Susan Strasser, *Satisfaction Guaranteed: The Making of the American Mass Market* (New York: Pantheon, 1989), 5.

5. Fox, *Mirror Makers*, 79–81.

6. Kathy Peiss, *Hope in a Jar: The Making of America's Beauty Culture* (New York: Henry Holt, 1998), 119.

7. Gar Schmidt, Helen Lansdowne Resor's obituary, Resor biography file, JWT Archives, Duke University Library, Durham, North Carolina.

8. Peiss, *Hope in a Jar*, 119–20.

9. Sharon Hartman Strom, *Beyond the Typewriter: Gender, Class, and the Origins of Modern American Office Work, 1900–1930* (Urbana: University of Illinois Press, 1992), 327, quoted in Scanlon, *Inarticulate Longings*, 180. Also see Juliann Silvulka, *Ad Women: How They Impact What We Need, Want, and Buy* (New York: Prometheus Books, 2008).

10. Strom, quoted in Scanlon, *Inarticulate Longings*, 173. Also see Angel Kwolek-Folland, *Incorporating Women: A History of Women and Business in the United States* (New York: Palgrave, 2002).

11. Strom, quoted in Scanlon, *Inarticulate Longings*, 173.

12. Rosalind Rosenberg, *Beyond Separate Spheres: The Intellectual Roots of Modern Feminism* (New Haven: Yale University Press, 1982), 213–15.

13. Wallace Boren, Staff Meeting Minutes, January 7, 1936, JWT Archives.

14. Cynthia Swank, "Not Just another Pretty Face: Advertising Women in the 1920s," (presentation to the Philadelphia Club of Advertising Women, March 9, 1982, JWT Archives). For advertising women's salaries, also see Silvulka, *Ad Women*, 47–81.

15. Scanlon, *Inarticulate Longings*, 183.

16. Peiss, *Hope in a Jar*, 97–100.

17. Helen Resor, Stockholder's Affidavit, 69, JWT Archives, Duke University Library, Durham, North Carolina.

18. Howard Henderson Papers, October 17, 1916, JWT Archives, Duke University Library, Durham, North Carolina.

19. Sidney Bernstein Papers, Copy Department, October 27, 1925, JWT Archives, Duke University Library, Durham, North Carolina.

20. Ibid.

21. I write about the most prominent women in JWT's Women's Editorial Department. The JWT archives hold detailed employment applications, and there are other materials that mention the more prominent women by name as well as the accounts on which they worked. I read job applications beyond the ones of the most prominent and found interesting pieces of information that I thought relevant to an understanding of the culture of JWT. Jennifer Scanlon included a chapter about these women in her book, *Inarticulate Longings*. Our findings regarding education, religion, and socioeconomic background are similar. See Scanlon, *Inarticulate Longings*, 169–96.

22. See Pierre Bourdieu and Jean-Claude Passeron, *Reproduction in Education, Society and Culture*, trans. Richard Nice. 2nd ed. (London: Sage, 1977).

23. Scanlon, *Inarticulate Longings*, 204.

24. Ibid.

25. Frances Maule, Personnel File, JWT Archives, Duke University Library, Durham, North Carolina.

26. Ibid.

27. Peiss, *Hope in a Jar*, 119–20.

28. Simone Weil Davis, *Living Up to the Ads: Gender Fictions of the 1920s* (Durham, NC: Duke University Press, 2000), 98–100.

29. Ruth Waldo Personnel File, JWT Archives, Duke University Library, Durham, North Carolina.

30. Ibid.

31. Ibid.

32. Ibid.

33. Russell Pierce, *Gringo-Gaucho: An Advertising Odyssey* (Ashland, OR: Southern Cross, 1991), 58.

34. Ibid., 56–57.

35. Sidney Berstein Papers, Waldo's Business Biography, JWT Archives, Duke University Library, Durham, North Carolina.

36. Ibid.
37. Scanlon, *Inarticulate Longings*, 201.
38. Sidney Berstein Papers, Waldo's Business Biography, JWT Archives, Duke University Library, Durham, North Carolina.
39. Ibid.
40. Ibid.
41. JWT News, Oversized Collection, JWT Archives, Duke University Library, Durham, North Carolina.
42. Ibid.
43. Aminta Casseres, Creative Staff Meeting Minutes, October 21, 1930, JWT Archives, Duke University Library, Durham, North Carolina.
44. "Minutes of a Representatives' Meeting," October 21, 1930, cited in Marchand, *Advertising the American Dream*, 34.
45. Aminta Casseres, Personnel File, JWT Archives, Duke University Library, Durham, North Carolina.
46. Edith Lewis, Personnel File, JWT Archives, Duke University Library, Durham, North Carolina.
47. Ibid.
48. Scanlon, *Inarticulate Longings*, 215.
49. "Early Important Women," Sidney Berstein Client Files: Chesebrough-Pond's, JWT Archives, Duke University Library, Durham, North Carolina.
50. Judith Schwartz, Kathy Peiss, and Christina Simmons, "We Were a Band of Willful Women," in *Passion and Power*, ed. Kathy Peiss and Christina Simmons (Philadelphia: Temple University, 1989), 118.
51. Carolina Ware, *Greenwich Village, 1920–1940, A Comment on American Civilization in the Post-War Years* (Berkeley: University of California Press, 1994).
52. Biographical Information, Thumbnail Sketch, JWT Archives, Duke University Library, Durham, North Carolina.
53. Evelyn Dewey, Personnel File, JWT Archives, Duke University Library, Durham, North Carolina.
54. Esther Eaton, Annette Anderson, Ann Blackshear, Helen Brown, Mary Loomis Cook, Margaret Brown, Helen Buckler, Monica Berry O'Shea, Mary Tucker, Personnel Files, JWT Archives, Duke University Library, Durham, North Carolina.
55. Agnes Foote, Lucille Platt, Therese Olzendam, Helen Thompson, Gertrude Coit, Personnel Files, JWT Archives, Duke University Library, Durham, North Carolina.
56. Margaret Finnegan, *Selling Suffrage: Consumer Culture and Votes for Women* (New York: Columbia University Press, 1999), 1–13. Also see Diane Atkinson, *Suffragettes in the Purple, White, and Green, London, 1906–1914* (London: Museum of London, 1992), for an analysis of how the British suffragists (or suffragettes) turned consumerism into political advantage.
57. Helen Lansdowne Resor, Biographical File, JWT Archives, Duke University Library, Durham, North Carolina.

58. Diane Atkinson notes in *Suffragettes in the Purple, White, and Green, London, 1906–1914* (London: Museum of London, 1992) that the color scheme was devised by Mrs. Pethick-Lawrence, treasurer and co-editor of the weekly newspaper *Votes for Women*.
59. William Leach, "Transformations in a Culture of Consumption: Women and Department Stores, 1890–1925," *Journal of American History* 71 (1984): 336–42.
60. Ibid., 338–39.
61. Ibid., 339.
62. Ibid., 339–40.

Chapter 2

1. Chandler Owen coined the phrase "Good Looks Supremacy," *Messenger* 6 (March 1924): 80, quoted in Kathy Peiss, *Hope in a Jar*, 203.
2. Edward H. Clarke, *Sex in Education; or, A Fair Chance for the Girls* (Boston: J. R. Osgood, 1873), quoted in Margaret A. Lowe, *Looking Good: College Women and Body Image, 1875–1930* (Baltimore: Johns Hopkins University Press, 2003), 1–2, 15–16.
3. Lowe, *Looking Good*, 20–21.
4. Ibid., 164. This term wasn't used until 1934, when psychologist Paul Schilder attempted to define the concept of body image. See Paul Schilder, "Localization of Body Image," *Proceedings of the Association for Research in Nervous and Mental Disease* 13, no. 5 (1934): 466, cited in Lowe.
5. In Foucault's theory of surveillance, the panopticon is a model prison that induces a "state of conscious and permanent visibility that assures the automatic functioning of power . . . the prisoner is constantly observed by an inspector." Michel Foucault, *Discipline and Punish: The Birth of the Prison* (New York: Vintage Books, 1995), 195–228.
6. Ruth Waldo, Personnel File, JWT Archives, Duke University Library, Durham, North Carolina.
7. *JWT News Bulletin*, March 1922, JWT Archives, Duke University Library, Durham, North Carolina.
8. Mary Tucker, Personnel File, JWT Archives, Duke University Library, Durham, North Carolina.
9. Carolyn Kitch, *The Girl on the Magazine Cover: The Origins of Visual Stereotypes in American Mass Media* (Chapel Hill: University of North Carolina, 2001), 3.
10. Ibid., 15.
11. Cynthia Swank (former director of the JWT Archive), presentation to the Philadelphia Club of Advertising Women, March 9, 1982, JWT Archives, Duke University Library, Durham, North Carolina.

12. Lois Banner, *American Beauty: A Social History . . . Through Two Centuries of the American Idea, Ideal, and Image of the Beautiful Woman* (Los Angeles: Figueroa, 2005).

13. Ibid., 69–82.

14. Ibid., 70.

15. Ibid.

16. Martha Banta, *Imaging American Women: Idea and ideals in Cultural History* (New York: Columbia University Press, 1987).

17. Kitch, *The Girl on the Magazine Cover*, 8.

18. See Banta, *Imaging American Women*; Banner, *American Beauty*; and Umberto Eco, ed., *History of Beauty* (New York: Rizzoli, 2004).

19. *JWT Company News* (internal company newsletter), no author, January 10, 1964, JWT Archives, Duke University Library, Durham, North Carolina.

20. Ibid.

21. *JWT News Bulletin*, March 1922, JWT Archives, Duke University Library, Durham, North Carolina.

22. Creative Staff Meeting Minutes, May 25, 1932, JWT Archives, Duke University Library, Durham, North Carolina.

23. Account History Files, Lever Brothers, JWT Archives, Duke University Library, Durham, North Carolina.

24. Ibid.

25. Howard Henderson Papers, "JWT Accounts, 1918," JWT Archives, Duke University Library, Durham, North Carolina.

26. Creative Staff Meeting Minutes, May 25, 1932, JWT Archives, Duke University Library, Durham, North Carolina. Also see Timothy Burke, *Lifebuoy Men, Lux Women: Commodification, Consumption, and Cleanliness in Modern Zimbabwe* (Durham: Duke University Press, 1996).

27. "Sales in the United States," Account History Files, Lever Brothers, JWT Archives, Duke University Library, Durham, North Carolina; Robert Lovett, "Francis A. Countway and 'The Lever Way,'" *Harvard Library Bulletin* 18, no. 1 (1970): 84–93; Ellen Gartrell, "More About the Lever Brothers Lux Collection," JWT Archives Web site: Emergence of Advertising in America, http://library.duke.edu.digitalcollections/eaa/lver.html (accessed April 22, 2009).

28. Creative Staff Meeting Minutes, May 25, 1932, JWT Archives, Duke University Library, Durham, North Carolina.

29. Banta, *Imaging American Women*, 89–91.

30. See Banta, *Imaging American Women*; Banner, *American Beauty*; Kitch, *The Girl on the Magazine Cover*; and Peiss, *Hope in a Jar*, for a discussion on physiognomy, beauty, and consumer culture.

31. Roland Marchand's concept of social tableaux is based on ad images in which "people are depicted in such a way as to suggest their relationship to each other or to a larger social structure." These scenes, however, only reflect "one very narrow stratum of American society." Roland Marchand, *Advertising the American Dream: Making Way for Modernity, 1920–1940* (Berkeley: University of California Press, 1985), 166.

32. Creative Meeting Minutes, May 25, 1932, JWT Archives, Duke University Library, Durham, North Carolina.
33. Ibid.
34. Ibid.
35. *JWT News Bulletin*, April 5, 1963, JWT Archives, Duke University Library, Durham, North Carolina.
36. Ibid.
37. Mireille. *French Women Don't Get Fat: The Secret of Eating for Pleasure*. New York: Alfred A. Knopf, 2004.
38. *JWT News Bulletin*, April 5, 1963, JWT Archives, Duke University Library, Durham, North Carolina.
39. Peiss, *Hope in a Jar*, 40–41.
40. Daphne Brooks, in Noliwe Rooks's *Ladies' Pages: African American Women's Magazines and the Culture that Made Them* (New Brunswick, NJ: Rutgers University Press, 2004), 17.
41. Rooks, *Ladies' Pages*, 22–24.
42. Kitch, *The Girl on the Magazine Cover*, 40.
43. Naomi Wolf, *The Beauty Myth: How Images of Beauty are Used Against Women* (New York: Morrow, 1991), 7.
44. Wolf, *The Beauty Myth*, 13–14.
45. Peiss, *Hope in a Jar*, 135.

Chapter 3

1. *JWT News*, January 10, 1964, JWT Archives, Duke University Library, Durham, North Carolina.
2. Juliann Sivulka, *Stronger Than Dirt: A Cultural History of Advertising Personal Hygiene in America, 1875–1940* (New York: Humanity Books, 2001), 137. As early as 1904, Walter D. Scott's article "The Psychology of Advertising," which appeared in the *Atlantic*, called attention to the method of using this softer selling style—a style that used suggestion or association to convey the impression of integrity, quality, and prestige. Scott's writings on this topic were compiled in *The Theory and Practice of Advertising* and *The Psychology of Advertising*.
3. Judith Williamson, *Decoding Advertisements: Ideology and Meaning in Advertising* (London: Marian Boyers, 1979).
4. Historian Grace Elizabeth Hale explores the making of whiteness in the South and shows how the creation of modern whiteness was taken up by the rest of the country (beginning in the 1920s) as a way of enforcing a new social hierarchy while, at the same time, creating the illusion of a national, egalitarian, consumerist democracy. Grace Elizabeth Hale, *Making Whiteness: The Culture of Segregation in the South, 1890–1940* (New York: Pantheon, 1998). The ad men and ad women at JWT, however, were contributing to this social hierarchy prior to the 1920s.
5. *JWT News Bulletin*, April 1923, JWT Archives, Duke University Library, Durham, North Carolina.

6. William O'Barr, *Culture and the Ad: Exploring Otherness in the World of Advertising* (Boulder, CO: Westview, 1994), ix.

7. John Uri Lloyd and John Thomas Lloyd, "History of Hamamelis (Witch Hazel), Extract and Distillate," *Journal of the American Pharmaceutical Association* 14, no. 3 (March 1935): 220–24.

8. "History: Pond's Extract Company," JWT Public Relations, March 1960, JWT Archives, Duke University Library, Durham, North Carolina.

9. "The Pond's Extract Company," September, 27, 1923, Information Center, JWT Archives, Duke University Library, Durham, North Carolina.

10. Thomas Lamont, of the Lamont Corliss Company, was a famous financier in railroads and banking, and his family had made a reputation as philanthropists as well. His brother-in-law, W. Corliss, served as the president of the company. In addition to Pond's Extract Company, the Lamont Corliss Company owned O'Sullivan Rubber Heels, Peter's Chocolate, Cailler's Chocolate, Nestlé Chocolate, Libby's Extract of Beef, and Cream of Wheat. "Account Histories: Pond's Extract Company," January 16, 1926, Inactive Account File, Chesebrough-Pond's, and "Pond's Case History," May 5, 1959, Howard Henderson Papers, JWT Archives, Duke University Library, Durham, North Carolina.

11. "Pond's Case History," Account Files, May 5, 1959, JWT Archives, Duke University Library, Durham, North Carolina.

12. Ibid.

13. "History: Pond's Extract Company," Regina Rohrman, JWT Public Relations Department, March 1960, JWT Archives, Duke University Library, Durham, North Carolina.

14. Ibid.

15. "Pond's Case History," May 5, 1959, Howard Henderson Papers, JWT Archives Duke University Library, Durham, North Carolina.

16. Ibid.

17. Geoffrey Jones, *Renewing Unilever: Transformation and Tradition* (New York: Oxford University Press, 2005).

18. "Pond's Case History," Account Files, May 5, 1959, JWT Archives. Duke University Library, Durham, North Carolina.

19. The emphasis on "normal" skin is an important element in creating the product meaning. This psychological appeal implied that Pond's was associated with "normal" women. In this case, normal skin can be read as "acceptable," white skin, the only type of skin shown in Pond's ads.

20. "Pond's Case History," Account Files, May 5, 1959, JWT Archives, Duke University Library, Durham, North Carolina.

21. Ibid.

22. This strategy is reminiscent of a relatively recent change in directions on the back of shampoo bottles—by adding the directive "repeat," sales of shampoo dramatically increased as consumers used double the amount.

23. Ibid.

24. Pond's Extract Company Account History, January 18, 1926, JWT Archives, Duke University Library, Durham, North Carolina.

25. Ibid.

26. It was not long before the Federal Trade Commission (FTC) took an interest in testimonial advertising (also called "personality" advertising). In a staff meeting at JWT (with [Ruth] Waldo, [Aminta] Casseres, [Augusta] Nicoll, —— Bell, —— King in attendance) in 1931, company executives discussed the implications of the investigation by the FTC into testimonial advertising. The FTC claimed that any endorser who had received payment had made a false and fraudulent statement. At the time of the meeting, and pending a court decision, the people working on testimonial ad campaigns were cautioned: "If Mrs. Vanderbilt says, in an endorsement, that Ponds Creams have made her beautiful, we do not have to prove either that she is beautiful or that the products are the cause of her beauty; but we must be prepared to show that she has used the creams for an appreciable period of time." "Staff Meeting Minutes," August 4, 1931, JWT Archives, Duke University Library, Durham, North Carolina.

27. Alva Johnston, *Outlook and Independent*, Consumers' Research, 340 West 23rd Street, New York City, no date (but probably six years after Pond's began testimonial ads), Pond's Extract Company Account History, January 18, 1926, JWT Archives, Duke University Library, Durham, North Carolina.

28. In Frank Comrie's lecture at Northwestern University, December 18, 1930, "Fundamental Appeals in Advertising," he says that Lansdowne was responsible for the testimonial type of ad in its modern form. JWT Archives, Duke University Library, Durham, North Carolina.

29. Cynthia Swank, "Not Just Another Pretty Face: Advertising to Women in the 1920s," presentation to the Philadelphia Club of Advertising Women, March 9, 1982.

30. "How Well Do You Know Your JWT'ers?" Thumbnail Sketch, January 3, 1947, JWT Archives, Duke University Library, Durham, North Carolina.

31. Ibid.

32. "Pond's Case History," Account Files, May 5, 1959, JWT Archives, Duke University Library, Durham, North Carolina.

33. "Pond's Extract Company Account History," September 18, 1926, JWT Archives, Duke University Library, Durham, North Carolina.

34. Ibid.

35. It is not clear from archival material how much of this decision was based on Lansdowne and the Women's Editorial Department staff's input. They had some experience, however, in securing endorsements for clients' products and may have even been responsible for suggesting that Pond's take this appeal further.

36. Pond's Extract Company Account History, January 18, 1926, JWT Archives, Duke University Library, Durham, North Carolina.

37. Christine Lunardini, *From Equal Suffrage to Equal Rights: Alice Paul and the National Women's Party, 1910–1928* (New York: New York University Press, 1986), 7–8.

38. "Pond's Case History," Account Files, May 5, 1959, JWT Archives, Duke University Library, Durham, North Carolina.

39. Special Production and Representatives' Meeting, April 9, 1928. Representatives' Meeting Minutes, JWT Archives, Duke University Library, Durham, North Carolina.

40. Information Center Records, Box 4, February, 26, 1930, JWT Archives, Duke University Library, Durham, North Carolina.

41. Ibid.

42. "Pond's Extract Company Account History," January 18, 1926, JWT Archives, Duke University Library, Durham, North Carolina.

43. Ibid.

44. Ibid.

45. Ibid.

46. Dorothy Dwight Townsend, "Mrs. Wilkins reads the *Ladies' Home Journal*," *JWT News Bulletin*, June 1923, JWT Archives, Duke University Library, Durham, North Carolina.

47. Ibid.

48. "Creative Staff Meeting Minutes," June 8 (no year), JWT Archives, Duke University Library, Durham, North Carolina.

49. Ibid.

50. Kathy Peiss, *Hope in a Jar* (New York: Henry Holt, 1998).

51. Ibid., 175.

52. Ibid.

53. Ibid., 174.

54. Simone Weil Davis, *Living Up to the Ads: Gender Fictions of the 1920s* (Durham, NC: Duke University Press, 2000), 81.

55. *Vogue*, January 15, 1916, JWT Archives, Duke University Library, Durham, North Carolina.

56. Roland Barthes, *Mythologies* (1964; reprint, New York: Noonday Press, 1990), 100. Similarly, JWT management claims a consumer universality in justifying its international expansion, which has a certain resonance with Marx's claim that the capitalist class represents its interests as universal. See Karl Marx and Frederick Engels, *The German Ideology* (London: Lawrence & Wishart, 1970), 64.

57. *Cosmopolitan*, 1943, JWT Archives, Duke University Library, Durham, North Carolina.

58. Ibid.

59. This message that promises self-confidence and inner glow is what cultural anthropologist William O'Barr refers to as "secondary discourse"—ideas about society and culture contained in the ad. This is different from "primary discourse," which refers solely to the product and its uses.

60. Antonio Gramsci, *Selections From the Prisons Notebooks*, ed. Quintin Hoare and Geoffrey Nowell Smith (New York: International, 1971).

Chapter 4

1. According to archival records, it appears as though Lansdowne coordinated a group of women who helped her with marketing research for Woodbury's Soap in 1914, around the same time she coined the slogan "The Skin You Love To Touch." Most of the more prominent women who worked for Lansdowne, and for whom significant archival materials exists, started in the late 1910s. (Ruth Waldo was the exception, she started in 1915.) In the Woodbury's account files, however, the group of earlier women (1910–15) were referred to as the Women's Editorial Department.

2. This slogan was copyrighted in 1914, three years after Lansdowne was promoted to the JWT New York City (JWT/NYC) office. Lansdowne also worked on the Crisco shortening account starting in 1909 or 1910; Crisco was introduced to the public in 1911. Stanley Resor started to spend more time at the JWT/NYC office, and, in 1912, Resor moved permanently to the NYC office. In 1916, a group headed by Resor bought JWT for $500,000. Resor became president of JWT, and the following year (1917), he and Lansdowne married. Stephen Fox, *Mirror Makers: A History of American Advertising and Its Creators* (Chicago: University of Illinois Press, 1997), 82.

    At JWT/NYC, Resor and Lansdowne continued to divide tasks as before. In general, Resor tended to administration and client services while Lansdowne concentrated on the creative work of ads. But informally, they discussed all aspects of the business, over the dinner table or on the commuter train to Greenwich, so decisions typically emerged with no clear line of accountability to either one (ibid.).

3. Woodbury Facial Soap Account History, Account Files, April 12, 1926, JWT Archives, Duke University Library, Durham, North Carolina.

4. Anne McClintock, "Soft-Soaping Empire: Commodity Racism and Imperial Advertising," in *The Gender and Consumer Culture Reader*, ed. Jennifer Scanlon (New York: New York University Press, 2000), 129.

5. Ibid., 130.

6. Juliann Sivulka, *Stronger Than Dirt: A Cultural History of Advertising Personal Hygiene in America, 1875–1940* (New York: Humanity Books, 2001), 18–19.

7. Ibid., 19.

8. It is difficult to tell how much input Lansdowne had on the institutionalization of science at JWT. She did, however, appropriate and incorporate "science" into her ad campaigns such as Crisco and Woodbury's, among others.

9. Peggy J. Kreshel, "The 'Culture' of J. Walter Thompson, 1915–1925." *Public Relations Review* 16, no. 8 (Fall 1990): 81.

10. Juliann Sivulka, *Stronger Than Dirt*, 72.

11. Ibid., 73.

12. Ibid., 74.

13. Woodbury's Account Files, JWT Archives, Duke University Library, Durham, North Carolina.

14. With the success of the U.S. Sanitary Commission, formed during the Civil War, as a model, thousands of women organized to deal locally with social problems though women's clubs, settlement houses, and public institutions. Juliann Sivulka, *Stronger Than Dirt*, 64–65.
15. Woodbury's Account Files, JWT Archives, Duke University Library, Durham, North Carolina.
16. Ibid.
17. Woodbury Account History, April 12, 1926, JWT Archives, Duke University Library, Durham, North Carolina.
18. Ibid.
19. Woodbury's Account History, Account Files, April 12, 1926, JWT Archives, Duke University Library, Durham, North Carolina.
20. Woodbury's Account File, Stanley Resor's speech to a JWT class, April 12, 1920. JWT Archives, Duke University Library, Durham, North Carolina.
21. Ibid.
22. Woodbury's Account Files, JWT Archives, Duke University Library, Durham, North Carolina.
23. Information Center Records, JWT Archives, Duke University Library, Durham, North Carolina.
24. Woodbury's Account Files, JWT Archives, Duke University Library, Durham, North Carolina.
25. Woodbury's Account Files, Stanley Resor's speech to JWT class (part of the JWT "University" training program he instituted), April 12, 1920, JWT Archives, Duke University Library, Durham, North Carolina.
26. Woodbury's Account Files, JWT Archives, Duke University Library, Durham, North Carolina.
27. Ibid.
28. Ibid.
29. Ibid.
30. Woodbury's Account File, Stanley Resor's speech to a JWT class, JWT Archives, Duke University Library, Durham, North Carolina. The classes, to which Stanley Resor was speaking, were part of the training program Resor instituted at JWT. In his talks, he does not credit Lansdowne or the Women's Editorial Department with the success of Woodbury's Soap. In fact, he never mentions either.
31. Woodbury's Account File, Stanley Resor's speech to a JWT class, JWT Archives, Duke University Library, Durham, North Carolina.
32. Laura Mulvey, "Visual Pleasure and Narrative Cinema." *Screen* 16, no. 3 (Autumn 1975): 27.
33. Ibid.
34. Dawkins Papers, 1937, "JWT: International Advertising Agency," JWT Archives, Duke University Library, Durham, North Carolina.
35. Woodbury's Account File, 1901–29, JWT Archives, Duke University, Durham, North Carolina.

36. Woodbury's Account Files, *Woman's Home Companion*, February 1929, JWT Archives, Duke University, Durham, North Carolina.
37. Ibid.
38. Ibid.
39. Ibid.
40. Ibid.
41. Fern Johnson, *Imaging in Advertising: Verbal and Visual Codes of Commerce* (New York: Routledge, 2008), 4.
42. Creative Staff Meeting Minutes, October 26, 1932, JWT Archives, Duke University Library, Durham, North Carolina.
43. Creative Staff Meeting Minutes, October 6, 1931, JWT Archives, Duke University Library, Durham, North Carolina.

Chapter 5

1. Kathy Peiss, *Hope in a Jar: The Making of America's Beauty Culture* (New York: Henry Holt and Company, 1998), 97–100.
2. Jennifer Scanlon, *Inarticulate Longings: The Ladies Home Journal, Gender and the Promise of Consumer Culture* (New York: Routledge, 1995), 174.
3. Information Center Records, JWT Archives, Duke University Library, Durham, North Carolina.
4. Sam Meek Papers, n.d., JWT Archives, Duke University Library, Durham, North Carolina.
5. During the depression years, however, JWT would find that other accounts such as Pond's and Lever Brothers (Unilever) would consistently provide revenue while other large accounts cut back international operations.
6. For a classic example of the masculine "modern business enterprise," defined by Alfred Chandler, Jr., see *The Visible Hand: The Managerial Revolution in American Business* (Cambridge: Harvard University Press, 1977). See also Mira Wilkins's *The Emergence of Multinational Enterprise: American Business Abroad from the Colonial Era to 1914* (Cambridge: Harvard University Press, 1970).
7. JWT International, January 8, 1957, no author, James Webb Young Papers, JWT Archives, Duke University Library, Durham, North Carolina.
8. Jeffrey Merron, "Putting Foreign Consumers on the Map: JWT's Struggle with General Motors International Advertising Account in the 1920s," *Business History Review* 73, no. 3 (Autumn 1999): 465–503.
9. See the Catalyst research report titled "2008 Catalyst Census of Women Board Directors of the Fortune 500," updated January 12, 2009, http://www.catalyst.org/publication/282/2008 (accessed March 10, 2009).
10. Pond's did not become part of Chesebrough until 1955.
11. From "The J. Walter Thompson Company: An Advertising History, authored by members of the Company," n.d., quoted in Merron, "Putting Foreign Consumers on the Map."

12. London Office, Sidney Ralph Berstein Company History Files, n.d., JWT Archives, Duke University Library, Durham, North Carolina.

13. Ibid.

14. Therese Olzendam's Personnel File, and "How Well Do You Know Your JWT'ers?" Thumbnail Sketch, September 20, 1948, JWT Archives, Duke University Library, Durham, North Carolina.

15. London Office, Sidney Ralph Berstein Company History Files, n.d., JWT Archives, Duke University Library, Durham, North Carolina.

16. Ibid.

17. JWT Newsletter Collection, Main Series, February 7, 1926, JWT Archives, Duke University Library, Durham, North Carolina.

18. Creative Staff Meeting Minutes, May 18, 1932, JWT Archives, Duke University Library, Durham, North Carolina.

19. Ibid.

20. Stockholder's Affidavit, Helen Resor, March 20, 1924, JWT Archives, Duke University Library, Durham, North Carolina.

21. Sidney Ralph Berstein Company History Files, as told by Howard Kohl, n.d., JWT Archives, Duke University Library, Durham, North Carolina.

22. Ibid.

23. Aminta Casseres's Personnel File, JWT Archives, Duke University Library, Durham, North Carolina.

24. Gladys Phelan's Personnel File, JWT Archives, Duke University Library, Durham, North Carolina.

25. Russell Pierce, *Gringo-Gaucho: An Advertising Odyssey* (Ashland, OR: Southern Cross, 1991).

26. Ibid., 91–100.

27. Ibid., 92.

28. James Woodard uses the term "managerial elite" to describe a new group in Brazilian society and the modernization of Brazilian advertising by JWT in his article "Marketing Modernity: The J. Walter Thompson Company and North American Advertising in Brazil, 1929–1939." *Hispanic American Historical Review* 82, no. 2 (May 2002): 215–56.

29. JWT News, no author, June 24, 1946, Sam Meek Papers, JWT Archives, Duke University Library, Durham, North Carolina.

30. Stanley Resor's introduction in the *J. Walter Thompson News Bulletin*, July 1928, Foreign Issue, JWT Archives, Duke University Library, Durham, North Carolina.

31. Julio Moreno, *Yankee Don't Go Home: Mexican Nationalism, American Business Culture, and the Shaping of Modern Mexico, 1920–1950* (Chapel Hill: University of North Carolina Press, 2003).

32. JWT Company History, n.d., Metters Papers, JWT Archives, Duke University Library, Durham, North Carolina.

33. "Join Thompson, See the World? Well, Almost," *Advertising Age*, March 16, 1959.

34. Alfred Chandler, Jr., *The Visible Hand*, 368.

35. Representatives' Meeting Minutes, August 6, 1929, JWT Archives, Duke University Library, Durham, North Carolina.
36. Russell Pierce refers to Ricketts in his memoir *Gringo-Gaucho*, as a research consultant who worked for JWT in Argentina, Uruguay, and Brazil. Pierce does not mention Ferguson in his memoir.
37. "What Does South America Offer the American Advertiser," *J. Walter Thompson News Bulletin*, Foreign Issue, July 1928, JWT Archives, Duke University Library, Durham, North Carolina.
38. Ibid.
39. Representatives' Staff Meeting Minutes, August 6, 1929, JWT Archives, Duke University Library, Durham, North Carolina.
40. Representatives' Staff Meeting Minutes, 1927–1929, letter dated May 11, 1927 (letters from international offices were often shared during the Representative Staff Meetings), JWT Archives, Duke University Library, Durham, North Carolina.
41. Mr. Baille, Representatives' Meeting Minutes, May 7, 1929, JWT Archives, Duke University Library, Durham, North Carolina.
42. Ibid.
43. Sam Meek Papers, JWT Archives, Duke University Library, Durham, North Carolina.
44. "Join Thompson, See World? Well, Almost," *Advertising Age*, March 16, 1959.
45. Pierce, *Gringo-Gaucho*.
46. Ibid., 233.
47. George Butler, "Bush House, Berlin and Berkeley Square: George Butler Remembers JWT 1925–1962," unpublished manuscript, JWT Archives, quoted in Merron, "Putting Foreign Consumers on the Map."
48. Representatives' Meeting Minutes, n.d., JWT Archives, Duke University Library, Durham, North Carolina.
49. Annette Kolodny analyzes "virgin land" as metanarrative, in both its conception and deployment, an ideological cover-up for Indian removal, frontier violence, government theft, land devastation, class cruelty, racial brutality, and misogyny. Annette Kolodny, *The Lay of the Land: Metaphor as Experience and History in American Life and Letters* (Chapel Hill: University of North Carolina Press, 1975).

Chapter 6

1. Woodbury's British Market Study, July 7, 1922, Reel 225 (16mm), JWT Archives, Duke University Library, Durham, North Carolina; William M. Peniche, "Beauty From Bangor to Bangkok: A Brief Review of Chesebrough-Pond's World-Wide Advertising," a presentation before an International Seminar, April 18, 1961, Sam Meek Papers, JWT Archives, Duke University Library, Durham, North Carolina.
2. JWT served General Motors in its international offices (only) for approximately five years. Pond's, on the other hand, was an important client for

decades both in the United States and internationally with steady and consistent sales.

3. William M. Peniche, "Beauty From Bangor to Bangkok: A Brief Review of Chesebrough-Pond's World-Wide Advertising," April 18, 1961, Sam Meek Papers, JWT Archives, Duke University Library, Durham, North Carolina.
4. Ibid.
5. "Pond's Case History," May 5, 1959, JWT Archives, Duke University Library, Durham, North Carolina.
6. Ibid.
7. "Beauty From Bangor to Bangkok."
8. JWT Company History, n.d., Metters Papers, JWT Archives, Duke University Library, Durham, North Carolina.
9. "JWT Breaks World's Record for Third Time," *JWT News Bulletin,* June 4, 1925. JWT Archives, Duke University Library, Durham, North Carolina.
10. "Saturday Evening Post, International Circulation," Curtis Publishing Company Records, Rare Book and Manuscript Library, University of Pennsylvania.
11. Dawkins Papers, Group Meeting Minutes, New York City, July 29, 1930, JWT Archives, Duke University Library, Durham, North Carolina.
12. "Foreign Circulation Figures, October 1913," Curtis Publishing Company Records, Rare Book and Manuscript Library, University of Pennsylvania.
13. In 1915, *Ladies' Home Journal* circulation numbers for Alaska, Cuba, the Canal Zone, Hawaii, the Philippines, and Puerto Rico totaled 3,032. "Distribution, March, 1915," Curtis Publishing Company Records, Rare Book and Manuscript Library, University of Pennsylvania.
14. Oceania is a region that includes Melanesia, Micronesia, Polynesia, Australia, and New Zealand. United Nations Statistics Division, http://milleniumindicators .un.org (accessed April 20, 2009).
15. "Looking Ahead, 1930 (Survey B)," Curtis Publishing Company Records, Rare Book and Manuscript Library, University of Pennsylvania.
16. "Beauty From Bangor to Bangkok."
17. Microfilm Collection, 35mm, foreign proofs previous to 1934, JWT Archives, Duke University Library, Durham, North Carolina.
18. The microfilm reel with JWT's international ads are all prior to 1934; many are not dated.
19. Microfilm Collection, 35 mm, foreign proofs previous to 1934, JWT Archives, Duke University Library, Durham, North Carolina.
20. Ibid.
21. Ibid.
22. Stanley Resor, Representatives' Meeting Minutes, December 13, 1928, JWT Archives, Duke University Library, Durham, North Carolina.
23. Creative Staff Meeting Minutes, May 25, 1932, JWT Archives, Duke University Library, Durham, North Carolina.
24. See Figure 6.1. Treasurer's Office Records, JWT Archives, Duke University Library, Durham, North Carolina.
25. Ibid.

Bibliography

Abelson, Elaine. *When Ladies Go A-Thieving*. New York: Oxford University Press, 1989.

Adams, James Truslow. *The Tempo of Modern Life*. Freeport, NY: Books for Library Press, 1970.

Althusser, Louis. "Ideology and Ideological State Apparatus." In *Lenin and Philosophy and Other Essays*, 85–126. New York: Monthly Review Press, 2001.

Anderson, Benedict. *Imagined Communities: Reflections on the Origin and Spread of Nationalism*. London: Verso, 1995.

Banner, Lois. *American Beauty: A Social History . . . Through Two Centuries of the American Idea, Ideal, and Image of the Beautiful Woman*. Los Angeles: Figueroa, 2005.

Banta, Martha. *Imaging American Women: Idea and Ideals in Cultural History*. New York: Columbia University Press, 1987.

Bartel, Diane. *Putting on Appearances: Gender and Advertising*. Philadelphia: Temple University Press, 1998.

Barthes, Roland. *Mythologies*. 1964. Reprint, New York: Noonday, 1990.

———. *The Pleasure of the Text*. Translated by Richard Miller. London: Jonathan Cape, 1976.

———. "The Rhetoric of the Image." In *Image, Music, Text*, 32–51. New York: Hill & Wang, 1964.

Baudrillard, Jean. *Towards a Critique of the Political Economy of the Sign*. St. Louis, MO: Telos, 1981.

Bell, Daniel. *The Cultural Contradictions of Capitalism*. New York: Basic Books, 1976.

Benjamin, Walter. "The Work of Art in the Age of Mechanical Reproduction." In *Illuminations*, edited by Hannah Arendt, 217–52. New York: Schocken, 1969.

Benson, Susan Porter. *Counter Cultures: Saleswomen, Managers and Customers in American Department Stores, 1890–1940*. Urbana: University of Illinois Press, 1986.

Berger, John. *Ways of Seeing*. New York: Penguin, 1972.

Berry, Sarah. *Screen Style: Fashion and Femininity in 1930s Hollywood*. Minneapolis: University of Minnesota Press, 2000.

Boorstin, Daniel. *Americans: The Democratic Experience*. New York: Random House, 1973.

Bourdieu, Pierre. "The Aesthetic Sense as the Sense of Distinction." In *The Consumer Society Reader*, edited by Juliet Schor and Douglas Holt, 205–11. New York: The New York Press, 2000.

———. *Distinction: A Social Critique of the Judgement of Taste*. Translated by Richard Nice. Cambridge: Harvard University Press, 1987.

Bourdieu, Pierre, and Jean-Claude Passeron. *Reproduction in Education, Society and Culture*. 2nd ed. Translated by Richard Nice. London, 1997.

Bowby, Rachel. *Shopping With Freud*. London: Routledge, 1993.

Brewer, John, and Roy Porter, eds. *Consumption and the World of Goods*. New York: Routledge, 1993.

Bronner, Simon J. "Reading Consumer Culture." In *Consuming Visions: Accumulation and Display of Goods in America, 1880–1920*, edited by Simon J. Bronner, 13–53. New York: Norton, 1989.

Brown, Kathleen. *Good Wives, Nasty Wenches, and Anxious Patriarchs: Gender, Race, and Power in Colonial Virginia*. Chapel Hill: University of North Carolina Press, 1996.

Burke, Timothy. *Lifebuoy Men, Lux Women: Commodification, Consumption, and Cleanliness in Modern Zimbabwe*. Durham, NC: Duke University Press, 1996.

Chandler, Alfred, Jr. *The Visible Hand: The Managerial Revolution in American Business*. Cambridge: Harvard University Press, 1977.

Clark, Christopher. *The Roots of Rural Capitalism*. Ithaca, NY: Cornell University Press, 1990.

Clarke, Edward Hammond. *Sex in Education; or, a Fair Chance for the Girls*. New York: Ayer, 1972.

Con Davis, Robert, and Ronald Schleifer. *Contemporary Literary Criticism: Literary and Cultural Studies*. 2nd ed. New York: Longman, 1989.

Cook, Blance Wiesen. "Female Support Networks and Political Activism: Lillian Wald, Crystal Eastman, Emma Goldman." *Chrysalis* 3 (1977): 43–61.

Cott, Nancy. *The Grounding of Modern Feminism*. New Haven: Yale University Press, 1987.

Cronin, Anne. *Advertising and Consumer Citizenship: Gender, Images and Rights*. London: Routledge, 2000.

Damon-Moore, Helen. *Magazines for the Millions: Gender and Commerce in the "Ladies' Home Journal" and the "Saturday Evening Post," 1880–1910*. Albany: State University of New York Press, 1994.

Daunton, M. J. *House and Home in the Victorian City*. London: E. Arnold, 1983.

Davis, Simone Weil. *Living Up to the Ads: Gender Fictions of the 1920s*. Durham, NC: Duke University Press, 2000.

De Grazia, Victoria, and Ellen Furlough, eds. *The Sex of Things: Gender and Consumption in Historical Perspective*. Berkeley: University of California Press, 1996.

De Lauretis, Teresa. *Alice Doesn't: Feminism, Semiotics, and Cinema*. Bloomington: Indiana University Press, 1984.

———. *Technologies of Gender: Essays on Theory, Film, and Fiction*. Bloomington: Indiana University Press, 1987.

Derrida, Jacques. *Writing and Difference*. Chicago: University of Chicago Press, 1978.

Deutsch, Sarah. "Reconceiving the City: Women, Space and Power in Boston, 1870–1910." *Gender & History* 6, no. 2 (1998): 202–23.

Dill, Bonnie Thorton. "The Dialectics of Black Womanhood." In *Feminism & History*, edited by Joan Scott, 34–47. New York: Oxford University Press, 1996.

Domosh, Mona. *American Commodities in an Age of Empire*. New York: Routledge, 2006.

———."Pickles and Purity: Discourses of Food, Empire, and Work in Turn-of-the-Century United States." *Social and Cultural Geography* 4, no. 1 (2002): 7–26.

Douglas, Ann. *The Feminization of American Culture*. New York: Knopf, 1977.

———. *Terrible Honesty: Mongrel Manhattan in the 1920s*. New York: Pan Macmillan, 1996.

Douglas, Susan. *Where the Girls Are: Growing Up Female with the Mass Media*. New York: Times Books, 1994.

Eckert, Charles. "The Carole Lombard in Macy's Window." *Quarterly Review of Film Studies* 3, no. 1 (1978): 1–21.

Eco, Umberto, ed. *History of Beauty*. New York: Rizzoli, 2004.

Englis, Basil, ed. *Global and Multinational Advertising*. Hove, UK: Lawrence Erlbaum, 1994.

Enloe, Cynthia. *Bananas, Beaches, and Bases: Making Feminist Sense of International Politics*. Berkeley: University of California Press, 1989.

Ewen, Stuart. *All Consuming Images: The Politics of Style in Contemporary Culture*. New York: Basic Books, 1988.

———. *Captains of Consciousness: Advertising and the Social Roots of the Consumer Culture*. New York: McGraw-Hill, 1976.

Ewen, Stuart, and Elizabeth Ewen. *Channels of Desire: Mass Images and the Shaping of American Consciousness*. Minneapolis: University of Minnesota Press, 1982.

Faderman, Lillian. *Odd Girls and Twilight Lovers: A History of Lesbian Life in Twentieth Century America*. New York: Penguin, 1991.

Finnegan, Margaret. *Selling Suffrage: Consumer Culture and Votes for Women*. New York: Columbia University Press, 1999.

Fiske, John. *Introduction to Communication Studies*. New York: Routledge, 1990.

Forgacs, David. *The Antonio Gramsci Reader: Selected Writings, 1916–1935*. New York: New York University Press, 2000.

Fox, Richard Wrightman, and T. J. Jackson Lears, eds. *The Culture of Consumption*. New York: Pantheon, 1983.

Fox, Stephen. *Mirror Makers: A History of American Advertising and Its Creators*. Chicago: University of Illinois Press, 1997.

Frisby, C. "Does Race Matter?: Effects of Idealized Images on African American Women." *Journal of Black Studies* 34 (2004): 324–47.

Fuss, Diana. *Essentially Speaking: Feminism, Nature and Difference*. New York: Routledge, 1989.

Gamman, Lorraine, and Margaret Marshment, eds. *The Female Gaze: Women as Viewers of Popular Culture*. Seattle: Real Comet Press, 1989.

Garvey, Ellen Gruber. *The Adman in the Parlor: Magazines and the Gendering of Consumer Culture, 1880s–1910s*. New York: Oxford University Press, 1996.

Geraghty, Christine. "Feminism and Media Consumption." In *Cultural Studies and Communications*, edited by James Curran, David Morley, and Valerie Walkerdine, 306–22. London: Arnold, 1996.

Goffman, Erving. *Gender Advertisements*. Cambridge: Harvard University Press, 1976.

Goldman, Robert. *Reading Ads Socially*. New York: Routledge, 1992.

Goldstein, Judith. "The Female Aesthetic Community." In *The Traffic in Culture: Refiguring Art and Anthropology*, edited by George Marcus and Fred Myers, 310–29. Berkeley: University of California Press, 1995.

Goodrum, Charles, and Helen Dalrymple. *Advertising in America: The First 200 Years*. New York: Harry N. Abrams, 1990.

Gordon, Lynn D. "The Gibson Girl Goes to College: Popular Culture and Women's Higher Education in the Progressive Era, 1890–1920." *American Quarterly* 39, no. 2 (Summer 1987): 211–30.

Hahn, Steve, and Jonathan Prude, eds. *The Countryside in the Age of Capitalist Transformation*. Chapel Hill, NC: University of North Carolina Press, 1985.

Hale, Grace Elizabeth. *Making Whiteness: The Culture of Segregation in the South, 1890–1940*. New York: Pantheon, 1998.

Hall, Stuart. "Encoding/Decoding." In *Culture, Media, and Language*, edited by Stuart Hall, 128–38. London: Hutchinson, 1980.

Haltunnen, Karen. *Confidence Men and Painted Women: A Study of Middle-class Culture in America, 1830–1870*. New Haven: Yale University Press, 1982.

Hamburger, Estelle. *It's a Woman's Business*. New York: Vanguard, 1939.

Haskill, Thomas, and Richard Teichgraeber. *The Culture of the Market*. New York: Cambridge University Press, 1993.

Hawkins, Margaret A., and Thomas K. Nakayama. "Discourse on Women's Bodies: Advertising in the 1920s." In *Constructing and Reconstructing Gender: The Links among Communication, Language, and Gender*, edited by Linda A. M. Perry, Lynn H. Turner, and Helen M. Sterk, 61–71. Albany: State University of New York Press, 1992.

Hoganson, Kristin. *Consumers' Imperium: The Global Production of American Domesticity, 1865–1920*. Chapel Hill: University of North Carolina Press, 2007.

Ikuta, Yasutoshi. *American Romance: The World of Advertising Art*. Tokyo: Heibonsha, 1988.

"The Inside of the Testimonial Racket." *Advertising & Selling*, January 7, 1931.

Isherwood, Baron, and Mary Douglas. *The World of Goods: Towards an Anthropology of Consumption*. New York: W. W. Norton, 1978.

"J. Walter Thompson Company." *Fortune*, November 1947, 94–202, 205–6, 210, 212, 214, 218, 220, 226, 228, 230, 233.

Jewell, Karen Sue. *From Mammy to Miss America and Beyond: Cultural Images and the Shaping of U.S. Social Policy*. New York: Routledge, 1993.

Johnson, Fern L. *Imaging in Advertising: Verbal and Visual Codes of Commerce*. New York: Routledge, 2008.

Jones, Geoffrey. *Renewing Unilever: Transformation and Tradition*. New York: Oxford University Press, 2005.

Kang, Myung Koo. "Postmodern Consumer Culture Without Postmodernity: Copying the Crisis of Signification." *Cultural Studies* 13, no. 1 (1999): 18–33.

Keding, Ann Maxwell. "Helen Lansdowne Resor." In *The Ad Men and Women—A Biographical Dictionary of Advertising*, edited by John Applegate et al., 268–70. Westport, CT: Greenwood Press, 1994.

Kerber, Linda. "Separate Spheres: Female Worlds, Woman's Place: The Rhetoric of Women's History." *Journal of American History* 75, no.1 (June 1988): 9–39.

Kessler-Harris, Alice. *Out to Work: A History of Wage-Earning Women in the United States.* New York: Oxford University Press, 1982.

Kilbourne, Jean. *Can't Buy My Love: How Advertising Changes the Way We Think and Feel.* New York: Simon & Schuster, 1999.

———. *Killing Us Softly 3*, DVD. Northampton, MA: Media Education Foundation, 2000.

Kimmel, Michael. *Manhood in America: A Cultural History.* New York: Free Press, 1996.

Kitch, Carolyn. *The Girl on the Magazine Cover: The Origins of Visual Stereotypes in American Mass Media.* Chapel Hill: University of North Carolina Press, 2001.

Kolodny, Annette. *The Lay of the Land: Metaphor as Experience and History in American Life and Letters.* Chapel Hill: University of North Carolina Press, 1975.

Kreshel, Peggy J. 1990. "The 'Culture' of J. Walter Thompson, 1915–1925." *Public Relations Review* 16, no. 8 (Fall 1990): 80–93.

Larson, Magali Sargatti. *The Rise of Professionalism: A Sociological Analysis.* Berkeley: University of California Press, 1977.

Lasch-Quinn, Elisabeth. *Black Neighbors: Race and the Limits of Reform in the American Settlement House Movement, 1890–1945.* Chapel Hill: University of North Carolina Press, 1993.

Leach, William. *Land of Desire: Merchants, Power and the Rise of a New America.* New York: Pantheon, 1993.

———. "Transformations in a Culture of Consumption: Women and Department Stores, 1890–1925." *Journal of American History* 71 (1984): 317–42.

Lears, T. J. Jackson. *Fables of Abundance: A Cultural History of Advertising in America.* New York: Basic Books, 1994.

———. "From Salvation to Self-Realization: Advertising and the Therapeutic Roots of Consumer Culture, 1880–1930." In *The Culture of Consumption: Critical Essays in American History, 1880–1980*, edited by Richard Wrightman Fox and T. J. Jackson Lears, 1–38. New York: Pantheon, 1983.

Lewis, Edith. *Willa Cather Living: A Personal Record.* Lincoln: University of Nebraska Press, 2000.

Lowe, Margaret. *Looking Good: College Women and Body Image, 1875–1930.* Baltimore: Johns Hopkins University Press, 2003.

Lunardini, Christine. *From Equal Suffrage to Equal Rights: Alice Paul and the National Women's Party, 1910–1928.* New York: New York University Press, 1986.

Lynd, Robert, and Helen Lynd. *Middletown.* New York: Harcourt Brace and World, 1929.

Manring, M. M. *Slave in a Box: The Strange Career of Aunt Jemima*. Charlottesville: University of Virginia Press, 1998.

Marchand, Roland. *Advertising the American Dream: Making Way for Modernity, 1920–1940*. Berkeley: University of California Press, 1985.

Marx, Karl, and Frederick Engels. *The German Ideology*. London: Lawrence & Wishart, 1970.

Mattlelart, Armand. *Advertising International: The Privatisation of Public Space*. London: Routledge, 1991.

Mattlelart, Michele, and Keith Reader. "Women and the Cultural Industries." In *Media, Culture and Society* 4 (1982): 133–51.

Maule, Frances. *She Strives to Conquer: Business Behavior, Opportunities, and Job Requirements for Women*. New York: Funk and Wagnall's, 1934.

Mays, Lary. *Screening Out the Past: The Birth of Mass Culture and the Motion Picture Industry*. New York: Oxford University Press, 1980.

McClintock, Anne. *Imperial Leather: Race, Gender and Sexuality in the Colonial Contest*. New York: Routledge, 1995.

———. "Soft-Soaping Empire: Commodity Racism and Imperial Advertising." In *The Gender and Consumer Culture Reader*, edited by Jennifer Scanlon. New York: New York University Press, 2000.

McCracken, Ellen. *Decoding Women's Magazines: From "Mademoiselle" to "Ms."* New York: St. Martin's, 1993.

McCracken, Grant. *Culture and Consumption: New Approaches to the Symbolic Character of Consumer Goods and Activities*. Bloomington: Indiana University Press, 1991.

McKendrick, Neil, John Brewer, and J. H. Plumb. *The Birth of Consumer Society: The Commercialization of Eighteenth-Century England*. Bloomingdale: Indiana University Press, 1985.

McRobbie, Angela. *Feminism and Youth Culture*. London: Macmillan, 1991.

Meyers, Marian, ed. *Mediated Women: Representations in Popular Culture*. Cresskill, NJ: Hampton, 1999.

Miller, Daniel. *Material Culture and Mass Consumption*. Oxford: B. Blackwell, 1987.

Miller, Michael Barry. *The Bon Marche: Bourgeois Culture and the Department Store, 1869–1920*. Princeton, NJ: Princeton University Press, 1981.

Miller, Zane. *The Urbanization of Modern America: A Brief History*. New York: Harcourt, Brace, Jovanovich, 1973.

Mitchell, W. J. T. *Iconology: Images, Text, Ideology*. Chicago: University of Chicago Press, 1986.

Moeran, Brian. *A Japanese Advertising Agency: An Anthropology of Media and Markets*. Honolulu: University of Hawaii Press, 1996.

Mohanty, Chandra Talpade. "Under Western Eyes: Feminist Scholarship and Colonial Discourses." In *Third World Women and the Politics of Feminism*, edited by Chandra Talpade Mohanty, Ann Russo, and Lourdes Torres, 51–80. Bloomington: University of Indiana Press, 1991.

Moi, Toril. *Sexual Textual Politics: Feminist Literary Theory*. London: Routledge, 1991.

Moog, Carol. *"Are They Selling Her Lips?": Advertising and Identity*. New York: Morrow, 1990.

Morgan, Richard. *J. Walter Takeover: From Divine Right to Common Stock*. Homewood, IL: Business One Irwin, 1991.

Mukerji, Chandra. *From Graven Images: Patterns of Modern Materialism*. New York: Columbia University Press, 1983

Mulvey, Laura. "Visual Pleasure and Narrative Cinema." *Screen* 16, no. 3 (Autumn 1975): 6–18.

Muncy, Robin. *Creating a Female Dominion in American Reform, 1890–1935*. New York: Oxford University Press, 1991.

Nava, Mica, Andrew Blake, Iain MacRury, and Barry Richards. *Buy This Book: Studies in Advertising and Consumption*. London: Routledge, 1997.

Norris, James. *Advertising and the Transformation of American Society, 1865–1920*. New York: Greenwood, 1990.

O'Barr, William. *Culture and the Ad: Exploring Otherness in the World of Advertising*. Boulder, CO: Westview, 1994.

Ohmann, Richard. *Selling Culture: Magazines, Markets, and Class at the Turn of the Century*. London: Verso, 1996.

Pease, Donald, and Amy Kaplan, eds. *Cultures of United States Imperialism*. Durham, NC: Duke University Press, 1993.

Pease, Otis. *The Responsibilities of American Advertising*. New Haven, CT: Yale University Press, 1958.

Peirce, C. S. *Collected Papers*. Cambridge, MA: Harvard University Press, 1931–1958.

Pierce, Russell. *Gringo-Gaucho: An Advertising Odyssey*. Ashland, OR: Southern Cross, 1991.

Peiss, Kathy. *Hope in a Jar: The Making of America's Beauty Culture*. New York: Henry Holt, 1998.

Perkins, Teresa E. "Rethinking Stereotypes." In *Ideology and Cultural Production*, edited by Michele Barrett, Philip Corrigan, Annette Kuhn, and Janet Wolff, 135–59. New York: St. Martin's, 1979.

Pieterse, Jan P. Nederveen. *White on Black: Images of Africa and Blacks in Western Popular Culture*. New Haven: Yale University Press, 1992.

Pope, Daniel. *The Making of Modern Advertising*. New York: Basic Books, 1983.

Potter, Daniel. *People of Plenty: Economic Abundance and the American Character*. Chicago: University of Chicago Press, 1954.

Presby, Frank. *History and Development of Advertising*. New York: Doubleday, Doran, 1929.

Radway, Janice. *Reading the Romance*. Chapel Hill: University of North Carolina Press, 1984.

Rapp, Rayna, and Ellen Ross. "The Twenties' Backlash: Compulsory Heterosexuality, the Consumer Family, and the Waning of Feminism." In *Class, Race, and Sex: The Dynamics of Control*, edited by Amy Swerdlow and Hanna Lessinger, 93–107. Boston: G. K. Hall, 1983.

Roediger, David. *The Wages of Whiteness: Race and the Making of the American Working Class*. London: Verso, 1991.

Rooks, Noliwe. *Ladies' Pages: African American Women's Magazines and the Culture that Made Them*. New Brunswick, NJ: Rutgers University Press, 2004.

Rosen, Marjorie. *Popcorn Venus: Women, Movies and the American Dream*. New York: Coward, McCann & Geoghegan, 1973.

Rosenberg, Emily. *Spreading the American Dream: American Economic and Cultural Expansion, 1890–1945*. New York: Hill & Wang, 1982.

Rosenberg, Rosalind. *Beyond Separate Spheres: The Intellectual Roots of Modern Feminism*. New Haven: Yale University Press, 1982.

Roy, Abhik. "Images of Domesticity and Motherhood in Indian Television Commercials: A Critical Study." *Journal of Popular Culture* 32, no. 1 (Winter 1998): 117–34.

Ryan, Mary P. "The Projection of a New Womanhood: The Movie Moderns in the 1920s." 2nd ed. In *Our American Sisters: Women in American Life and Thought*, edited by Jean E. Friedman and William G. Shade, 366–85. Boston: Allyn and Bacon, 1976.

———. *Womanhood in America: From Colonial Times to the Present*. New York: New Viewpoints, 1975.

Saussure, Ferdinand. *Course in General Linguistics*. Translated by Roy Harris. London: G. Duckworth, 1983.

Scanlon, Jennifer. *Inarticulate Longings: The "Ladies' Home Journal," Gender and the Promise of Consumer Culture*. New York: Routledge, 1995.

Schudson, Michael. *Advertising, the Uneasy Persuasion: Its Dubious Impact on American Society*. New York: Basic Books, 1986.

Schwartz, Judith, Kathy Peiss, and Christina Simmons. "We Were a Little Band of Willful Women: The Heterodoxy Club of Greenwich Village." In *Passion and Power: Sexuality in History*, edited by Kathy Peiss and Christina Simmons, 118–37. Philadelphia, Temple University, 1989.

Scott, Joan Wallach, ed. *Feminism & History*. New York: Oxford University Press, 1996.

Schor, Juliet B., and Douglas B. Holt, eds. *The Consumer Society Reader*. New York: The New Press, 2000.

Shammus, Carole. *The Pre-Industrial Consumer in England and America*. New York: Oxford University Press, 1990.

Sivulka, Juliann. *Ad Women: How They Impact What We Need, Want, and Buy*. New York: Prometheus Books, 2008.

———. *Soap, Sex, and Cigarettes: A Cultural History of American Advertising*. New York: Wadsworth, 1998.

———. *Stronger Than Dirt: A Cultural History of Advertising Personal Hygiene in America, 1875–1940*. New York: Humanity Books, 2001.

Smith-Rosenberg, Carrol. *Disorderly Conduct: Visions of Gender in Victorian America*. New York: Oxford University Press, 1985.

———. "The Female World of Love and Ritual: Relations Between Women in Nineteenth-Century America." In *Feminism & History*, edited by Joan Scott, 366–97. New York: Oxford University Press, 1996.

Spigel, Lynn, and Denise Mann, eds. *Private Screenings: Television and the Female Consumer*. Minneapolis: University of Minnesota Press, 1992.

Stage, Sarah. *Female Complaints: Lydia Pinkham and the Business of Women's Medicine*. New York: W. W. Norton, 1979.

Strasser, Susan. *Satisfaction Guaranteed: The Making of the American Mass Market*. New York: Pantheon, 1989.

Sussman, Warren I. *Culture as History: The Transformation of American Society in the Twentieth Century*. New York: Pantheon, 1984.

Sutton, Denise Hardesty. "Globalizing Modern Beauty: The Women's Editorial Department at the J. Walter Thompson Advertising Company, 1910–1945." PhD diss., Clark University, 2004.

Thomas, Richard. *The Commodity Culture of Victorian England*. Stanford, CA: Stanford University Press, 1990.

Tickner, Lisa. *The Spectacle of Women: Imagery of the Suffrage Campaign, 1907–1914*. London: Chatto and Windus, 1987.

Tobin, Joseph, ed. *Re-Made in Japan: Everyday Life and Consumer Taste in a Changing Society*. New Haven: Yale University Press, 1992.

Tomes, Nancy. *The Gospel of Germs: Men, Women, and the Microbe in American Life*. Cambridge: Harvard University Press, 1998.

Trolander, Judith Ann. *Professional and Social Change: From the Settlement House Movement to Neighborhood Centers, 1886 to the present*. New York: Columbia University Press, 1987.

Tuchman, Gayle, Arlene Kaplan Daniels, and James Benet, eds. *Hearth and Home: Images of Women in the Mass Media*. New York: Oxford University Press, 1978.

Twitchell, James. *Adcult USA: The Triumph of Advertising in American Culture*. New York: Columbia University Press, 1991.

Waller, May Ellen. "Popular Women's Magazines, 1890–1917." PhD diss., Columbia University, 1987.

Ward, Douglas B. "Tracking the Culture of Consumption: Curtis Publishing Company, Charles Coolidge Parlin, and the Origins of Market Research, 1911–1930." PhD diss., University of Maryland, 1996.

Ware, Carolina. *Greenwich Village, 1920–1940, A Comment on American Civilization in the Post-War Years*. Berkeley: University of California Press, 1994.

Weinbaum, Alys Eve, Lynn M. Thomas, Priti Ramamurthy, Uta G. Poiger, Madeleine Yue Dong, and Tani E. Barlow, eds. *The Modern Girl Around the World: Consumption, Modernity, and Globalization.* Durham, NC: Duke University Press, 2008.

Wexler, Laura. *Tender Violence: Domestic Visions in an Age of U. S. Imperialism*. Chapel Hill: University of North Carolina Press, 2000.

Wicke, Jennifer. *Advertising Fictions: Literature, Advertisement and Social Reading*. New York: Columbia University Press, 1988.

Wilkinson, Endymion. *Japan Versus the West: Image and Reality*. London: Penguin, 1990.

Williams, Raymond. "Advertising: The Magic System." In *Problems in Materialism and Culture*, 170–95. London: Verso, 1980.

Williams, Rosalind. *Dream Worlds: Mass Consumption in Late Nineteenth-Century France*. Berkeley: University of California Press, 1991.

Williamson, Judith. *Decoding Advertisements: Ideology and Meaning in Advertising*. London: Marian Boyers, 1979.

Willis, Susan. "I Shop Therefore I Am: Is There a Place for Afro-American Culture in Commodity Culture?" In *Changing Our Own Words: Essays on Criticism, Theory and Writing by Black Women*, edited by Cheryl Wall, 173–95. New Jersey: Rutgers University Press, 1990.

Wilson, E. *The Sphinx in the City: Urban Life, the Control of Disorder, and Women.* Berkeley: University of California Press, 1991.

Wolf, Naomi. *The Beauty Myth: How Images of Beauty Are Used Against Women.* New York: Morrow, 1991.

Young, Iris Marion. "The Ideal of Community and the Politics of Difference." In *Feminism/Postmodernism*, edited by Linda J. Nicholson. New York: Routledge, 1990, 300–23.

Zuckerman, Mary Ellen. *A History of Women's Popular Magazines in the United States, 1792–1995.* Westport, CT: Greenwood, 1979.

Index

CPSIA information can be obtained at www.ICGtesting.com
Printed in the USA
BVOW020927010612

291564BV00003B/1/P